The Future of Rural America

Rural Studies Series

The Future of Rural America: Anticipating Policies for Constructive Change, edited by Kenneth E. Pigg

Rural Policies for the 1990s, edited by Cornelia B. Flora and James A. Christenson

Electric Power for Rural Growth: How Electricity Affects Rural Life in Developing Countries, by Douglas F. Barnes

The Rural South in Crisis: Challenges for the Future, edited by Lionel J. Beaulieu

Research, Realpolitik, and Development in Korea: The State and the Green Revolution, by Larry L. Burmeister

Women and Farming: Changing Roles, Changing Structures, edited by Wava G. Haney and Jane B. Knowles

Whose Trees? Proprietary Dimensions of Forestry, edited by Louise Fortmann and John W. Bruce

My Own Boss? Class, Rationality, and the Family Farm, by Patrick H. Mooney

Agriculture and Community Change in the U.S.: The Congressional Research Reports, edited by Louis E. Swanson

Small Farms: Persistence with Legitimation, by Alessandro Bonanno

Family Farming in Europe and America, edited by Boguslaw Galeski and Eugene Wilkening

Studies in the Transformation of U.S. Agriculture, edited by A. Eugene Havens with Gregory Hooks, Patrick H. Mooney, and Max J. Pfeffer

Technology and Social Change in Rural Areas: A Festschrift for Eugene A. Wilkening, edited by Gene F. Summers

The Future of Rural America

Anticipating Policies for Constructive Change

edited by Kenneth E. Pigg

Westview Press

BOULDER • SAN FRANCISCO • OXFORD

Rural Studies Series, Sponsored by the Rural Sociological Society

This Westview softcover edition is printed on acid-free paper and bound in library-quality, coated covers that carry the highest rating of the National Association of State Textbook Administrators, in consultation with the Association of American Publishers and the Book Manufacturers' Institute.

Copyright © 1991 by the Rural Sociological Society

Published in 1991 in the United States of America by Westview Press, Inc., 5500 Central Avenue, Boulder, Colorado 80301, and in the United Kingdom by Westview Press, 36 Lonsdale Road, Summertown, Oxford OX2 7EW

Library of Congress Cataloging-in-Publication Data
The Future of rural America : anticipating policies for constructive
    change / edited by Kenneth E. Pigg.
        p. cm.—(Rural studies series)
    Includes bibliographical references and index.
    ISBN 0-8133-8364-1
    1. Rural development—United States. 2. United States—Economic
policy—1981–   . 3. Agriculture—Economic aspects—United States.
4. Rural renewal—United States. I. Pigg, Kenneth E. II. Series:
Rural studies series of the Rural Sociological Society.
HN90.C6F88 1991
307.1′412′0973—dc20   91-16084
                                                                    CIP

Printed and bound in the United States of America

⊚ The paper used in this publication meets the requirements
    of the American National Standard for Permanence of Paper
    for Printed Library Materials Z39.48-1984.

10   9   8   7   6   5   4   3   2   1

Contents

Tables and Figures

Foreword

The claim that rural areas in the United States are being left behind or passed by has become a cliche. This image is fostered by overwhelming evidence that many rural residents, when compared to their more urban counterparts, are increasingly facing a wide array of problems, including those of employment, health care, education, and earnings. However, being left behind implies a dislocation from the economic and social mainstream of America, a situation certainly not applicable to rural areas any more than it is to central cities. The fortunes of rural America are inextricably tied to national and global socioeconomic trends. While it may not be accurate to say that rural America literally is being left behind, the fact remains that many policy makers approach rural problems as artifacts of the past, a past which no longer seems relevant to current social and economic forces. The chapters in this volume are important not only because they debunk the image of a rural society that is independent of larger socioeconomic conditions, but because they offer prescriptions for moving rural America into the future.

Kenneth Pigg has assembled an excellent collection of original works by an impressive cadre of experts on rural social and economic organization. The selection of chapters achieve a nice balance between conceptualization and application; they provide a timely and much-needed discussion of rural policy and the socioeconomic context within which such policy must operate. This volume in the Rural Studies Series of the Rural Sociological Society is an important contribution to the literature on rural development in the United States; hopefully it will be a catalyst for other works of this caliber.

Forrest A. Deseran, Community Editor
Rural Studies Series, Rural Sociological Society

Acknowledgments

It has been my pleasure to work with a distinguished, committed, and cooperative group of contributors to this volume. They have taught me how to perform the editing role and put up with innumerable and probably insufferable suggestions. I have been privileged to work with exceptionally fine individuals in this endeavor and will count that among my many blessings.

I must also acknowledge a considerable debt to George W. Nickolaus, formerly Dean of the College of Public and Community Service at the University of Missouri. As one who is committed to courage in the redress of intolerable situations, George provided me the opportunity, means, and support to complete this volume. Originally, it was his idea to address the future of rural America and the means by which that future might be secured. He extended me the professional courtesy and personal encouragement to pursue this endeavor. Thank you, George.

Finally, such a work cannot be accomplished without exemplary and patient staff support. Wendy Larson provided editorial assistance that produced an intelligible collection from a disparate assortment. Josie Wright and Jody Strutz produced both draft and final typescript with forgiving spirits and considerable technical skill.

Kenneth E. Pigg

1

Introduction:
The Future of Rural America

Kenneth E. Pigg

Somewhere in rural America, where one of the interstate highways crosses a state boundary, there is an exit to a small rural community. The sign there reads "Exit 0." The highway designers obviously meant this as an alphabetical designation, but one cannot help reading it as a literal zero. Is this the interpretation we are to apply to rural America today? Have most observers and policy makers, in fact, "written off" rural America?

It is ironic that this metaphor should become connected with the massive investment in rural development represented by the interstate highway system. The federal government, at least partly in the name of a better rural life for Americans who chose to live there, poured billions into this transportation infrastructure. These highways, along with utilities, communications, water and sewer systems, etc., have been touted as the means by which the quality of rural life has been improved, the economies of rural communities strengthened, and health care made accessible to rural residents.

Yet today the benefits attributed to the infrastructure enterprise seem illusory. Rural poverty is depressingly extensive. Not only are the traditionally poor still poor, but we are suddenly sensitive to a "new rural poor," represented by farm families displaced by rapid deflation and technological change. The forces certain to change the nature of agriculture over the next several decades have unknown human ramifications.

In north Missouri nearly a century ago, the promise of new economic opportunity led a small group of people to establish a new community—Economy, Missouri. Today the place that represented the promise more accurately represents the failure of the economy of self-sufficiency in an economic system strongly tied to international fiscal flows and product competition. The town of Economy is a few disheveled structures without a productive resident population. Economy is a shambles.

While the economy of most of rural America is not in the same dire straits as Economy's, the linkages between rural economic enterprise and that of the rest of the world have changed dramatically. Only where local communities and enterprises have adjusted to changing socioeconomic conditions will we find, today or in the future, a healthy "Economy."

The purpose of this volume is to provide first, a broadening of the perspectives for the future basis of rural policy; and, second, to provide a beginning point for rethinking the rural problem that confronts policy makers. It is admittedly difficult to overcome rhetorical posturing in complex political situations. Nevertheless, both the direct and opportunity costs of any federal rural development program are likely to be extremely high, thus discouraging Congressional action in a period when budget constraints make any new program initiative politically risky. Unless there are compelling reasons to offset these costs, necessary rural development actions are unlikely.

The organization of the volume emphasizes several themes which are addressed by contributors. The first theme addresses the question of the essential elements of "ruralness." The second theme is a critique of commonly accepted remedies for rural problems, namely economic development and technological change. These two strategies for change are rapidly being relegated to the category of "silver bullets" as we recognize that the tacit prescription for action involved with each is inappropriate in many instances and their perceived benefits carry numerous and significant costs. The third theme has direct programmatic implications, calling for institutional restructuring. These themes were not originally established by the editor but emerged from the final compilation of chapters. While other topics are also addressed, and some contributors address more than one theme, the volume accomplishes the purposes set forth above. The contributors provide a rich set of concepts and practical approaches to addressing the future of rural America in constructive ways.

A Historical Perspective

Frequently, it is instructive to remind ourselves of historical precedents. Arguably the appointment of the Commission on Country Life by President Theodore Roosevelt in 1910 marked the first systematic assessment of rural conditions and explicit rural policy recommendations. The Commission's report was responsible for many changes, including establishment of the Extension Services of the state agricultural colleges and construction of farm-to-market roads. Perhaps it could be best remembered for providing a basis for concerted action by a "centralized national agency" for the betterment of rural conditions, especially farming.

The Commission report also is replete with references to the importance of the rural value system to which could be attributed the development of a productive urban workforce. Commission members argued that, if there was to be a viable future rural economy, a larger share of this workforce should be retained on the farm and in rural communities. Finally, the report stated that "local initiative is (to be) relied on to the fullest extent and that federal and even state agencies do not perform what might be done by the people in the communities (Commission 1911: 113)." The role of external agencies was to be "stimulative and directive, rather than mandatory and formal (Commission 1911: 113)." The development of "native resources," both human and physical, was to be the focus of all activity.

Part of the compelling nature of the 1910 Commission's policy statement was the simple vision provided for rural America at the turn of the century. In the words of Liberty Hyde Bailey, Chairman of the Commission,

> The philosophy of the situation requires that the disadvantages and handicaps that are not a natural part of the farmer's business shall be removed, and that such forces shall be encouraged and set in motion as will stimulate and direct local initiative and leadership. (Commission 1911: 112)

With the farming population so central to rural life and conditions at that time, it was only natural to focus remedial actions on farm families and enterprises.

Forty years later President Nixon appointed the Task Force on Rural Development which issued its report, "A New Life for the Country," in 1970. In the first chapter of its report the Task Force implies that previous efforts to prepare rural migrants for productive work in urban areas had apparently been so successful that the "large cities are slowly strangling themselves" (Task Force 1970: 1). The report notes the extensive urban decay resulted in the "tearing apart (of the) fabric of family and society," in deteriorated housing, increased crime rates and environmental pollution. The rationale for rural development had shifted in just 40 years from preservation and improvement of rural conditions for their own sake, to prevention of the likelihood that "the social and economic ills of the Nation's inner cities may worsen and spread over the entire nation" (Task Force 1970: 1). The answer to the "problem" of rural migration to the cities was "rural development," the creation of more economic opportunities and a better environment in countryside America. The Task Force called for a modest investment in rural development to forestall the need for an estimated $100 billion investment to correct the problems of the inner cities.

The Task Force report dealt with more than farming, calling for public policy to address the concerns of developing a better quality of life in rural areas. The report affirmed the importance of local initiative and leadership as well as calling for increased responsibility for the private sector. However, the Task Force report marked a shift from targeted rural programs to the benefits to be derived from the "total economic and social development of the Nation" (Task Force 1970: 11).

The Task Force called for a permanent Commission on Rural Development. It recommended a national policy on the geographic distribution of population and economic growth as well as numerous "procedural" changes including the organization of rural development efforts around "growth centers," increased federal research support, and simplification and streamlining of procedures for applying for assistance. It listed a number of specific actions in economic development (such as the establishment of a Rural Development Credit Bank), and in education, nutrition and welfare, housing, health care, natural resource development, and transportation.

While the recommendations presented in 1970 were more comprehensive in scope than those of the Commission on Country Life, the success of the effort to change public policy was minimal. It is clear that the Commission succeeded in formulating a more compelling public policy argument for the rural America of its time than that of the Task Force on Rural Development. It is also clear that without a similarly compelling rationale future policy changes will fare little better than that of "New Life for the Country." Further, complications such as the intrusion of global economic effects, the effects of a number of social trends on rural institutions, the declining farm population and changing political stature of Congressional representatives from rural America have made the public policy formation process far more complex.

Buttel and Gillespie in "Rural Policy in Perspective: The Rise, Fall, and Uncertain Future of The American Welfare State," extend our historical understanding in a critical essay. They review the more general policy concepts which underlay the welfare state initiated in Western nations in the mid twentieth century. Unlike the Country Life Commission, the recommendations from the President's Task Force on Rural Development reflect the typical dependence on general welfare betterment policies rather than policies targeted on the rural population. Buttel and Gillespie argue that this approach represented a "disguised" rural development policy which present conditions indicate has not been effective, nor is it likely to be considering the "new social structure of accumulation" which characterizes present global trends. Their analysis contradicts the common view that rural development policy has been subjugated by farm and agriculture policy, placing it instead in a larger context.

If present and future discussions on rural development policy are to override the sterility of political rhetoric, a vision for rural America similar in its precisely perceptive regard for existing conditions must be formulated and forcefully presented. It is self-evident that a stable and sustainable future for rural residents is preferable to continued economic and social deterioration. A host of documentaries and studies, such as *America II* (Louv 1983), bear witness to its urgency. In a world where American leaders are forceful in their insistence on acceptable "human rights" actions in other countries, it is ironic that human rights are an insufficient basis for public policy for Rural America.

What Is Rural?

This question continues to haunt research scientists and policy makers alike. Portions of this volume argue that it is still a critically important question, especially for policy purposes. Much of what was considered characteristically unique or special about rural areas has recently taken on different meaning. Farming involves such a small proportion of the rural population that rural status often does not have much to do with the farm enterprise. Another factor historically associated with rural areas is an economy heavily dependent on the natural resource base and the extraction of raw materials to supply the industrial sector. The proportion of final cost attributed to raw materials' costs is now so low in many finished goods that the extractive industries are depressed and employment is declining as these industries struggle to stay competitive by further mechanization. A deeper understanding of this question is necessary if constructive rural development policy is to be formulated.

In this volume, Castle, Blakely and Wilkinson address the question of ruralness. For Castle, "The Benefits of Space and the Cost of Distance," the *essential* feature of ruralness is the economic relationship between space and distance. Castle argues that population density is the distinguishing characteristic between rural and urban, and provides a framework for rural development policy which begins with the question "What is the economic function performed by space and population sparsity?" The related policy considerations Castle discusses under the general categories of non-traditional rural area goods and services and resource mobility and adaptability. What is new about what Castle is saying is that it is now inadequate to target rural development to the improvement of material conditions *in specific places*.

Blakely, "The Emerging Global Economy and Rural Communities: A New Perspective," is concerned with previous rural development policies that have been "place-focused," as in federal financial assistance for infrastructure. He addresses this characteristic by noting that, for many rural residents, "community" is no longer spatially bound. Rather, one's community context may change with certain issues and concerns such as child abuse or environmental degradation. In this formulation the effects of the technology embodied in the telephone, mass media, automobile and freeway travel have transcended the rural community as a spatial setting for social interaction and institution-building.

Wilkinson, in "The Future of the Community in Rural Areas," addresses ruralness as a spatial concept and notes that the social costs of space may outweigh the economic. While the economic costs may contribute significantly to the high incidence of rural poverty and unemployment, the social costs are directly reflected in dependency, economic depression, internal conflict and extreme individualism.

The significant features that constitute ruralness may be analyzed, at least in the policy context, as social problems. To be rural today often means tolerating a lower quality of life as measured by restricted access to quality health care, education, social services and economic opportunity. It means existing on significantly lower family income than that of urban families. It means lower-quality housing and a rapidly deteriorating and inappropriate physical infrastructure. Successful and meaningful rural development policy must address the fact that, for many Americans, living in areas of low population density is not an attractive alternative.

Silver Bullets in the Sheaves[1]

Economic development and technological change may seem to be silver bullets possessing magical results for rural America. Judging by the spate of recent publications on the promise of economic and technological development for rural areas, policy makers might well conclude that economic and technological change will provide ample opportunity for rural development. Accordingly, the most appropriate policy actions are those that support such change and/or intervene to make progress more efficient in addressing rural conditions. While such a political stance may be effective in areas like the Northeast or parts of the West where metropolitan development has spilled over into adjacent rural areas, for most of the rest of the countryside the prescriptive actions suggested by these two "silver bullets" offer little constructive opportunity without direct intervention.

Drabenstott, in "Developing the Farm-Dependent Rural Economy: The Policy Choices," outlines the difficulties involved with continuing present policies when conditions solicit different economic strategies. He considers whether the needs are for assistance in adjusting to current trends or remaking the economic systems of rural areas. Gillis, in "Encouraging Economic Development in Rural America," takes this a step further with a critique of conventional industrial attraction strategies by presenting practical, workable approaches to rural economic development that target more appropriate opportunities. It is important to note that many interventions he proposes—as do others such as Jones (1989)—deal with establishing more satisfactory rural conditions to support local economic development efforts, such as investment in human capital and physical infrastructure, rather than in economic development activities directly. This indicates the need for comprehensive review of existing policies in agencies such as the U.S. Departments of Agriculture and Commerce as well as parallel state agencies.

"The Role of Community in Rural Economic Development" by Wade and Pulver points out that the economy and the community cannot be separately addressed. Indeed, without community-focused approaches and community action, economic development is unlikely to benefit local residents. With this premise, based on many years' experience in fieldwork, they illustrate the fundamentally difficult relationship between national and local policy. National policy makers must resist the temptation to develop specific programs, which tend toward specific prescriptive actions, and work instead toward providing an environment to support the efforts of local policy making. Only at the local level can appropriate, workable action be formulated and carried out.

According to Goe and Kenney, in "The Restructuring of the Global Economy and The Future of U.S. Agriculture," agriculture is faced with dilemmas similar to those of other domestic industries even though agricultural change has lagged behind. They contend that agriculture will be shaped by a number of factors which underlie the current changes in other sectors. Almost everyone is aware of the economic restructuring now in progress. Manufacturing employment is stable but declining in the proportion of the total number of persons employed. Employment in service industries is growing rapidly. As noted earlier, the natural resource industries—mining, forestry, and related processing—are declining in employment. The standard export base model used by most analysts of economic growth has been modified to include passive income from dividends, interest and rent, as well as transfer payments (Shaffer, et al. 1988). Transportation and communications changes have opened most markets to international competition. Advances in technology, specifically the commercialization of developments in information technology, biotechnology and new materials such as polymers and ceramics are a mechanism for future economic growth. According to Goe and Kenney, information technology and biotechnology hold the most promise for increasing the productivity and profitability in agriculture production and processing enterprises, even though newly developed technologies have not yet been widely applied in agriculture.

Increased development and application of new technologies in agriculture will be important in rural America. Their use is likely to be directly tied to further increases in the size of the farm enterprise. According to a recent analysis by USDA's Economic Research Service, there are perhaps 740 counties in the U.S. "leaning toward" large farm status, classified according to the percentage of farms which had 1982 sales of over $40,000 (Carlin and Green 1989). With an additional 750 counties already classified as being in the large farm category, slightly over half the counties in the U.S. are likely to benefit from increased income to agriculture enterprises due to technological change. Goe and Kenney are quick to point out that factors underlying the present economic restructuring may be more important than technological changes itself. The "shift toward flexibility in production," "fragmentation of mass markets," and "the need for environmentally sound production practices" may have greater effect in agriculture.

Institutional Restructuring

As noted above, technology tends to fragment rural areas spatially. The antidote to this is "community." Just as the economy is being restructured, the community is acquiring different meaning for rural residents. They often do not work where they live. They are affected by forces other than local. In fact, one's choice of residence may be influenced today more by social and environmental concerns than by economic or educational factors. Even though the meaning attached to "community" is changing, there is considerable evidence that it is still significant for rural residents (Bellah, et al. 1985). Perhaps the most important task is to understand the meaning and significance attached to "community" by rural residents and to be sensitive to these factors as public policy is formulated.

While community is the fundamental institution undergoing essential restructuring in rural areas, other institutions face similar challenges. Salamon, "Families in the New Rural Community," addresses the

10

changing nature of the family as a rural institution. She finds new family "models" being developed as surrogates for the functions historically performed by traditional family units. Garkovich, "Individual and Social Problems in Rural Community Life," extends the discussion to include other human service providing institutions such as social and educational institutions. The inseparability of economic and social changes are explicitly addressed in these treatments.

On yet another front, Donald and Doris Littrell in "Civic Education, Rural Development and the Land Grant Institutions," and Seroka and Subramaniam, "Governing the Countryside: Linking Politics and Administrative Resources," address the institutions of rural governance. The contrast of these two treatments is instructive. The Littrells focus attention on the problems of local governance, arguing for a new approach to civic education to prepare rural residents to more effectively establish and implement local policy. Seroka and Subramaniam address the institutional structure itself. That is, they analyze the shortcomings of administrative structures as presently configured and argue for a more rational combination of resources to improve efficiency and effectiveness. It is unlikely that either approach alone will be sufficient.

In the past, central interventions have played a major role in the success of rural development efforts. Rural electrification, housing, education, and economic development represent only some of the areas in which national efforts resulting in institutional innovations have been highly beneficial. New efforts in this context will be essential; institution-building is an important future role for the federal government. Notwithstanding this, another federal (and state) role is to be "stimulative and directive" in its relationships with local individuals as they attempt to seize control of their own institutions, restructuring those whose resources are important for future benefits and retiring those whose utility is exhausted.

A Proleptic Note

An undertaking such as intended in this volume requires a bit of audacity. In the words of Victor Ferkiss,

> Any proposal for change must be reasonably specific about how to get to where we want to go from where we are. . . .The process of reordering society so as to achieve the promise of tomorrow

will take place in a future of contingencies no one can foresee, but (we) must do more than suggest an alternative future. . . .We must at least try to understand the nature of the metamorphosis and how it takes place (1974: 260).

Such a challenge is a formidable one and has not been taken lightly. The nature of the changes needed, however, are extremely complex, demanding simplicity in a world full of constraints.

The two final chapters of this volume provide examples of the kind of simple but compelling visions Ferkiss must have in mind. Rodale and Lehman, "Regenerating Rural America," offer a vision of change analogous to the ecological concept of regeneration. They discuss the ecological aspects of regeneration in detail and then present some examples of its application to rural communities. Busch, in "Waking The Owl of Minerva: Constructing a Future for Rural America," provides a different kind of vision based on new forms of social organization. After a convincing argument that social scientists have a challenging role to play in helping communities understand the nature and implications of their image of the future, he traces the sources of those images. Finally, Busch provides some examples of ways in which rural communities can put the images they value into action.

This volume is but a beginning, a prolepsis. The contributors have anticipated action by federal, state and local decision makers. In fact, a number of states and localities have already initiated such action, and the governors of the nation have assembled a blueprint for even broader change (John, Batie and Norris 1988). In anticipating such action, the authors offer a broader perspective on both the nature of the necessary changes and the process for making those changes most constructively.

Those actions suggested by the contributors in this volume which offer the greatest promise should not come as a surprise. Economic improvements are needed to reduce the burden and incidence of poverty and create an environment of opportunity. The rural community needs help to fashion a more attractive quality of life with better education, health care, social and cultural activities, and less psychological isolation. Institutional innovations which provide vehicles for initiating and managing change can not be overlooked. Furthermore, one of the neglected aspects of change is the *process* by which it is implemented. The term "partnership" is often misused, but the concept cannot be overemphasized. Only a collaborating set of leadership roles, with major and appropriate activities developed and pursued jointly by federal, state and local decision makers, will suffice to produce the kind of long-term changes necessary to secure a future for rural America and fulfill the expectations of rural citizens.

Notes

1. This section title employs two metaphors combined with which some readers may not be familiar. The first is a references to a widely used publication by John Fernstrom of USDA, Extension on industrial development, *Bringing in the Sheaves* (1970). This publication has been successfully employed by many communities in their industrial recruitment and attraction programs. The second refers to a publication by Jack McCall, *Small Town Survival Manual* (1988), in which he discusses several "parables" which get in the way of community action. One of these is the story of the "hired gun" (cf. expert in economic development) who comes to "save the community" and leaves them a "silver bullet" to take care of the next problem they have. McCall argues that such experts are often "false prophets" and provide little help to the community.

References

Bellah, Robert N., R. Madsden, W.M. Sullivan, A. Swidler and S. Tipton. 1985. *Habits of the Heart*. New York: Harper and Row.

Carlin, Thomas A., and Bernal L. Green. 1989. "Farm Structure and Nearby Communities." *Rural Development Perspectives*, 5: 16-20.

Commission on Country Life. 1911. *Report of the Commission on Country Life*. New York: Sturgis and Walton Company.

Ferkiss, Victor C. 1974. *The Future of Technological Civilization*. New York: G. Braziller.

Fernstrom, John. 1970. *Bringing in the Sheaves*. Washington, D.C.: United States Department of Agriculture, Extension Service.

John, DeWitt, Sandra S. Batie, and Kim Norris. 1988. *A Brighter Future for Rural America? Strategies for Communities and States*. Washington, D.C.: National Governors' Association, Center for Policy Research.

Jones, Sue H. (ed.) 1989. *Focus on the Future: Options in Developing a New National Rural Policy*. College Station, TX: Texas Agricultural Extension Service.

Louv, Richard. 1983. *America II*. New York: Penguin Books.

McCall, Jack. 1988. *Small Town Survival Manual*. Columbia, MO: University Extension, University of Missouri, Community Economic Development Program.

President's Task Force on Rural Development. 1970. *A New Life for the Country*. Washington, D.C.: U.S. Government Printing Office.

Shaffer, Ron E., Priscilla Salant, and William Saupe. 1988. "Rural Economies and Farming: The Link," in Gene F. Summers, Leonard E. Bloomquist, Thomas A. Hirschl and Ron E. Shaffer (eds.). *Community Economic Vitality: Major Trends and Selected Issues*. Pp. 13-16. Ames, IA: North Central Regional Center for Rural Development.

2

Rural Policy in Perspective:
The Rise, Fall, and Uncertain Future of
the American Welfare-State[1]

Frederick H. Buttel and Gilbert W. Gillespie, Jr.

Policy directed specifically to achieving *non*farm community and rural-regional development and institution-building is a relatively new phenomenon in the advanced countries. Prior to the Great Depression, when farm households were still a majority of the rural population, rural policy was largely implemented through agricultural policy (Rasmussen 1985; 1986).[2] In the U.S. and elsewhere in the industrial world, the Great Depression ushered in some tentative steps toward rural development policy, principally through Depression relief efforts. But rural development policy per se did not emerge until after World War II, under the aegis of vibrant post-War economic expansion, the development of the modern welfare-state, and American dominance of geopolitics and the world economy. Ironically, in the U.S. and elsewhere in the "developed" countries, rural development policies did not emerge until the rural population had decisively declined and after rural-urban differentials in incomes and levels of living had narrowed or were no longer diverging.

U.S. rural development policy, however, has over the past decade entered a period of uncertainty. Rural-urban or, more precisely, nonmetropolitan-metropolitan,[3] income disparities have begun to widen again, as have disparities among nonmetro households and among nonmetro regions (Henry, et al. 1986). Most importantly, there has been a dearth of comprehensive ideas for addressing the rural development problems of the late 1980s and beyond.

This chapter provides a fresh perspective on this new era of rural development policy by developing three major arguments. First, rural (and regional) development policy, as conventionally understood in the post-World War II period, has been integrally connected to a set of post-War institutions—state expansion in general and the welfare-state in particular—which were made possible by sustained, rapid economic expansion and the concomitant surpluses governments were able to appropriate, redistribute, and invest. Second, America's welfare-state (as it developed in the Depression and the post-War period) has been a relatively unique one by Western standards, and accordingly, U.S. rural development policy has had distinctive components. Finally, it is suggested that a number of factors that have led to a slow, but steady demise of the welfare-state over the past decade may well require entirely new ideas and policies to enhance the well-being of rural America.

Regional Polarization, the Welfare-State, and Rural-Urban Disparities

It is useful to begin by noting that the most fundamental taproot of rural problems lies in the tendency toward *regional polarization and divergence* that is essentially universal among market economies.[4] In fact, unfavorable levels of economic activity owing to regional polarization are one of the two defining characteristics of "rural" in advanced industrial societies, the second being the dependence of such regions on extractive-primary industries (Buttel and Gillespie 1988). The regionally uneven pattern of capital accumulation and economic expansion in market economies has been widely acknowledged by theorists from a diversity of perspectives (Holland 1976a: Chapters 1-3). Nonetheless, there is wide agreement that the most fundamental antecedent of rural development problems is spatially unequal patterns of economic development.

Spatial unevenness should not be viewed as a simple developed/less-developed or core/periphery continuum. There are a number of factors that shape this development pattern as well as compensatory processes that mitigate unevenness. For example, spatial polarization and rural underdevelopment can be based on factors such as unfavorable natural resource endowments, heavy dependence on declining industries, geographical isolation, high transportation costs to markets, and generalized market processes. Also, as in the case of the U.S. South, rural underdevelopment can be a longstanding reflection of economic structures and archaic social relationships, such as slavery, sharecropping, racial discrimination, and political dominance of merchant and agrarian capital, that inhibit economic development (Billings 1979; 1988; Falk and Lyson 1988). Finally, a number of factors may modify or mitigate regional polarization. Neoclassical regional theorists, for example, posit a tendency for *growth poles*—typically, medium-sized cities—to become established in the midst of peripheral regions. These growth poles or centers become an economic force which blunts the polarizing impact of the regional economy and raises rural-peripheral levels of economic activity and levels of living above what they would otherwise be. Neoclassical regional economists have also posited a tendency for regional disparities to exhibit convergence once national economies move into their mature, mass-consumption phases (Williamson 1975).

Further, as higher rates of unemployment and lower wage rates are among the principal concomitants of spatial polarization for rural-peripheral economies and labor markets, these factors may become a "relative advantage of backwardness." The availability of large pools of low-wage labor (or relatively cheap nonlabor inputs) may make these areas attractive for investments in labor-intensive, low-profit, technologically-mature manufacturing industries (Markusen 1985). The rapid growth of the U.S. Sunbelt, although strikingly uneven (Falk and Lyson 1988; Lyson 1989), has been a particularly dramatic instance of how regional underdevelopment and low wage scales may make a peripheral region attractive for large-scale investments at a particular juncture in the overall economic development process.

The Rise of the Modern Welfare-State

Although regional polarization and rural-urban economic disparities have characterized the advanced countries for centuries, the means for addressing these inequalities were not readily available until about 1890-1930. These means were two-fold. First, late nineteenth and early twentieth century industrialization led to the emergence of mass working classes, comprising near-majorities of the population and electorate in most industrial countries (Przeworski 1985; Przeworski and Sprague 1986). The growing strength of labor, and of worker consciousness that state policy should enhance its well-being, led to the establishment of militant labor, socialist, and communist parties in most countries in Western Europe; these left parties played the key political role in securing legislation that led to social-democratic, welfare-state systems (Stephens 1979). Second, industrialization, capital accumulation, and the growing fiscal, administrative, and intervention capacities of modern states provided the material basis for capturing surpluses through taxation and for deploying these surpluses to reduce socioeconomic inequalities.

The beginnings of the modern welfare-state were in England. Following passage of the initial legislation in 1897—an industrial accident insurance act—further legislation (instituting a disability coverage plan) was passed in 1906, followed by major breakthroughs in old age pension programs (in 1908) and by health and unemployment insurance in the National Insurance Act of 1911. By 1920 England was the world's leader in "welfare-state development" (Orloff and Skocpol 1984). Among the reasons for England's leadership were the political power of its labor unions and the fact that, as the world's hegemonic industrial power, the state had access to sufficient economic surpluses to fund welfare-state programs.

By the 1920s most of the world's industrial countries had begun to establish social insurance programs and had passed major items of protective labor legislation. The U.S. was among the world's latecomers in this regard. This was partially due to the absence of the two major conditions that have been associated historically with welfare-state development in the west. First, labor in the U.S. was relatively weak because of the ambiguous legal status of unions (until passage of the Wagner Act during the Great Depression), disunity among national labor organizations along craft vs. industrial lines, and the ethnic heterogeneity of the working class (Levine 1988). Second, the U.S. state itself was very weak prior to 1935 (Skowronek 1982).

The initial piece of modern welfare-state legislation in the U.S. was the Social Security Act of 1935.[5] By comparison with old age pension programs in most European countries, the U.S. social security program was quite conservative, since it tied social insurance benefits to labor force participation and left administration of public assistance programs to the states (Quadagno 1984). Mid-1960s data on social security programs show the distinctiveness of the U.S. variant of the social-democratic welfare-state. In 1966, U.S. social security expenditure as a percent of gross national product was 7.9 percent, compared to 21.0

percent in Austria, 19.6 percent in West Germany, 18.5 percent in Belgium, 18.3 percent in the Netherlands, 18.3 percent in France, and 17.5 percent each in Sweden and Italy. Among the industrial countries, only Japan had a lower percent of GNP (6.2) devoted to social security spending (Wilensky 1975: 30-31). The U.S. and Japan have continued to exhibit the lowest levels of welfare-state development; these two countries remain the only two advanced industrial states that lack a comprehensive pension plan and national health insurance and in which state social spending is not redistributive (Stephens 1979).

This is not to imply that overall U.S. federal spending has been as small as comparative data on social security expenditures would imply. Indeed, beginning with the tentative embracement by the federal government during the Roosevelt era of a generalized "social Keynesian" fiscal and monetary policy, U.S. government spending grew rapidly and has continued to exhibit a general "nontargeted" (as well as a strong military-dominated) character. That is, domestic programs have tended not to be targeted to specific subordinate social classes, as in the European social-democratic welfare-states, or, as we will see below, to particular regions.

Rural-Regional Policies and the Rural Welfare-State

Policies aimed at redressing regional and rural-urban economic imbalances were initiated in the post-World War II period. Generally rural policy followed patterns set forth in the development of welfare-state policies over the preceding four decades. England is generally seen as having been among the first nation-states to embrace regional policy instruments designed to bolster levels of economic activity and well-being in peripheral regions. Like many of the allies after the end of the War, England found that the surge of wartime manufacturing activity had occurred largely in major cities and had led to depopulation and stagnation in underdeveloped rural regions. The British government initiated a set of policies—chiefly controls on investment in core cities, subsidies to firms locating in low-income regions, and infrastructural investments in peripheral regions— designed to reduce regional disparities (MacLennan and Robertson 1969). These policies were made possible in large part by the Labor Party's strong presence in England's underdeveloped regions and by the support of Labor Party politicians from other regions who saw regional policy as being consistent with redistributive agendas. Other European countries followed suit. By the late 1950s essentially all western European countries had significant regional policies, the strength and funding of which tended to parallel that of the more conventional welfare-state measures (Holland 1976a; 1976b).

The U.S. was likewise a latecomer to regional policy, and the regional policies it implemented were similarly modest and nonredistributive in nature. U.S. regional policies essentially date from the Kennedy-Johnson Administrations in the 1960s (Hansen 1970), well after regional policies were common elsewhere in the industrial world. U.S. regional policy has been more circumscribed, considerably less interventionist, and less redistributive than policies in other western countries. U.S. regional policy instruments that were targeted have largely consisted of modest programs for funding public works and infrastructural improvements in poor regions. There has been relatively little effort by the federal government to directly influence industrial location decisions so as to lead to greater investment in underdeveloped or rural regions than would otherwise have been the case.[6]

This is not to suggest, however, that federal spending has been of minor importance or has failed to have a significant impact on patterns of regional polarization and rural development. Indeed, large—though typically nontargeted or weakly targeted—federal domestic spending and economic development programs were implemented in the 1960s and early 1970s. In FY 1985, federal expenditures that could be traced to counties averaged over $3,000 for each man, woman, and child—hardly a small sum (Bradshaw and Blakely 1987: 11-17). Moreover, these domestic spending programs have had major rural development implications despite the fact that they were generally not intended to benefit disproportionately rural or peripheral (or metropolitan or core) regions.

Table 2.1, taken from Bradshaw and Blakely (1987: 11-17), provides a general indication of how federal outlays are currently distributed among metropolitan and nonmetropolitan counties. These data show the dramatic role that federal defense and space expenditures have come to play in contributing to the pronounced advantage that metropolitan counties currently enjoy over their nonmetro counterparts in per capita federal outlays. The roughly $700 per capita difference in mean per capita federal expenditures on defense and space between metro ($1,011) and nonmetro counties ($303) in FY 1985 essentially accounts for the $714 per capita difference in total outlays that could be traced to county

TABLE 2.1 Per capita federal expenditures in metro and nonmetro counties, fiscal year 1985

Function	All Counties	Metro Counties	Nonmetro Counties
All Functions	$3,022	$3,192	$2,478
Agriculture & Natural Resources	49	21	137
Community Resources	116	117	113
Defense & Space	842	1,011	303
Human Resources	27	26	31
Income Security	1,545	1,516	1,637
National Functions	444	502	258

Note: The data in this table refer only to the 93 percent of Federal expenditures that could be traced to county levels. Federal obligations for other programs such as direct or guaranteed loans, and interest on the national debt, are excluded. Detail may not add to totals due to rounding.

Source: Government and Development Policy Section, Economic Research Service, U.S. Department of Agriculture. (Bradshaw and Blakley 1987:11-17).

levels ($3,192 vs. $2,478, respectively). By comparison, nonmetro counties received $1,845 per capita in FY 1978, as against $2,007 per capita for metro counties, and the nonmetro-metro differential in federal defense and space outlays was less than $300 per capita (Hendler and Reid 1980). Total federal spending that can be traced to counties increased slightly in real terms from FY 1978 to FY 1985. The composition of this funding, however, changed in two important respects. The proportion of military and space funding has increased significantly while nondefense funding decreased. Second, due to the tendency for military and space funding to go mainly to metropolitan counties, nonmetro counties now receive only about 70 percent of the per capita federal outlays that metro counties currently enjoy. Thus the status of rural development funding has been adversely affected not only by the selective dismantling of the welfare-state, but also by the rise of the "warfare state."

The Current Context of American Rural Development

The Rise and Fall of Rural America, 1965-1990

Undergirded by rapid economic growth and growing strength of organized labor and the Democratic Party in the 1960s, the U.S. government rapidly expanded its domestic spending programs. As with earlier social security legislation, these domestic spending programs were not strongly targeted—either to poor households or poor regions—and were implemented more as a Keynesian demand expansion and stabilization strategy than as a means to redistribute wealth and income. Nonetheless, as these Great Society programs were launched in the 1960s and continued under the three administrations of the 1970s, the socioeconomic condition of rural America exhibited unprecedented progress. Metropolitan-nonmetropolitan disparities in per capita incomes narrowed substantially from 1965 to 1969, and exhibited particularly dramatic convergence from 1969 to 1973. From 1969 to 1973, nonmetropolitan per capita incomes increased at an astounding rate of 5.9 percent per year, compared to 2.7 percent annually for metropolitan counties. The disparities began to widen very slightly in the period from 1973 to 1979, but by and large the federal domestic policies that led to improvement in the condition of rural America in the preceding years remained intact (albeit with some funding declines in real terms). These improvements in rural economic conditions, while they resulted in nonmetropolitan per capita incomes being only 78 percent of metropolitan county incomes at their peak, did nonetheless represent significant progress (Henry, et al. 1986; 1987). This period will no doubt be remembered for some time as the golden age of rural America.

Despite the clear overall improvements in the well-being of rural regions as a result of Great Society programs, several caveats deserve mention. First, overall economic expansion clearly was as (or more) important than domestic spending programs in stimulating rural development. Nevertheless, these spending programs, particularly those focused on infrastructure and services, were of decisive importance in enabling rural regions and communities to take advantage of the opportunities for economic growth. Second, the nonmetropolitan "deep" South, which has long had the highest incidence of persistent poverty, fared less well than did the somewhat less disadvantaged border-South region in access to Great Society funding. Third, the nonmetropolitan "Blackbelt" South exhibited little development even at the apex of the Great Society; the small improvements in aggregate levels of living observed there were probably more due to mass outmigration of the rural poor than to structural upgrading of the nonmetropolitan deep South economy. Fourth, the bulk of what is here taken to be "rural development spending" in the late 1960s and early 1970s was not labeled as such when spending programs were authorized. Little of this funding has been in the form of rural development programs per se. Federal spending in rural regions was derived from a myriad of programs—water pollution abatement, old-age assistance, occupational training, infrastructural development, and housing programs; health services subsidies; small business development and so on—that were implemented in metro and nonmetro counties alike. This pattern of federal policy and intervention essentially represented a "disguised" rural development policy—in essence, a disguised rural welfare-state—even though most of these programs were not premised on benefiting rural America.

The condition of rural America has changed dramatically since the late 1970s, principally as a result of two factors. First, as suggested earlier, successive Presidential administrations since the early 1980s have progressively dismantled major components of American social democracy that together constituted the heart of the country's rural development program (and which, among other things, contributed to reduced overall poverty rates and convergence of white and nonwhite incomes in the late 1960s and early 1970s). Second, the deepening global recession, which began in 1973-74 but which worsened in the early and mid-1980s, has served to undercut the fiscal basis of federal rural development efforts and has contributed to a nascent restructuring of the world economy that has potentially adverse consequences for the well-being of nonmetropolitan America. From 1979 to 1984 nonmetropolitan per capita incomes declined slightly in real terms (−0.1 percent annually), while metropolitan per capita incomes increased modestly (0.9 percent annually; Henry et al. 1986).

There are several features of rural development program successes in the 1960s and 1970s that deserve mention. One is to reiterate a point mentioned in passing several times earlier: the connection between what has historically been America's major rural development success story and the current phasing out of America's variant of social democracy. The U.S. variant largely took the form of combining broad, nontargeted domestic public investment, social services, and retirement/public assistance programs with Keynesian fiscal and monetary policy. The nontargeted nature and the absence of a "rural" identity of these programs may have been a blessing in disguise for rural development in two ways. First, since much of federal "rural development" spending was actually a patchwork of nontargeted programs that benefited both metropolitan and nonmetropolitan regions, rural America did not have to mobilize politically to receive access to these programs. Second, many of these programs took the form of grants to local units of government for the construction of infrastructure and operation of service facilities, which arguably led to longer term benefit than if these programs had been focused primarily on income redistribution.

A further aspect of federal rural development funding that is just now being appreciated is how the selective dismantling of the American welfare-state has affected rural development. This dismantling has been centered on the broad economic development and service delivery programs that accrued largely to *places and local organizations* (rather than to individuals; Hardy 1983). For example, the Presidential administrations in the 1980s have not appreciably reduced cash transfer programs to individuals (e.g., social security, medicare and medicaid, government employee retirement programs, food stamps, supplemental security income, aid to families with dependent children, and so on: King 1989). Government cash transfers remain very important to the economic base of rural America and have no doubt mitigated the dislocations caused by the dismantling of other aspects of the welfare-state. Retirement programs, especially social security and medicare, have become especially important to rural America as the rural population continues to age (Hirschl and Summers 1985). "Retirement counties" now have the highest levels of per capita income of all types of nonmetropolitan counties (Bender, et al. 1985). In addition, one out of every six nonmetropolitan counties derives 25 percent or more of its labor-proprietor income from federal, state, and local governmental payrolls; these counties, which generally had per capita incomes above the average for nonmetro counties, are referred to as "government counties" (Bender, et al. 1985).

Before returning to the theme of the historical and future role of the welfare-state in rural development, it is useful to identify three other factors that combined fortuitously to bolster the socioeconomic condition of rural America in the 1970s. One was the temporarily favorable situation of several raw materials industries, particularly agriculture, oil, coal, and other energy resources. Following the 1973-74 OPEC oil embargo and the later Iranian oil embargo, the energy sectors prospered handsomely. Spearheaded by rapid expansion of exports, American farmers experienced one of their most prosperous decades in American history. The agricultural sector benefited (albeit temporarily) in the form of rapid appreciation of land and other capital assets, through very low interest rates and through tax and trade policies that encouraged an agricultural investment boom.

The impact of the favorable circumstances of the primary materials sectors is indicated clearly by the differential rates of growth in per capita income among various categories of nonmetro counties from 1970 to 1980. Agricultural counties (Bender, et al. 1985) experienced particularly dramatic increases in per capita income in 1971-73 (a time of tightening world grain markets and the take-off of the 1970s export boom), and until 1979 continued to enjoy mean per capita incomes well above the average for nonmetro counties. Mining counties, which prior to 1970 had the lowest mean per capita incomes of all categories of nonmetro counties, experienced substantial increases in per capita incomes from 1970 to 1975 and stable per capita incomes until the end of the decade.

The fortunes of agricultural and mining counties, however, were to be dramatically reversed after 1981. Triggered by the deepening national and global recession, raw materials prices began to plummet. Many nonmetro energy extraction facilities were abandoned, and new exploration was virtually halted. The decline in agricultural exports beginning in 1981, combined with rapid increases in real interest rates, led to a deepening farm crisis and severe economic distress in agricultural counties. Per capita incomes of agricultural and mining counties began to decline rapidly after this point, contributing disproportionately to the overall decline in nonmetro real per capita incomes from 1979-84.

A second factor was the onset of national and global economic stagnation that began roughly at the time of the Arab oil embargo. Ironically, the emerging crisis of American industry and Keynesian economic policies in the 1970s proved to be a temporary boon for the rural economy. Sagging profit levels and the maturation of traditional industrial products through the "product life cycle" (Markusen 1985) led to capital mobility from metropolitan to nonmetropolitan places (and from "rustbelt" to the "sunbelt") in search of cheap labor (Falk and Lyson 1988). From 1969 to 1984 the nonmetro share of wage and salary manufacturing employment rose from 19 to 22 percent (Brown and Deavers 1987), even though the nonmetro share of the total U.S. population declined from 31 to 24 percent over this period (Wimberley 1986). Currently the proportion of the nonmetro labor force in manufacturing exceeds that of the metro labor force, and 40 percent of nonmetro residents live in manufacturing counties (Bender, et al. 1985). Brown and Deavers (1987) have referred to these changes as the "industrial transformation of the rural economy." But apparently because of the generally low wage scales paid by manufacturing firms in nonmetro counties, the rapid growth of nonmetropolitan manufacturing during the 1970s led to only a tiny increase in the per capita incomes of nonmetro manufacturing counties during the decade (Henry, et al. 1986; Skees and Swanson 1988). Triggered by stagnant productivity, the overvalued dollar, high real interest rates, and formidable competition from Third World (especially East Asian) firms, there was a rapid loss of low-wage industrial jobs as the 1980s unfolded. American firms facing profitability squeezes increasingly found nonmetro labor no longer cheap enough and began to shift their factories to Third World countries (Froebel, et al. 1980; Sanderson 1985).[7] Nonmetro counties, because of their disproportionate share of low-wage manufacturing jobs, were hurt most by the demise of America's traditional industrial base (Brown and Deavers 1987).

The third factor in the apparent renaissance of nonmetro America in the 1970s was the *population turnaround*—a temporary reversal of the longstanding historical tendency for metro areas to gain population at the expense of nonmetro counties through net migration. Whereas in 1965-69 nonmetro counties experienced a small net loss of population, they exhibited a 1.4 percent annual rate of population increase from 1973-79 (compared to 1.1 percent for metro counties: Henry, et al. 1986). Nonmetro population growth during this period likely had positive impacts in terms of stimulating employment, particularly in the trade and other service sectors.[8] More recent data show, however, that while nonmetro population growth still continues, these counties are now growing more slowly than their metropolitan counterparts (1.2 vs. 1.4 percent per year, respectively) due to the reappearance of net nonmetro-to-metro migration (Henry, et al. 1986). The likelihood is that nonmetro counties as a whole will no longer enjoy the disproportionate stimulus of net in-migration that they experienced in the preceding decade, even though some nonmetropolitan counties, especially those whose economies are based on government services and retirement locations, will continue to exhibit growth in population (Henry, et al. 1987).

In sum, we can now see that the many factors that contributed to improvement of living standards in nonmetro areas in the late 1960s and 1970s have been transformed or negated over the last decade. Moreover, these factors—especially the fortuitous combination of the "rural welfare-state," the prosperity of the primary materials sectors, and metro-to-nonmetro capital mobility in the initial phase of global economic stagnation during the 1970s—have generally received little attention in the mainstream rural development literature. In the early 1980s it was still conventional wisdom that the future of nonmetro America was bright—that ongoing trends "point to a convergence of nonmetro and metro sectors" (Hawley and Mazie 1983). The supersession of these social forces in the 1980s by more powerful forces was unanticipated and insufficiently appreciated.

Rural America in the Context of International Restructuring and Fiscal Crisis

One of the major implications of defining "rural" as we have done earlier is to call attention to the fact that American rural regions, because of their historical and contemporary rooting in primary production sectors, have intimate connections with the world economy and, in particular, to Third World development and underdevelopment. Thus primary raw materials, the principal commodities produced in rural America, tend to be those that have long been internationally traded and are the major focus of Third World production. Thus, rural regions in an advanced country will tend to be in actual or potential competition with Third World zones. Over the past 15 years, with the increasing tendency for industrial capital to be highly mobile in search of cheap labor, American rural regions have found themselves competing more directly with Third World countries for low-wage, low-skill industrial employment (Froebel, et al. 1980; Lyson 1988). Likewise, the increasingly international and market-oriented nature of the world food economy has subjected American food and feed grain producers to competition with a multitude of Third World countries seeking to expand exports in order to service their high debt loads.

Against a backdrop of rapid economic growth in Japan and in the Asian "gang of four" (Singapore, Hong Kong, Korea, and Taiwan) and apparent "economic recovery" in the U.S., it is not often appreciated that the world economy as a whole has been in a state of chronic stagnation since the early 1970s. For example, while aggregate GNP in the OECD countries increased by 5.1 percent annually in 1960-68 and 4.7 percent annually in 1968-73, the growth rate declined to 2.6 percent in 1973-79 and 2.2 percent in 1979-85. Aggregate growth in the OECD economies increased to about 2.8 percent per annum in 1986-87, but OECD anticipates another decline by the end of the decade (Greenhouse 1987). U.S. trends have closely paralleled those for the OECD countries as a whole. Nonetheless, current growth rates are clearly inferior to those which prevailed for nearly three decades after World War II. Further, despite the rapidly rising fortunes of the Asian NICs (newly-industrializing countries) and a handful of other late-industrializing countries, most of the remainder of the Third World remains mired in a crisis of high external debt, balance of payments problems, declining real incomes, and capital flight.

Chronic global economic stagnation, albeit highly selective and differentiated in its incidence and impacts, has come to be the major parameter affecting the prospects for rural development in the U.S. and elsewhere in the developed world. We have already discussed one of the most crucial ways in which chronic stagnation has affected American rural development. A second way in which stagnation has begun to affect rural America has been by setting in motion a prolonged phase of global industrial restructuring (Buttel and Gillespie 1988). Some of the more important implications of international restructuring for rural America are indicated by placing the rise and fall of rural America in the historical context of economic policy.

The heyday of American rural development occurred in a distinctive political-economic context of rapid national and global growth. The OECD countries were characterized by the political-economic logic of linking mass production with mass consumption. A triad of institutions—collective bargaining, Keynesian economic policies, and the welfare-state and, in some European countries, corporatist systems of wage determination—ensured rapid growth in demand for manufactured goods, sustained high profit levels, enabled wage increases in tandem with productivity growth, and yielded essentially full employment. Third World countries had manageable debts and many exhibited rapid economic growth, providing growing markets for OECD exports. Third World development strategies continued to revolve around import substitution so that the low-income countries were not yet major competitors in manufactured goods. The U.S. was the world's dominant economic power, and U.S. economic policy could stimulate the global economy alone.

These conditions were to change dramatically in the 1970s. Triggered by massive inflation owing to the Arab oil embargo and the effects of the monetization of U.S. government debt associated with deficit financing of the Vietnam War, economic stagnation dominated the economy. This was followed in the 1980s by a period of reduced inflation, but with anemic and/or socially unequal GNP growth. Other factors that pushed the world economy into stagnation include: (1) the technological maturation, productivity stagnation, and declining profitability of the major industries that undergirded post-World War II growth (chemicals, plastics, autos, petroleum, and electronics) (Roobeek 1987); (2) the monetary imbalances caused by the massive diversion of American dollars to the OPEC countries and their "recycling" through Eurobanks and off-shore financial institutions to Third World countries; (3) the increased emphasis of Third World economic policy on exports—particularly of manufactured goods, food and feed grains, agroindustrial inputs, and luxury food commodities—in order to service loans and diversify their economies, providing competition for OECD producers; and, (4) the increased internationalization of the world economy, led by off-shore financial institutions and global capital markets, which preempted much of the autonomy of national governments in making economic policy (Lipietz 1987).

Rural Policy Implications of Global Economic Stagnation, Fiscal Crisis, and the New International Division of Labor

Important for understanding the implications of global economic changes for American rural policy is that the factors that have undermined the "rural welfare-state" and have caused rural economic dislocation are not merely cyclical in nature. Rather, these factors appear to reflect a fundamental disintegration of the political-economic arrangements that undergirded post-War expansion and rural-urban convergence. Gordon, et al. (1982) and others have referred to these arrangements as the "social structure of accumulation." The dominant political-economic institutions of post-War expansion—collective bargaining, Keynesian economic management, and the welfare-state —are undergoing irreversible eclipse in the dominant OECD countries (Lipietz 1987). Collective bargaining between capital and labor has been progressively undermined by the declining share of the industrial working classes in the OECD countries' class structures, by the declining political power of the labor movement, and by increasing capital mobility to Third World countries. Keynesian economic policies have been rendered ineffective by fiscal crises and the fact that, with an increasingly global economy, demand stimulation and its economic benefits can no longer be confined within national borders. The welfare-state has also fallen victim to fiscal crises. When and if the world economy exhibits a renewed pattern of rapid accumulation and per capita income growth, the political-economic institutions that undergird this expansion will likely be far different than those of the post-War era.

The specific outlines of the new social structure of accumulation that will buttress a renewed cycle of expansion are by no means clear. Nonetheless, there is emerging agreement (see for example, Lipietz 1987; Gordon, et al. 1982; Roobeek 1987; Castells and Henderson 1987; Hausermann and Kramer-Badoni 1989) that new information technology industries will be among the major components. The world economy of the future will likely be based on "high-technology" production techniques and new products. To the degree that economic dominance in the world economy is associated with successful international competition in high-technology innovation, states will be unwilling to leave their countries' positions in high-technology to the vagaries of the market and private entrepreneurship. Thus research and development (R&D) and investment in the new technologies will be heavily shaped by state subsidies and other forms of state intervention such as military contracting, state R&D corporations, and negotiated interstate trade in high-technology products. The engines of capital accumulation in the new international division of labor will be the high-technology industries and the high-technology-related "information society" sector. The information sector will become increasingly important in consumption of high-technology products and in establishing the conditions (e.g., through credit, insurance) for high-technology production.

Though there is likely to be increased concentration in the ownership of industrial capital, this may be accompanied by the deconcentration of industrial locations, smaller factories, and complex patterns of subcontracting, often directed toward small firms (Piore and Sabel 1984; Cohen and Zysman 1987). Production will be increasingly geared toward highly differentiated consumer lifestyles, rather than toward mass consumption, because of more flexible production techniques and growing economic inequality. There will also be continued expansion of the "hidden" economy—production organized under extra-legal or illegal auspices (Portes, et al. 1989; Therborn 1986). The hidden economy will expand as an "adaptive strategy" of workers to the decreasing coverage of the welfare-state, and will essentially serve as a substitute for state employment-stimulation and welfare programs (Roobeek 1987).

The following would seem to be among the more important implications of this future transition for rural-regional policy in the U.S.

(1) Rural development progress of the magnitude achieved from the late 1960s to the mid-1970s will be seriously impeded by slow aggregate national and global growth and by state fiscal austerity. Slow, unstable aggregate growth tends to lead to greater dislocation and instability in nonmetro than in metro counties (Malley and Hady 1987). Therefore, rural development gains will be difficult to register until and unless there is expanded national and global accumulation.

(2) Slow, unstable growth has undermined the fiscal basis of the welfare-state which has historically been the bulwark of rural development progress in the advanced countries by bolstering rural infrastructure and services, providing old-age assistance and unemployment insurance, and placing a floor under wages. The phasing back of many welfare-state and associated domestic spending programs will undermine the traditional means by which rural improvement has been achieved. New formulas for national rural development policy will be necessary. The most likely strategy will be to focus government spending on infrastructural improvement[9] and education, though such strategies have obvious limits.

(3) Depressed raw materials sectors and pronounced capital mobility have brought rural America into more direct competition with developing countries, especially in mining, agriculture, and manufacturing. Nonmetro counties are not likely to fare well in international competition with Third World counterparts that enjoy cheaper land and labor. Technological and managerial strategies for "increased competitiveness"

of rural America's farms, mines, and factories will be ineffective in restoring nonmetro employment and income levels. Rural development strategy will likely need to hinge on *insulating* rural America from international competition through, for example, selective protectionism, support for worker or community enterprise ownership, or national policies to encourage the flow of capital into rural areas (Green and McNamara 1988).

(4) While the emergent world economy has clearly been characterized by "internationalization" and the decreasing importance of national economies as self-contained units, there are also political limits to the free sway of global commodity markets. As Gilpin (1987) stresses, all of the major industrial powers have reasons to fear a complete internationalization of the world economy. Thus it is likely that the future will be some combination of internationalization of markets on one hand, and selective protectionism of politically powerful or "strategic" industries, interstate negotiation of trade, and regionalization of trade on the other. Many U.S. rural industries will continue to produce behind tariff walls and other nontariff barriers. Others will decline or disappear as a result of competition with cheap-labor zones and subsidized producers overseas. Rural America does not have a monolithic interest in protectionism, since some rural producers benefit from overseas market access. The evolving matrix of protectionism vs. internationalization will be pivotal in shaping the economic opportunities available to particular rural regions in the U.S. Likewise, several rural-based industries, such as grain and meat producers and textile firms, may play an important political role in shaping U.S. government trade policies.

(5) Rural America can expect to receive little benefit from the deployment of new "high-technologies." Nonmetro regions will be almost totally bypassed in R&D and initial commercialization of the information and new materials technologies and of biotechnology (Markusen 1985). The mass deployment of these new technologies is likely to accelerate labor displacement in the primary production sectors that are most important in nonmetro regions (Roobeek, 1987). At the mass production stage high-technology production facilities are likely to locate in low-wage Third World zones, as much of semiconductor and computer production has already done (Markusen, et al. 1986). The major exception to these generalizations may be with respect to biotechnology; the expansion of industrial bioprocessing will likely

stimulate demand for starches and lignocellulose materials, which could be a boon to the domestic agricultural and forestry sectors (Buttel 1987). Other than increased demand for biotechnology feedstocks, the only bright spot for nonmetropolitan America in high-technology development is that many colleges and universities, which might serve as incubators for high-technology investments, are located in small towns and rural areas.

(6) The hidden economy, which has been researched mainly in large urban places close to major streams of immigrant labor, is likely to spread to the low-wage zones of nonmetro America. These production arrangements will be a viable adaptive strategy for many rural workers, but will reinforce a productive structure with little possibility of dynamism (Portes, et al. 1989). Little is known, however, about the current role of the hidden economy in U.S. nonmetro regions, though some have suggested that this type of production has long played a major role and has exhibited a recent surge in the form of industrial "home work."

(7) Rural America will be adversely affected as long as the militarization of the federal budget and the strongly military cast of high-technology development remain in effect. Military and space outlays tend to go disproportionately to metro counties. Also, military programs have largely been financed through cutbacks of domestic spending programs (many of which are rural-development related) as well as through federal borrowing and deficit spending. Redressing the military-domestic balance of federal spending would contribute to rural development.

(8) Should the dismantling of the welfare-state in the U.S. become extended to old-age assistance programs, especially social security, the impacts on rural America would be particularly devastating. Preserving old-age assistance programs is integral to the economic future of rural America.

(9) There will be an increased need for rural people to mobilize to salvage federal domestic programs which benefit nonmetro America. Mobilization of this sort has two major limits, however. First, the nonmetro population is a declining proportion of the total U.S. population, and each time legislative boundaries are redrawn the political clout of rural America declines. Second, rural residents have traditionally been politically conservative, and the federal policy measures

outlined above that may be necessary for rural improvement have not traditionally received strong support among the nonmetro electorate.

(10) State and local policy will become more important in achieving rural development because of the likelihood of a declining federal role, even as the leverage of local policy declines in the face of an increasingly internationalized world economy. Subnational rural development policy must transcend the traditional emphasis on attracting new manufacturing industry. New directions, such as encouraging reinvestment by financial institutions in local communities, placing more emphasis on capturing federal and state infrastructural development and service delivery funds, and on creating service sector employment (Green and McNamara 1988) are needed.

Conclusion

This chapter sought to accomplish a number of objectives in relation to rural development and rural policy. A historical analysis of rural development policy was presented which has emphasized that the traditional means of rural development have been integrally related to the rise of the modern welfare-state. Specifically, the fiscal basis for achieving convergence of nonmetro and metro incomes and living standards has primarily been that of federal domestic spending programs, most of which were neither labeled as "rural development" nor targeted for nonmetropolitan regions. It has also been demonstrated that American rural development policy has been distinctive by western standards and that the origins of our unique rural development policies can be found in the limited development and the nonredistributive nature of the American welfare-state. Further, the selective dismantlement of the American welfare-state, which began in the late 1970s but which has been rapidly accelerated in the 1980s, has begun to undermine rural development progress and traditional rural development policy. In addition to the diminution of rural-development-related federal domestic spending, other components of the early 1970s renaissance of rural America—the agricultural export boom, tight raw materials markets, and the population turnaround—have ceased to exist.

Finally, some of the more important parameters of rural development policy in the future have been identified. Particular emphasis has been given to: (1) the expected continuation of state fiscal austerity and the decline of the welfare-state, (2) the likelihood of increased competition between low-income (rural) regions in the advanced countries and low-income countries (the Third World), and (3) the likely outlines of a new social structure of accumulation. Each of these factors suggests the need for entirely new strategies to bolster the socioeconomic position of nonmetropolitan America. The suggestions for new national rural policy directions are modest and limited, as is the knowledge base on how rural development has been related to the historical and contemporary evolution of the dominant political-economic institutions in the western countries. Nonetheless, the scope of analysis opened in this chapter has promise for a more detailed elaboration of the prospects and limits of alternative rural development policies for the future.

Notes

1. This chapter has benefitted from the comments of Kenneth Pigg, Thomas A. Lyson, David Brown, Thomas Hirschl, Gary Green and Louis Swanson.

2. It is typically taken as common knowledge that rural areas prior to the twentieth century were largely agricultural in composition. This, in our view, is a simplistic, empirically untenable position deriving from evolutionary rural-urban continuum reasoning. Rural communities prior to and during the early stages of the industrial revolution, in fact, tended to be characterized by high levels of artisinal and other nonfarm forms of production. Also, many major American cities, such as Chicago, were strongly agricultural in nature because the bulk of their industries were based on providing inputs to farmers and processing agricultural outputs.

3. In this chapter we will use the expressions rural and nonmetro synonymously. It should also be stressed at the outset that rural America is *strikingly diverse* and that many regions of nonmetro America—particularly those with large urban places and those outside of the South—are socioeconomically privileged (Killian and Hady 1987). These relatively privileged, urban-like nonmetro zones will not generally be of concern here. We will focus primarily on the *more remote, less densely-settled, socioeconomically disadvantaged rural regions,* such as those that predominate in much of the South and portions of the western Corn Belt, Great Plains, Southwest, Mountain West and Upper New England.

4. See Friedmann and Alonso (1975) for an especially comprehensive collection of papers on regional problems and policies in a wide range of world nations, including state-socialist countries.

5. Orloff and Skocpol (1984), however, have noted that there were rudiments of welfare-state policies in the U.S. before passage of the Social Security Act. These policies included civil war pensions, which for a time served as a functional equivalent for old-age pensions, as well as workers' compensation and mothers' pensions programs in a number of states.

6. It should be noted, of course, that state and local governments have long attempted to influence industrial location, mainly by competing with other states and localities through providing tax, service, and infrastructural subsidies and via wage rates. Though national rural policy is emphasized here, subnational policies are of considerable importance.

7. The notion of the "new international division of labor" (Froebel, et al. 1980), while it has helped to capture important aspects of international restructuring, can nonetheless be said to oversimplify these dynamics. In particular, this notion primarily stresses the mobility of traditional industrial capital (e.g., textiles, electronics) to the Third World and has given little attention to the role of the new high-technology industries and to the mobility of money capital (Jenkins 1984; see also the articles in Gottdiener and Komninos 1989).

8. See McGranahan (1987) for a discussion of the importance of population growth in contributing to growth in the construction and service sectors of the nonmetro economy.

9. There must, however, be a shift in infrastructural priorities, i.e., away from roads and sewers to the telecommunication infrastructure necessary for full rural integration into the "information society" and the service economy.

References

Bender, L. D., and others. 1985. *The Diverse Social and Economic Structure of Nonmetropolitan America.* RDRR-4. Washington, DC: Economic Research Service, U.S. Department of Agriculture.

Billings, D. B. 1979. *Planters and the Making of a "New South."* Chapel Hill: University of North Carolina Press.

_____ 1988. "The rural South in crisis: a historical perspective," in L. B. Beaulieu (ed.), *The Rural South in Crisis.* Pp. 13-29. Boulder, CO: Westview Press.

Bradshaw, T. K., Jr., and E. J. Blakely. 1987. "Unanticipated consequences of government programs on rural economic development," in *Rural Economic Development in the 1980s*. Pp. 11/1-11/17. Washington, DC: Economic Research Service, U.S. Department of Agriculture.

Brown, D. L., and K. L. Deavers. 1987. "Rural change and the rural economic policy agenda for the 1980s." *in Rural Economic Development in the 1980s*. Pp. 1/1-1/31. Washington, DC: Economic Research Service, U.S. Department of Agriculture.

Buttel, F. H. 1987. "Biotech tradeoffs in the rural economy." *Rural Development Perspectives*. 3: 11-15.

Buttel, F.H. and G. W. Gillespie, Jr. 1988. "The changing bases of rural development: international restructuring, disguised institutions, and the future of rural America." Unpublished manuscript, Department of Rural Sociology, Cornell University.

Castells, M., and J. Henderson. 1987. "Techno-economic restructuring, socio-political processes and spatial transformation: a global perspective." in J. Henderson and M. Castells (eds.), *Global Restructuring and Territorial Development*. Pp. 1-17. Beverly Hills, CA: Sage.

Cohen, S. S., and J. Zysman. 1987. *Manufacturing Matters*. New York: Basic Books.

Falk, W. W., and T. A. Lyson. 1988. *High Tech, Low Tech, No Tech*. Albany: State University of New York Press.

Friedmann, J., and W. Alonso (eds.). 1975. *Regional Policy*. Cambridge: MIT Press.

Froebel, F., J. Heinrichs, and O. Kreye. 1980. *The New International Division of Labour*. Cambridge: Cambridge University Press.

Gilpin, R. 1987. *The Political Economy of International Relations*. Princeton: Princeton University Press.

Gordon, D. A., R. Edwards, and M. Reich. 1982. *Segmented Work, Divided Workers*. New York: Cambridge University Press.

Gottdiener, M., and N. Komninos, eds. 1989. *Capitalist Development and Crisis Theory*. London: Macmillan.

Green, G. P., and K. T. McNamara. 1988. "Traditional and nontraditional opportunities and alternatives for local economic development." in L. B. Beaulieu (ed.), *The Rural South in Crisis*. Pp. 288-303. Boulder, CO: Westview Press.

Greenhouse, S. 1987. "When the world's growth slows." *New York Times* (27 December, Section 3):1, 24.

Hansen, Niles M. 1970. *Rural Poverty and the Urban Crisis*. Bloomington, IN: Indiana University Press.

Hardy, D. F. II. 1983. "Federal assistance for rural development: the train that passed in the night?" *The Rural Sociologist* 3: 392-398.

Hausermann, H., and T. Kramer-Badoni. 1989. "The change of regional inequality in the Federal Republic of Germany." in M. Gottdiener and N. Komninos (eds.), *Capitalist Development and Crisis Theory*. Pp. 331-347. London: MacMillan.

Hawley, A. H., and S. M. Mazie. 1983. "An overview." in A. H. Hawley and S. M. Mazie (eds.), *Nonmetropolitan America in Transition*. Pp. 3-23. Chapel Hill: University of North Carolina Press.

Hendler, C. I., and J. N. Reid. 1980. *Federal Outlays in Fiscal 1978: A Comparison of Metropolitan and Nonmetropolitan Areas*. Rural Development Research Report No. 25. Washington, DC: Economics, Statistics, and Cooperatives Service, U.S. Department of Agriculture.

Henry, M., M. Drabenstott, and L. Gibson. 1986. "A changing rural America." *Economic Review* 71: 23-41.

Henry, M. Drabenstott, and L. Gibson. 1987. "Rural growth slows down." *Rural Development Perspectives* 3: 25-30.

Hirschl, T. A., and G. F. Summers. 1985. "Shifts in rural income: the implications of unearned income for rural community development." *Research in Rural Sociology and Development* 2: 127-141.

Holland, S. 1976a. *Capital Against the Regions*. New York: St. Martin's Press.

_____. 1976b. *The Regional Question*. New York: St.Martin's Press.

Jenkins, R. 1984. "Divisions over the international division of labor." *Capitaland Class* 22: 28-57.

Killian, M. S., and T. F. Hady. 1987. "The performance of rural labor markets." in *Rural Economic Development in the 1980's*. Pp. 8/1-8/23. Washington, DC: Economic Research Service, U.S. Department of Agriculture.

King, D. 1989. "Economic crisis and welfare state recommodification: a comparative analysis of the United States and Great England." in M. Gottdiener and N. Komninos (eds.), *Capitalist Development and Crisis Theory*. Pp. 237-260. London: MacMillan.

Levine, R. F. 1988. *Class Struggle and the New Deal*. Lawrence: University Press of Kansas.

Lipietz, A. 1987. *Mirages and Miracles: The Crises of Global Fordism*. London: Verso.

Lyson, T. A. 1988. "Economic development in the rural South: an uneven past—an uncertain future." in L. B. Beaulieu (ed.), *The Rural South in Crisis*. Pp. 265-275. Boulder, CO: Westview Press.

_____. 1989. *Two Sides to the Sunbelt*. Westport, CT: Greenwood Press.

Malley, J. R., and T. F. Hady. 1987. "The impact of macroeconomic policies on rural employment." in *Rural Economic Development in the 1980s*. Pp. 10/1-10/19. Washington, DC: Economic Research Service, U.S. Department of Agriculture.

Markusen, A. R. 1985. *Profit Cycles, Oligopoly, and Regional Development.* Cambridge: MIT Press.

Markusen, A.R., P. Hall, and A. Glasmeier. 1986. *High Tech America.* Boston: Allen and Unwin.

McGranahan, D. A. 1987. "The role of rural workers in the national economy." in *Rural Economic Development in the 1980s*. Pp. 2/1-2/3. Washington, DC: Economic Research Service, U.S. Department of Agriculture.

MacLennan, M. C., and D. J. Robertson. 1969. "Regional policy in the United Kingdom." in E. A. G. Robinson (ed.), *Backward Areas in Advanced Countries*. Pp. 37-51. London: MacMillan.

Orloff, A. S., and T. Skocpol. 1984. "Why not equal protection? explaining the politics of public social spending in England, 1900-1911, and the United States, 1880s-1920." *American Sociological Review* 49: 726-750.

Piore, M. J., and C. F. Sabel. 1984. *The Second Industrial Divide.* New York: Basic Books.

Portes, A., M. Castells, and L. A. Benton, eds. 1989. *The Informal Economy.* Baltimore: Johns Hopkins University Press.

Przeworski, A. 1985. *Capitalism and Social Democracy.* New York: Cambridge University Press.

Przeworski, A. and J. Sprague. 1986. *Paper Stones: A History of Electoral Socialism.* Chicago: University of Chicago Press.

Rasmussen, W. D. 1985. "90 Years of rural development programs." *Rural Development Perspectives* 1: 6-7.

_____. 1986. "Agricultural and rural policy: a historical note." *New Dimensions in Rural Policy.* Pp. 32-38. Washington, DC: Joint Economic Committee, U.S. Congress.

Roobeek, A. J. M. 1987. "The crisis in fordism and the rise of a new technological paradigm." *Futures* 19: 129-154.

Quadagno, J. S. 1984. "Welfare capitalism and the Social Security Act of 1935." *American Sociological Review* 49: 632-647.

Sanderson, S. (ed.). 1985. *The Americas in the New International Division of Labor.* New York: Holmes and Meier.

Skees, J. R., and L. E. Swanson. 1988. "Farm structure and local society well-being in the South." in L. B. Beaulieu (ed.), *The Rural South in Crisis.* Pp. 141-157. Boulder, CO: Westview Press.

Skowronek, S. 1982. *Building a New American State.* New York: Cambridge University Press.

Stephens, J. D. 1979. *The Transition from Capitalism to Socialism.* London: Macmillan.

Therborn, G. 1986. *Why Some Peoples Are More Unemployed Than Others.* London: Verso.

Wilensky, H. L. 1975. *The Welfare State and Equality.* Berkeley: University of California Press.

Williamson, J. G. 1975. "Regional inequality and the process of national development: a description of the patterns." in J. Friedmann and W. Alonso (eds.), *Regional Policy.* Pp. 158-200. Cambridge: MIT Press.

Wimberley, R. C. 1986. "Agricultural and rural transition." *New Dimensions in Rural Policy.* Pp. 39-45. Washington, DC: Joint Economic Committee, U.S. Congress.

3

The Benefits of Space
and the Cost of Distance[1]

Emery N. Castle

The rural-urban distinction relies on an arbitrary line of demarcation. Because human density is the distinguishing characteristic between that which is urban and that which is rural, a continuum rather than a distinct line of demarcation is involved. A general formulation of rural development or rural revitalization issues should give explicit attention to population density with recognition that the economic welfare of the more sparsely populated areas is linked with, and usually dependent upon, economic activity in those areas that are more densely populated. The rural areas that are the most prosperous are those that have close economic links with more densely populated areas, frequently large urban centers.

Greater population density, of course, does not automatically lead to more socially desirable results. Severe social maladjustments frequently occur at the extremes—in the inner cities and in the more isolated areas. Nor does such an argument necessarily deny that there may be undesirable side effects (negative externalities) associated with the concentration of population. Many nations have been convinced of this and have attempted, without notable success, to reduce the concentration of people (Mills n.d.).

There may well be a lack of overall system symmetry in the costs and benefits of decisions when people decide to live in highly concentrated areas. The perceived benefits of a particular location decision may accrue largely to the individual making that decision, but the costs of added density may be spread unevenly over the larger group. Higher income people may be better able to protect themselves from low quality air, crime, and other undesirable side effects stemming from high concentrations of people. And it is higher income people who often make decisions affecting the location of others. Public agencies also may fail to consider the social cost of concentrated populations in their decisions because the per unit costs of providing certain public services— some waste disposal activities, public transportation, and roads—decline as density increases.

If density of population is a continuum and if the less densely populated areas are dependent on the more densely populated areas for the generation of economic activity, it may be asked whether it is useful to consider "rural development" or "rural revitalization" as distinct from development generally. The answer is not self-evident, at least to me. Classifications based on arbitrary lines of demarcation may create mischief both in conceptual as well as in practical work, but it is also important to deal with manageable problems. For certain purposes it may be useful to distinguish between places that are sparsely settled and those that are densely settled. "Urban studies" and "urban economics" have yielded insights regarding the problems of metropolitan areas. Nothing comparable exists that might be labeled "rural studies." If it is discovered that population density is either not an important, relevant, or operational variable, it should be admitted and made known so that others need not travel the same unproductive path. But at this time such a conclusion is not warranted.

The application of economic reasoning to this formulation of rural issues leads to the title of this chapter—the benefits of space and the cost of distance. What is the economic function performed by space and population sparsity? Do the economic benefits of space change as development occurs and incomes improve? If so, this needs to be appreciated as people in areas of sparse population look to the future. Even as space may enter some production and consumption processes in a positive way, overcoming distance always involves a cost. Clearly the linkages provided by transportation and communication between the less and more sparsely populated areas are of crucial importance in this connection. Changes in the cost and availability of these services will affect the economic and social relations between and among regions.

Location economics has received considerable attention by those working in the discipline of economics; a review of this body of literature may be found in a recent article by Stevens (1985). This literature has been characterized by both theoretical developments as well as empirical investigations, but some contend this literature has not made major contributions to the formation of public policy. In his exhaustive study of the U.S. urban system, Edgar Dunn (1981, 1983) suggests two major explanations for this state of affairs. One is that the theoretical formulations do not adequately reflect the dynamics of technical change—space and distance are not static concepts in a social setting. The other is that the data available for the analysis of such problems are often inadequate. Definitions and classifications used for data collections in one social setting become obsolete when the social setting changes. For example, what constitutes a "central place" in one time period may not be a "central place" two decades later, even though it remains a major population center.

The Benefits of Space

Traditional farming and forestry activities have been space using, and those who obtained their livelihood from such activities typically have been residents of sparsely populated areas. For quite logical reasons, the more intensive of these enterprises, for example vegetable production, has been located closer to the urban or metropolitan center than those less intensive. Because land costs are higher near such centers, those farming and forestry activities that use less land per unit of output have an advantage. But this traditional view must now be modified greatly if it is to be in accordance with reality. The traditional extractive industries are no longer dominant economic activities in many rural or nonmetropolitan areas. On the other hand, a significant percentage of the income and employment from some of these extractive industries is generated within metropolitan areas (Weber, Castle, and Shriver 1987). Technical change has been of the nature that some extractive industry activities more nearly resemble manufacturing than traditional farming or forestry. Furthermore, environmental compatibility is becoming increasingly important in the location of extractive activity. For example, poultry production located near residential areas results in significant incompatibilities—the generation of odors and the attraction of insects. Recent research by Mills and Chodes (1988) has shown that occupational differences between the metropolitan and nonmetropolitan areas are not significant. But it does not necessarily follow that density of population is irrelevant if treated as a continuous rather than a discrete variable.

As income rises and the cost of distance is lowered, either in the movement of people and goods (transportation) or in the transmission of information (communication), the benefits of space and cost of distance will change. With increases in income, people have greater capacity to select those space attributes they prefer. Some may elect to spend some of their lives in densely populated areas to take advantage of those cultural amenities that are typically available only where density of population exists. Higher incomes may also permit them, at least partially, to protect themselves against low quality air and the kinds of crime that tends to be associated with population density. Others may view space, at least a certain amount of space, as desirable for residential purposes and choose the suburbs or a rural residence. And, of course, an increasing number are opting for a combination and spend part of each year or a part of their lives in densely as well as in sparsely populated areas. Just as fresh fruit and vegetables can now be consumed throughout the year, technical change and improved incomes permit many to "consume" the varying combinations of space attributes that are to their liking.

The way space enters production decisions also varies with the passage of time. Technical change modifies the proportion of labor, land, capital and, entrepreneurship. In agriculture, technical change generally has been land saving.

The Cost of Distance

Just as space is necessary for certain production and consumption activities, overcoming distance entails cost. A distinction needs to be made between geographic and economic distance. Our economic and social development has been such that the financial cost associated with overcoming space is no longer a linear function of geographic distance, if it ever was. It typically costs less to fly from one large urban center to another than it does from a large urban center to a hinterland city of less geographic distance. And, of course, financial outlay for transportation may not be the major economic cost of overcoming distance because the value of human time is not included. T.W. Schultz has taught us that the value of human time increases as economic progress occurs. When the cost of human time is included, the large urban centers may be even closer relatively than when financial outlays alone are considered. Thus, rapid transit by land and air and well-established communication networks can do a great deal to reduce the economic cost of geographic distance because they permit us to economize on the use of human time.

Historically, many U.S. institutions had the effect of lowering the cost of geographic distance. Cheap land and free land (land grants and the Homestead Act) encouraged the settlement of land. One of the objectives of the Reclamation Act was the creation of opportunity in space-using activities. Many state and local level public policies have had comparable impacts and effects. A comprehensive network of rural roads exists in most parts of the country, and rural mail service is provided for remote settlers. Clearly, conditions have changed. Until the early 1970s growth occurred more rapidly in areas of dense, not sparse, population. And there has been institutional adjustment. The land use legislation of the 1970s at the state level generally had the preservation of land for agriculture and other less intensive use as one of its objectives. There was recognition that the cost of public services tended to decline with density. Rural land use zoning appeared to serve the dual objectives of protecting the resource base for agriculture and forestry and reducing the cost of certain public services, as well.

There has been substantial literature on the "rural-urban turnaround" phenomenon of the 1970s. Although it would not serve the objectives of this paper to provide an exhaustive review of this material, one paper deserves special mention. Carlino (1985) has argued that the growth of rural areas during this period was led by growth in rural manufacturing that he attributes to technical change affecting transportation and communication. No doubt such technologies will continue to be developed, and new applications will be found for the technologies that exist, with the net effect that the economic cost of distance will be further reduced. This will have the effect of increasing returns to rural labor and land.

Other things being equal, a reduction in the real cost of economic distance will improve the economic prosperity of a less densely populated area. In this way, the less densely populated region can improve its terms of trade with those of greater density, although this is not necessarily a zero-sum game. If the relative efficiency of any area can be improved, the prospect exists for greater aggregate income.

How might this be accomplished? Most, of course, will happen because of private sector decisions. Private sector industries, entrepreneurs, and individual job seekers and holders, as well as consumers, adjust to new realities, sometimes with remarkable speed. But public policies do affect the real cost of economic distance as well, and deregulation of transportation and communication should be viewed from this vantage point. If there are externalities associated with density that are not reflected in those costs that affect individual decisions (a proposition that needs examination), and if there are social benefits associated with closer linkages among areas of varying population density, deregulated transportation and communication industries may not always be in the public interest even though aggregate transportation costs in the short run are reduced.

From the standpoint of rural development strategy, it may make sense to distinguish between the cost of economic distance within the rural area and the cost of economic distance between the area itself and other external places. As noted, lowering the cost of external linkages is favorable to economic development of an area. The economic cost of overcoming geographic distance within an area is another matter.

Traditional local area policies have reduced the cost of economic distance to the more sparsely settled outlying areas. Roads, mail service, and other public utilities have been subsidized in various ways, including the use of average, as contrasted to marginal, cost pricing for such services. In recent years some communities have attempted to change these policies. Antigrowth sentiments, public finance considerations, and the preservation of land for agricultural and other space-using purposes have been among the reasons.

Policy Implications

Numerous public policy implications flow from the systematic consideration of space and distance in rural development. The most obvious, perhaps, is the changed political power base from which rural people operate. The rural areas are so diverse that it is difficult for them to make their political power felt on the basis of their "ruralness" even though special interest groups within the rural areas, for example farmers, have organized and have been politically potent. A coalition of rural special interests is improbable, and even if one did come into existence, it would be unlikely to develop a comprehensive rural development policy. It is to be expected there will be a correlation between political power and density of population, with the more sparsely populated areas being at a disadvantage.

For the above reason, as well as others, development policies for the less sparsely populated areas are likely to become increasingly decentralized. Clearly there is a trend toward a greater role for state and local, relative to the federal, government even though many local and state government initiatives have not been notably successful. Nevertheless, there are policy options that are attractive for some areas related to fundamental considerations of space and distance as set forth at the outset of this paper. Two sets of issues emerge as important in this respect. I have chosen to label one "non-traditional rural area goods and services" and the other "resource mobility and adaptability."

Nontraditional Rural Area Goods and Services

As used in this paper, "nontraditional" means goods and services which have not been produced recently by a particular rural area; a nontraditional good or service in one region may be a traditional one for another. However, if rural economic change is to benefit rural areas generally, it cannot consist of increasing income and employment in one area by attracting them away from another, unless the resulting output can be produced more efficiently. Therefore, those nontraditional rural goods and services that will serve rural development objectives will be those that stem from change in society generally. Two major sources of change can be identified as being of major importance. One are those technical changes in transportation and communication that affect the cost of distance. The other is greater affluence in the society. As a society becomes more affluent, its members derive an increasing percentage of their satisfaction from those goods and services that enhance the quality of life (Castle 1981). Examples of nontraditional goods and services include rural residences, outdoor recreation, and waste disposal.

An important part of rural development strategy is to make the rural areas attractive as places to live. Place of residence no longer needs be near the place of principal occupation for a large part of the lives of many people. Footloose businesses may locate where they believe their employees or executives will be happy. To the extent that transportation and communication permit, residence and place of occupation may be separated by considerable distance. In addition, transfer payments, both on a per capita basis as well as a percentage of total income, have been increasing. As a percent of total income, transfer payments are higher for nonmetropolitan (17.8 percent) than for metropolitan-counties (13.04 percent) (Smith, Wills, and Weber 1987). Thus, the attraction of older people to rural areas becomes an important consideration for some rural areas. Many retirees have income stability if not high income, and this underwrites the demand for services of a particular kind. "Footloose consumers" need to be given attention as well as "footloose industries."

Two examples make the above paragraph less abstract. While Cummings Engine cannot be said to have located in Columbus, Indiana, because of quality of life considerations, quality of life considerations for their employees was a major factor in bringing outstanding architecture to that city. After World War II the company became concerned about the adequacy of public facilities, especially schools. Cummings entered into an arrangement with the local government and agreed to assist in bringing outstanding architects to Columbus for school design. One thing has lead to another, and architects now compete to design buildings in Columbus. Outstanding architecture can now be enjoyed in this small midwestern city, far from the urban centers of the nation. The other example pertains to Ashland, Oregon, which is the home of Southern Oregon College. Its main claim to fame is the Shakespearean festivals held at the college each year where, I am told, Shakespeare is done better than at any other place in the West. A number of airline pilots have chosen to make their homes in Ashland. Medford, Oregon, a few miles from Ashland, has an airport served by commercial airlines with nonstop service to San Francisco, Portland, and Seattle. In this case, several hundred miles separate place of residence and place of occupation because of the quality of life provided by the Ashland community and because of transportation.

The natural environment also may make a major contribution to the quality of life in many rural areas. It is a subject so complex and with so many ramifications that one almost despairs of dealing with it in a few paragraphs. The traditional attitude of the rural resident toward the natural environment has been one of multiple use. Traditionally, their livelihood has depended on the use of natural resources for food and fiber production or on some other form of natural resource extraction. But the out-of-doors has also provided entertainment and beauty for the rural resident. Hunting, fishing, hiking, and the observation of nature have always been sources of wonder, joy, and satisfaction for rural residents. Given this background, the annoyance of some farmers and foresters is understandable when they are assumed to be hostile to ecology and the natural environment.

Modern technology has, however, changed the traditional conditions of natural resource use. For example, hybrid seeds, fertilizers, chemical pesticides and machinery from outside the rural ecosystem have had profound environmental impacts. Understandably many now view farming, mining, and timber production as ecologically undesirable because these industries intervene in natural systems in a major way. But many traditionally rural residents simply cannot accept such a point of view. It is foreign to their traditions; their jobs and their businesses have depended on natural resource extraction and use.

One of the unfortunate features of U.S. environmental policy is that it has evolved into a confrontation of these two viewpoints, with political power too frequently deciding which view will prevail. Those interested in rural economic development need to assist in the development of a contemporary philosophy of multiple natural resource use. Natural resources need to be viewed in terms of what they contribute to the quality of life, as well as to the production of natural resource commodities. The importance of natural resources to the understanding of natural processes, outdoor recreation, and the provision of space and scenery may be just as important to the welfare of some rural areas as is the production of food, fiber, minerals, and energy. The need is to isolate those natural resource characteristics that contribute to the quality of life, as well as traditional production processes, and then develop compatible multiple use patterns.

Nontraditional products may be illustrated further by a consideration of the disposal of residuals. Nothing is more likely to raise the ire of rural residents than to have their areas become dumping grounds for the refuse of city residents. Nevertheless, the cost of space tends to be inversely associated with density of population, and waste disposal often utilizes space. Little is to be gained by permitting emotion to override reason in discussions of this issue.

An important element in the decision process is whether the location of residuals is imposed or voluntarily accepted in return for compensation. Waste disposal is a cost of density; on equity grounds, those who enjoy the benefits of density should pay the costs. The less densely populated areas are deserving of compensation if they accept residuals resulting from density. To repeat, voluntary transactions are much superior to coercion in matters of this kind (Carter 1987). The prospect that the disposal area will be rendered unfit for future use or unsafe for future habitation, needs to be considered regardless of density of population.

Resource Adaptability and Mobility

Resource adaptability and mobility is a cornerstone of growth and change in rural areas. That is, there is a need to be concerned about the flow of resources into as well as within rural areas, just as there needs to be concern about the loss of resources to other areas. It is clear that resource adaptability and mobility issues become crucial policy issues in many rural areas. The more adaptable and mobile the available resources are, the greater their capacity for minimizing the cost of space.

Consider, for example, the agricultural use of land and water. There has been a trend in recent years to "protect" agricultural uses from transfer to nonagricultural uses. This is often done by state or local government through the use of zoning or other devices. Such prohibitions are likely to do little to protect the viability of the traditional industries; the threats they face generally stem from external, macro forces. If such prohibitions are effective, they may not only inhibit rural area growth and change, but they may also prevent the owners of these resources from realizing returns associated with the highest economic use of those resources. Of course, this should not be taken as a general argument against zoning or group decision making in natural resource use.

Resource adaptability and mobility is of obvious importance in the consideration of educational policy. More than two decades ago, John M. Brewster, a philosopher who devoted his professional life to studying the problems of agriculture in rural America wrote:

> The first requisite of Jeffersonian principles bids us turn attention more directly to ways of expanding educational opportunities for rural areas and of creating more new nonfarm employment opportunities in both rural and urban sectors of the nation. Only as we move toward this objective of more abundant opportunities for all people do we open a realistic road to more rapid achievement of an agriculture of proficient

family farms for all who remain in farming. That, as I understand it, is the true relevance of the Jeffersonian Dream today (Brewster 1963: 130).

Education and the welfare of rural people have been closely related subjects in this country for nearly two centuries. Much has been written about Jefferson and the family farm, but he also was much concerned about the education of rural people. Although his interest in and promotion of the University of Virginia is well known, what is less well known is that Jefferson accepted the University of Virginia as a political compromise, and he was disappointed that provision was not made at that time for a more universal system of education (Malone 1977). Certainly the legislation creating the land grant colleges and universities in the 1860s was consistent with the Jeffersonian philosophy.

This legislation must be considered among the most pioneering educational efforts of any society. In his remarkable book *Economic and Social Development: A Process of Social Learning* (1971), Edgar Dunn writes of specializing and generalizing social adaptations through learning. The enormous effectiveness of the land grant colleges and universities stemmed from the fact that they provided for both. By the application of science to agriculture, they provided for specializing adaptations. These specializing adaptations were not limited to those who remained on the land and farmed. They benefitted many who served agriculture by providing inputs to agriculture and many who assisted in marketing agricultural products. But the land grant system provided also for generalizing adaptations. No one knows how many rural people were made more aware of the world in which they lived by resident and extension educational programs, but many were. Many attended land grant universities with a vague idea that they would study "agriculture" or "home economics." In such a pursuit they were exposed to the natural sciences, the social sciences and the humanities. While the land grants may have sidetracked some into remaining in agriculture who would have otherwise turned to other occupations, surely there were many whose horizons were broadened and whose adaptability was increased enormously by attendance at a land grant university.

It was possible to achieve this rare combination of specializing and generalizing adaptation by education often because agriculture provided the focus for this educational effort. The land grants were created to promote agriculture and the mechanic arts. Even though schools and colleges of engineering, as well as agriculture, were created at many land grants, engineering developed in a different way than did agriculture. The reasons are several, but perhaps the principal cause for the difference is that subsequent legislation provided considerable funding for agricultural research and extension. These activities made possible programs that were different than emerged from those that were able to emphasize mainly instruction in classrooms.

A broad view therefore needs to be taken of all of the educational resources available to rural areas. Rural area residents have long viewed education as an important device for social adaptations and social mobility. Nevertheless, to the extent that education emphasizes certain kinds of specializing adaptations, it can reinforce social rigidity rather than mobility.

Deavers (1987) has argued that many rural communities are unable to capture the benefits of spending on education because those who receive education may leave the area that provides the education. He justifies central spending on rural education on these grounds. Bryan (1981) notes that even though rural areas spend less on education than more densely populated areas, this is not necessarily because they value education less but rather because their incomes are lower. In his words, "The data show that the rural states indicate absolutely no tendency to be skimpy when it comes to education if we consider the funds with which they have to work." (Bryan 1981: 64)

Deavers also has called attention, as have others, to the changing informational requirements of rural decision makers. Because rural areas are highly diverse, these informational requirements or needs cannot be specified generally. Deavers has in mind a service not unlike that provided commercial agriculture by the schools and colleges of agriculture. This is surely an ambitious objective requiring a most imaginative program.

Enhancing the adaptive capacity of human resources in rural areas becomes an important part of rural development strategy. It should be viewed as a means for reducing obstacles and barriers to the outside world. Lowering such barriers will not ensure that resources will always flow in the direction of the rural community. But it will improve the prospects for attracting such resources by improving the quality of life, the quality of the labor force, and the indigenous entrepreneurial capacity.

Summary

This chapter has been concerned with space and distance as these concepts relate to rural areas. Rural is a relative concept, indicating that the density of population is less in some areas than it is in others. The consideration of space and distance as continuous rather than discrete variables permits important issues affecting rural areas to be uncovered.

Space is a necessary attribute for many production and consumption activities. By definition, that is by virtue of the sparsity of population, rural areas can provide space. If they wish to flourish, they must take advantage of this unique variable. The traditionally rural activities have been space using. As our society changes, the mix of space-using activities will also change. Tourism and outdoor recreation are but one example of space-using activities that have resulted from basic social trends—population growth, higher incomes, and greater leisure time, to be specific.

But, if space is a positive attribute for many producing and consuming activities, overcoming distance always comes at a cost. Thus it is not enough for a rural area to only make space available, access must also be provided. Access is made possible either by the physical movement of people and goods (transportation) or by the transmittal of information (communication).

Technical change and public policy affecting transportation and communication are of great importance to those who have concern with rural development, growth, and change.

In a dynamic national and international scene both the benefits of space and the costs of distance for particular areas will change. Those rural areas that are prepared to evaluate the offering of nontraditional goods and services are the most likely to prosper. This does not mean that the traditional industries in the rural areas will necessarily be abandoned—farming, forestry, and rural manufacturing, for example. But it does mean that the less-traditional activities need to be considered. Rural residences, outdoor recreation, and the export of services to more densely populated areas provide examples of activities that are nontraditional in many rural areas. How can these nontraditional activities be encouraged? No formula exists, but generally there needs to be greater attention paid to the attractiveness of rural areas as places to live.

54

Attention also needs to be given to the adaptability and mobility of resources in rural areas if nontraditional producing and consuming activities in rural areas are to be accommodated. This includes both natural and human resources. Land and water institutions need to be examined with respect to their capacity to accommodate nontraditional economic activities. Educational programs and facilities need to be evaluated both with respect to the migration of people away from the rural areas as well as to the attractiveness of the rural area to possible new settlers.

Notes

1. Some of the ideas expressed in this chapter may also be found in my chapter, "Policy Options for Rural Development in a Restructured Rural Economy: An International Perspective," in *Agriculture and Beyond: Rural Economic Development*. Madison, WI: University of Wisconsin, 1987.

References

Brewster, John M. 1963. "The Relevance of the Jeffersonian Dream Today." in Howard W. Ottoson (ed.). *Land Use Policy and Problems in the United States*. Pp. 86-136. Lincoln, NE: University of Nebraska Press.

Bryan, Frank N. 1981. *Politics in the Rural States: People, Parties and Processes*. Boulder, CO: Westview Press.

Carlino, Gerald A. 1985. "Declining City Productivity and the Growth of Rural Regions: A Test of Alternative Explanation." *Journal of Urban Economics*. 18: 11-27.

Carter, Luther J. 1987. "U.S. Nuclear Waste Program at an Impasse." *Resources*. No. 88. Washington, D.C.: Resources For the Future.

Castle, Emery N. 1981. "Agricultural Education and Research: Academic Crown Jewels or Country Cousin?" The 1980 Kellogg Foundation Lecture to the National Association of State Universities and Land Grant Colleges, Resources For the Future.

Deavers, Kenneth L. 1987. "Choosing a Rural Policy for the 1980s and 90s." *Rural Economic Development in the 1980s: Preparing for the Future*. Pp. 377-395. Washington, D.C.: United States Department of Agriculture.

Dunn, Edgar. 1971. *Economic and Social Development: A Process of Social Learning.* Baltimore, MD: Johns Hopkins University Press.

_____. 1981. *The Development of the U.S. Urban System. Volume I: Concepts, Structures, Regional Shifts.* Washington, D.C.: Resources For the Future.

_____. 1983. *The Development of the U.S. Urban System, Volume II: Industrial Shifts, Implications.* Washington, D.C.: Resources For the Future.

Malone, Dumas. 1977. *Jefferson and His Time: The Sage of Monticello.* Boston, Massachusetts: Little, Brown and Company.

Mills, Edwin S . N. D. "The Determinants of Small Area Growth." Corvallis, OR: The Oregon State University Press.

Mills, Edwin S. and Gary Chodes. 1988. "Non-Extractive Employment Outside Metropolitan Areas." Proceedings of the National Rural Studies Committee Conference, May 22-24. Pp. 29-36. Corvallis, OR: Oregon State University.

Smith, Gary W., David B. Wills and Bruce A. Weber. 1987. "The Aging Population, Retirement Income and the Local Economy." *Community Economics.* Corvallis, OR: Western Rural Development Center, Oregon State University.

Stevens, Benjamin H. 1985. "Location of Economic Activities: The JRS Contribution to the Research Literature." *Journal of Regional Science.* 25: 663-685.

Weber, Bruce A., Emery N. Castle and Ann L. Shriver. 1987. "The Performance of the Natural Resource Industries." *Rural Economic Development in the 1980s: Preparing for the Future.* Pp. 103-133. Washington, D.C.: United States Department of Agriculture.

4

The Emerging Global Economy and Rural Communities: A New Perspective

Edward J. Blakely

It is important for policymakers and academics to comprehend the altered context of rural communities. Rural areas are moving beyond their parochial and limited roles framed solely by their local economic base to communities with a genuine stake in the international economy. There is considerable evidence that rural areas are responding to forces and factors that lie outside their immediate economic circumstances. The capacity of rural communities to respond to these changed conditions will determine if rural communities can shape their own destiny rather than be shaped by the forces that surround them.

Rural development, by definition, is the altering of a current conception of community and developing an alternative view. *No community is ever fully developed.* Rural communities, like individuals, are always in the process of developing. It is this "process" in itself that is at the core of rural development initiatives. Yet, this process and the goals of development are now in doubt due the rapid changes in the economy. In many ways the current literature dismisses the notion of a rural/small town community as a social organization or as an institutional form.

One school of thought suggests that the rural community is *passé* because the increasing openness of the socioeconomic system removes all of the former spatial boundaries that defined a communal setting. The advent of the telephone and the ubiquity of the automobile and freeway have transcended rural community as a setting for social institutional development. As a result, we are faced with a new conceptualization of the rural community not as place but as a series of networks. These networks, recent theorists (Wellman 1980) suggest, have permanently replaced our territorial and narrow view of the status and form of the rural community. In essence, there is no longer any real relationship between spatial size of a community and the human relationships formed in that place or across the nation and around the world.

Another view is that the rural community as a separate identifiable socioeconomic and values unit is dying because of external events, too large in scale and too distant from the locality of influence. Global and not local controllable factors are influencing the pattern of communities to a far greater degree than resident action or inaction. This phenomenon can be seen in small cities and towns where once dying or marginal resource based communities spring to life because outside investors decide that the location is suitable for urban retirees, second homes, and hobby farms for urbanites, backroom offices, or new exploitations of natural resources. In many instances the existing rural identity was overwhelmed, left out, or left behind by these changing economic circumstances.

These two views of the demise of rural community form the basis of the global restructuring debate as it affects rural areas. It is manifest through such signs as the alteration of identity of once proud, small farm towns in Iowa, Minnesota and Wisconsin that have become components or cogs of international market forces. These communities are being marginalized in an international market system that no longer recognizes their locational resource attributes, their labor, or their industrial production systems as useful. Certainly, if entire nations are subject to forces beyond their control, smaller units such as the rural communities seem even less viable in this larger sphere.

The Search for the Rural Community in a Global Society

On the other hand, there is a new search for identity on a smaller and more personal scale. New books such as *Habits of the Heart* (Bellah et. al. 1985) mark the trail of Americans' search for the old rural communal spirit in their personal and, increasingly, in their professional lives. As a result, new forms of communities are being formed. These I term *insta-communities.* They are formed for the lifecycle instance of the person rather than the sustained purpose of human settlement and civic organization. They represent fragmented activities associated with the functions of personality rather than the holistic nurturing purposes associated with the rural *communal pattern.* Thus, instacommunities are formed for joggers, single parents, senior citizens, gays, and the like. Each of these fragments of a life system attempts to serve as the communal vehicle for the total system of relationships that were formerly the basis for larger community group identity. Moreover, many of the functions of the former rural community institutional system have been transferred to new "helping groups." The former role of the rural church is transformed and transfigured by "personal help" groups that assist in everything from overweight to acute mental crisis. Similarly, schools and 4-H youth group activities have been overwhelmed by a multitude of special interest centers that assist children in urbanizing them to baseball and ballet.

In every sense, the basic framework for rural development is being challenged by larger events. This story is not new. The tension between the larger societal influences and local issues has dominated rural community development discussions for more than a decade. Duane Gibson (1974) in a speech aptly entitled, "Our Stubborn Ounces," declared that the target for assisting individuals in the major transitions of society is through the community as a geographic as well as an institutional form. Besides Gibson, Cary (1970), Biddle and Biddle (1968), and many others writing before, after, and with them reached this conclusion on the basis that the formation of locally vigorous institutions can serve as the only real base for social and economic growth. As Warren stated in 1975, "there is good news and bad news" for rural development. The good news, according to Warren, is the fact that rural communities are open systems, not formal organizations, and mobilization in a more complex world has greater potential than ever before. The bad news is that rural development specialists have few skills to offer the changing circumstances because the rural development process is too frequently aimed at preserving the past rather than engaging in building the future.

This chapter is designed to place these real and important discussions and arguments into context for rural development policy makers and professionals. If we fail to see the reality associated with them and deny these forces, then we will fail to serve the rural communities well.

The New Global Realities

There are a series of new global realities that are so deeply affecting the nation that they are altering the understanding of rural development. The entire rural development process is being recast by a series of global realities that affect rural communities different ways. In large measure, these global realities are associated with specifically identifiable transformations, yet their impacts and implications are numerous and cross many conceptual areas in different ways. There are four new dimensions to the rural development process.

Restructuring Rural Wealth Generation

Wealth creation is no longer based on available rural based natural, physical, or human resources. At one time small rural communities with requisite natural wealth could depend on those resources, if properly managed, to produce sustained economic growth. The presence of iron ore, forests, or other natural resources were a key barometer of both local and national wealth. In fact, places derived their reputations and frequently their names from the wealth they generated. This natural wealth developed both an industrial form (for good or evil) as well as a community culture based on that pattern. It also developed a set of institutions designed to support this system of economic activity. In essence, this was a closed system in open competition with the rest of the world.

Similarly, communities with strategic locations, such as seaports, railheads, river access, and more recently international airports were the strongest in the economic system. These communities act as international gateways for the natural resource areas, as well as the finance and trade centers. Of course, an institutional system, including a social pattern, emerged in these centers that was clearly recognizable. Human resources provided a special set of assets for many rural communities that attracted capital and employment. This natural hierarchy of communities, combined with a rather predictable pattern of development, provided a conceptual base for rural development. Today, community assets in themselves are no longer wealth generators.

Rural wealth is created in today's financial environment through the recombination and the redesignation of capital financial assets rather than by producing products from the natural environment. As a result, money is the base asset. So, money alone is the determinant of the use of other assets, not the product of their use. The mobility of capital has created a new order of firms independent of places. A new order of international firms is emerging that is altering the development process in rural communities. A single community cannot control or alter that development process.

Community self-help schemes are stymied by this new system that may not recognize rural community (physical, natural, or human resources) as assets. While the old rural community economic development orientation was to build wealth on community resources, the new economic order relies on the ability of a community to attract capital.

Repositioning the Process of Nation State and Community Building

The United States, once the wealthiest and most powerful nation in the world, is now *one* of the powerful. In fact, it can be economically argued that the United States is a developing nation. It has the world's largest debt; it has an undereducated population; it has a declining standard of living; it has low and declining domestic productivity. This repositioning of the United States, combined with the rising economic power of other nations, creates a new development dilemma. The old development model for rural areas in the United States was based on the modernization model. That is, the ideal of community development was to assist in the transition to newly developed domestic products or processes. These products and processes were largely designed to meet the character and resources of the places in which they were to be used. They were not imports.

Yet today to modernize rural communities to achieve the success of our competitors would mean importing technical know-how from the Japanese, Koreans, Taiwanese, and Brazilians. This may seem ludicrous on its face, but it is instructive to note that in all previous rural development modes there was a cultural-technology transfer from the dominant model of development from the most advanced to the least advanced. The major import in this form of development has been the social ideology, not merely the technology. In some ways, the recent fad with respect to Japanese management systems is related to this form of cultural transfer. In addition, the major concept and context for community development is based on spreading "democratic processes." The economic miracles of some of the nations described have been achieved with little attention to community democracy. One might reasonably ask whether past rural development processes have anything to offer communities in this situation.

Not only is the order of nations changing, but so is the organization of small cities and towns. Information-dense large cities, not resource-based towns, are the major gateways for development. These cities operate outside the regional and even the nation state system. In their role as international centers of information and capital, cities like New York, Los Angeles, San Francisco, Boston, and Miami, operate on a different plane. They seldom need to interact with their surrounding communities or even the nation. This same pattern is emerging in rural areas such as Stevens Point, Wisconsin (as an insurance center), Trinidad, California (as the headquarters for the international cable news), and many other similar examples.

In essence, the entire hierarchy of towns to small cities to the metropolis has been permanently altered. Small cities no longer view themselves within a regional network. They are now asserting their global economic roles. Even small communities with the advent of new telecommunications technologies can play international roles. As a result, the interrelationships between communities that helped forge the community building block context for mutual development has broken down.

Rural development practice has not recognized the extent and the means to assist communities to reposition themselves. The focus of rural development has been on the microcommunity level rather than the macro forces changing communities' positioning in the international order.

The Uncoupled Professionals

Professions and professionals operating in rural areas, until recently, have played their roles in relatively clear and well-defined boundaries. An economist was expected to give economic advice and leave social and political systems to others. Today, the economist is one of several emerging professions that is not related to any institutional or similar base. This new free range of professionals includes people trained in law, medicine, accounting, urban planning, and many other fields. Their backgrounds are not as important as their roles . In some instances, they are called consultants. But in many cases they function as organizers, leaders and/or directors of a myriad of new activities in rural communities. These practitioners assist in designing economic plans for small towns, land-use models to protect the rural landscape, and computerized methods of producing farm products. They are powerful, unseen and scarcely ever accountable. Yet, they form a new breed of econocrats that have increasing power over the destiny of rural and urban groups and communities.

This new breed of professional is not bound by the past or by any form of professional ethic or institutional form. They are involved in almost every aspect of rural life. They make up the majority of senior level officials in almost all government agencies. The econocrats are pushing out rural community developers by fashioning new community economic development agencies that rely more on technical than human expertise. The econocrats now have effective ascendancy in state governments as directors of bureaus of commerce, finance, or economic development. If we look more closely at the corporate sector, we see these well-trained econocrats organizing and maximizing economic resources as if people didn't matter. The econocrats have created a notion of progress through their manifestos, such as *Megatrends* (Naisbett 1982) and *In Search of Excellence* (Peters 1982), combined with a whole group of futurists who are recodifying both individual and institutional relationships. In fact, the econocrats view rural communities as commodities. These communities are used until they are no longer useful. As a result of their influence, cities all over the world are uncertain of the loyalty of corporations and even corporate headquarters.

Econocrats are a special breed that view their activity as more important than the place or the employer. This new "professionalism" transcends the particular background of the person practicing it. Rural development has been slow to incorporate many of the econocratic skills. In essence, tension between community as human-fulfilling space and personal relationships is gradually being replaced by a new economic base model that views community in terms of its output rather than its processes. This change is troublesome because it fragments, rather than integrates, the rural community.

Uncoupling Work Roles from Rural Community Roles

Rural communities, as discussed earlier, were marked by the firms that inhabited them. That is no longer true today. Firms are footloose to a greater extent than they ever were in the past. This footloose quality is manifest not only in the way the firm uses its physical and financial assets but also in the way in which human assets are associated with the organization. Not only has work changed, but the relationship of the worker to the work has changed. The rural labor force, as many analysts have shown (Bradshaw and Blakely 1980), is increasingly like the urban-developed area's work force. The new work force is in the service sector rather than the production sector. Service work is not only work performed in restaurants and among retailers; service work is now the dominant form of production.

An interesting and provocative aspect of this transformation has been the need for many workers to mark the place—rural, small town, or a lifestyle area—as the boundary of their professions. As a consequence, firms have moved to the workers, or the workers have increasingly moved the work to wherever they choose to be in the world. In a real sense, the old attachment of firms to places has been replaced by a new attachment of skilled individuals to certain rural places. A rising number of professionals are opting for nonmetropolitan environments. It is this professional talent that can form the base for economic revitalization. A new form of industrial recruitment is based on attracting skilled people to a locality rather than attempting to attract firms to new localities. This change in the nature of firm development is a signal to rural areas to look to human capital in new ways in the development process. Rather than viewing humans as the victims of industrial forces, a different paradigm might be put in place that views human intellectual wealth as a new international commodity. This view of people in relationship to forming their environment, rather than being victimized by it, radically alters the perspective of the role of rural communities.

The Shape of Things to Come

The above factors influence the scale and scope of rural communities. Rural areas are reacting to forces that are rapidly transforming what we see and what we do. The shape of the social system that will emerge is already outlined by current trends. Harlan Cleveland (1987), a recognized authority on development trends, points out that the future is already here with respect to the dominant forms of economic activity. Nearly fifty percent of the developed world's labor force will be in the knowledge sector in only a few years. In essence, the shape of things to come is already here. The real issue is how rural communities can begin to shape their destiny by using new capacities of telecommunications and knowledge to create a set of natural resources that can enable rural areas to deal effectively in a global economic order. The components of this system are: (1) research as the central industrial form, (2) knowledge institutions as an engine of development, and (3) information as an industrial product.

Research as the Central Industrial Form
Rather Than Manufacturing

Research is now an industrial form. In fact, research is the leading industry in most of the United States and has been for many years, John McHale, author of *The Changing Information Environment (1982)*, shows that information is limitless and expandable. In fact, research expands as it is used. This, in turn, creates whole new industries based on the pursuit of knowledge. These industries are created to exploit scientific research, technology transfer, biotechnology, computer software, and the like. These new industrial forms have no conceptual or physical boundaries. This means rural communities are now competing for becoming headquarters or the central locations for many emerging industrial areas. They have no opportunity boundaries.

In essence, we have entered an era in which research is the base for a totally new central industrial system that is not an adjunct to industry but a new industrial activity. This activity depends on crossing all economic frontiers—local, state, national, physical, and intellectual.

Knowledge Institutions as Engine of Development

With the rise of a knowledge society, the role of all institutions is changing. The role of universities is most challenged in this context. Universities were once the custodians of knowledge. Now universities are the propagators and developers of new industrial wealth. The university is the center of economic development. It must be seen as such. University resources are being harnessed as part of economic development schemes and programs all over the nation.

The University of California is using its powerful resources to attract the Supercollider to California. The universities in North Carolina and, more recently, Texas are now famous for their role in stimulating the economic development of their states. In almost every state university, resources are being used directly to sponsor activities as wide ranging as the development of science and industrial parks, the operation of small business incubators, and the direct development of new firms. First, it means that the university is no longer an innocent or neutral bystander in the rural development process. University involvement with an area or community can have a marked impact on a rural community's economic survival. Second, the most important aspect of the growth in the university role is the significance of the use of university resources as basic infrastructure for economic development.

Information as an Industrial Product

Information is the most widely available and troublesome product in the world today. There is plenty of information in the world. In fact, industrial problem solving is now done on a worldwide basis.

Engineering projects now use the skills of the best engineers all over the world rather than concentrating on the internal skills of a single firm. For example, Boeing Aircraft can use engineering talent from an international pool to develop components of its new commercial aircraft, rather than depending entirely on a large internal staff of engineers to develop all of the complex components of a 747 aircraft. In essence, there is a worldwide storehouse of knowledge on almost every subject and a control system to facilitate its exchange.

It is true that there is an increasing gap between the information rich and the information poor. This gap is not a difficult technological gap to overcome. The computer will become as common as the telephone in rural areas. As these new systems come to play, what can a rural community developer add? What is the intervention point in a constant stream of information? Finally, why does anyone need the assistance of the local rural development professional when the knowledge and skills of community specialists all over the world are available?

As we approach the new century, the issue for rural development will be how to improve the information capacity of the most remote villages and arrange access to new information on a range of topics not available before. This is not to say that certain human process skills will not be important. However, the leading information-gathering and dissemination skill that was the central resource of the development specialist may become irrelevant.

Emerging Rural Community Dynamics

As the 1900s draw to a close, we are increasingly mindful of the contradictions of our times. On one hand, there is a greater search for localized small town identity. On the other hand, there is a far more internationally competent and interconnected community emerging. How are these contradictions working themselves out currently?

We see the resurgence of the past with a new vengeance and vitality. This is manifest in part in the new spiritual movements sweeping the world. At the community level several dimensions are emerging that seem to be kind of intellectual halfway houses on the way to major reforms. These include surrogates for social community and surrogate communal institutions.

Surrogates for Social Community

There is an increasing tendency to find new forms and forums to replicate the "communal" aspects of small towns. These should not be mistaken for a desire to move back to the old-fashioned community in all respects. The people who go back to nature still seem to drive Volvos. Nonetheless, there is a resurrection of some community institutional character. This can be observed in the redevelopment of many forms of local consultive mechanisms. The institutionalization of these community organs at the local government level has created a new career system for many community developers as promoters and monitors of these highly specialized community forums.

In addition, there is an identifiable social movement emphasizing the elements of small towns and neighborhoods. This movement has its roots in the information society, not in the past. The *urban villagers* are able to develop a "community" orientation almost entirely because they are not tied to the place for their livelihood. In a sense, the community in this perspective is a shallow portrayal of its earlier, deeper sociocultural binding quality.

Finally, there is the more universal community that is manifest in movements throughout the world. This community of movements can be observed either as a manifestation of interests, such as concern for the environment, or representations of lifestyles, such as senior citizens. Some of these groups are tightly bound, others less so. They are communities inasmuch as they have common notions and are bound together for a purpose.

These new communities are sometimes coterminus with certain a lifestyle or other attributes of place. However, they are not place centered. As these groups rise, there has been a corresponding tendency to spawn professionals to meet their needs. Therefore, we now train community developers to work with the aging, and health or issues groups as if they were separate communities, rather than a subset of the total community.

New Surrogate Rural Communal Institutions

A panoply of new institutions has emerged to replace the family and generic community's primary functions. These institutions assist in child rearing, social relationships, and personal development. The helping groups, as they are sometimes called, provide an number of long-term and short-term services that were previously found within the family or locally-based institutions, such as the school and church.

These institutions supply the interconnections or networks that allow human interrelationships to go on in a highly complex world. These new systems are growing both in size and areas of coverage, even in rural America. Almost every new problem is a candidate for the emergence of a "support group." The former role of community worker as an intermediary has been both enhanced and diminished by these new groups. In many ways these groups provide the one-to-one service that development specialists cannot or should not provide. On the other hand, these groups tend to develop their own community system boundaries, making it difficult for the generalist community developer to access.

Shaping the Future

Rural communities must begin to fashion new perspectives on their future. These perspectives will determine the goals rural communities will pursue and the tools they use in this pursuit. The following issues will determine how each community embarks on this process. Each community will have to:

(1) *Recognize that rural community is a global and not a parochial concept.* Rural communities must pioneer the use of new information systems to hook up the world. They must develop means for information sharing rather than information hoarding. The role of the community developer becomes the linking agent for new systems of community and an information organizer rather than a people organizer.

(2) *Develop new targets beyond spatial areas for rural development.* The targets for rural development must move beyond rural locality to have a credible future. New targets must include areas of social welfare for those left out of the information age as worldwide groups, rather than mere manifestations of local actions.

(3) *Find new intervention points.* The old intervention points based on the assumption of an indigenous local economic base must be revised. The new entry point for rural development is within a particular knowledge area rather than a local resource. Each community will have to learn to assess its place within the international knowledge system. This will mean that the skills of "econocrats" will be required in assisting local problem solving. Rural development specialists may be able to assist in forging links between communities with similar needs on a global rather than local basis.

(4) *Utilize research as a rural development tool.* For far too long rural developers have eschewed research as a useful tool. In part, it has been the result of the old research paradigm that was based on assessing what transpired in the past. A new, "real time" research paradigm is emerging that emphasizes obtaining information and organizing information for decision making. This research model is a necessary adjunct to a rural development approach. A practice that is based on assisting groups makes decisions based on the best available information in the world. This is a highly appropriate role for the development specialist. The "effective" or human communication role is not diminished by this new role of information gatherer. In fact, it is enhanced.

Conclusion

A new challenge faces rural America. The challenge is quite simply whether communities want to become part of shaping the future or be shaped by it. This is a difficult challenge because the scope of the challenge moves beyond the territorial and conceptual limits that formed the field. The current circumstances that liberate people and firms from places will persist. Therefore, rural communities must offer new skills and new tools to become engaged in forging a new future.

It is only by reconceptualizing the issues and designing a new paradigm that rural development can proceed. Modernity is here. Modern life has not solved all of rural America's problems. In some respects it has created new and more difficult ones. The direction of change is not toward re-establishing the rural past but toward *building a new future* for rural Americans as partners in the emerging global economy.

References

Bellah, Robert, Richard Madsen, William Sullivan, Ann Swidler and Steven Tipton. 1985. *Habits of the Heart.* Berkeley CA: University of California Press.

Biddle, William and Loureide J. Biddle. 1968. *Encouraging Community Development: A Training Guide for Local Workers.* New York: Holt, Reinhardt, and Winston, Inc.

Bradshaw, Ted K. and Edward J. Blakely. 1980. *Rural Communities in Advanced Industrial Society.* New York: Praeger.

Cary, Lee J. 1970. *Community Development as a Process.* Columbia, MO: University of Missouri Press.

Cleveland, Harlan. 1987. "The Twilight of Hierarchy: Speculation on the Global Information Society." *International Journal of Technology Management.* 2:2.

Gibson, Duane. 1974. "Our Stubborn Ounces: Enduring Dedication to Community." *Journal of the Community Development Society.* 5:2.

Naisbett, John. 1982. *Megatrends: Ten New Directions Transforming Our Lives.* New York: Warner Books

McHale, John. 1982. *The Changing Information Environment.* Boulder, CO: Westview Press.

Peters, Thomas. 1982. *In Search of Excellence: Lessons from America's Best Companies.* New York: Harper and Row.

Warren, Roland. 1975. "External forces Affecting Local Communities: The Bad News and the Good News." *Journal of the Community Development Society.* 6: 2-7.

Wellman, Barry. 1980. "Networks, Neighborhoods and Communities: Approaches to the Study of the Community Question." Research Paper No. 97. Toronto, Canada: Centre for Urban and Community Studies, University of Toronto.

5

The Future of the Community in Rural Areas

Kenneth P. Wilkinson

Recent economic and social trends pose serious problems for communities in rural areas, today and for the future. Rural deprivation, indicated by poverty, inadequate services, and many related conditions, already is prevalent in most countries (Bunce 1982), including such highly developed countries as the United States (Brown and Deavers 1987). Moreover, in the United States as in other countries, rural community development, which might be part of the solution (Summers 1986), faces an uphill struggle—a struggle against powerful forces now shaping economic and social structures throughout the world. An analysis of the future of the community in rural areas must begin with an appreciation of these trends and their likely consequences.

A useful approach to understanding the contemporary situation is to recognize that the community in rural areas is in flux and not necessarily in transition. Transition would imply a more or less orderly change from one stable form to another, such as from "traditional" to "modern." Rural areas today do not contain stable or traditional communities, and the cross-cutting forces in the present trends do not add up to a coherent process of transition. Flux gives a better description. In flux there are problems without solutions, and the outline of the future is not fixed. By the same token, of course, flux presents opportunities for intervention that might not occur in a process of transition.

This review examines major trends affecting rural areas, with particular attention to the rural areas of the United States. The trends and their likely effects are taken as background for identifying problems and opportunities for community development in the future in rural areas.

Economic and Social Trends

"Rural change" has been a central concern of the rural social sciences for many decades and a fact of life for many more. To be sure, crucial changes are under way in rural areas, and people are suffering because of them. But the same could have been said centuries ago. Change and suffering are enduring qualities of rural life. In a general sense, the reasons are obvious: change is ubiquitous and potentially disruptive, and the pace of change in society as a whole has been continuous and fairly rapid over virtually the entire course of modern history. It can be said without exaggerating that few things are as familiar in the rural experience as the winds of change. Still, today's trends have their own features, and many observers see in these trends a rural crisis gathering if not one already at hand—a crisis of rural well-being demanding quick and certain steps by government and other actors to avoid a rural disaster. The effects of recent trends can best be understood by recognizing patterns in the broad historical milieu from which they have developed.

Three historical patterns have been and are now altering the communities in rural areas. One is the "social cost of space." The second is the development of a "global economy." The third is a change in the relationship between territory and community. These merit brief mention as background for understanding specific contemporary forces of change.

Cost of Space

As to the social cost of space, there is no question that rural areas lag behind urban areas in social well-being. Myths aside, the social cost of space has been high and growing in all of the history of the American community (Kraenzel 1955). In an earlier era, perhaps, the fundamental features of rural settlement—small numbers, low density, and high distance from other settlements—were advantages for community solidarity. If a small rural settlement had good natural resources, it could survive as a self-sufficient community. The demise of traditional society, however, was well advanced in most of the world by the beginning of the eighteenth century.

Settlements in rural America, for example, have always depended upon ties to urban centers, first to those in Europe, then to the new ones along the eastern seaboard, and finally to those spread across the nation. Settlements of great distance from major centers, especially those lacking in density, have suffered the social cost of space. Carl Kraenzel (1955) first labeled the social cost of space and described its features—dependency, economic depression, internal conflict, and extreme individualism. The economic cost of space (i.e., transport cost) adds to the problems of rural living and contributes no doubt to high incidence of rural poverty and unemployment, but the social cost of space is more than an economic cost. It is a cost to the quality of life. Social relationships in small remote settlements often show the painful human experience of this cost, in sharp contrast to the romantic images of rural life that continue to influence national policy. The social cost of space in rural areas has increased over the years as the society has become increasingly urban.

Global Economy

The development of a global economy, the second background factor for understanding contemporary changes, also began many years ago. However, the effects of the truly global economy date to the twentieth century, particularly to the period since World War II when the United States and other industrial nations became major actors in the economic and political networks that now link all or nearly all nations.

Critical appraisals of the effects of this development on rural areas point to two of its important consequences. It has shifted the locus of decision making on many matters affecting local life away from the rural community and, indeed, away from the nearby urban centers to which rural areas have been linked in the past (Warner 1974). And it submits rural areas, as "peripheries," to the machinations of footloose power actors, such as multinational corporations, whose international activities in search of profits are not easily regulated by the government of any given nation (Howes and Markusen 1981). Clearly, the well being of rural people in the future will be bound up to no small extent with the changing positions of nations and the activities of large firms in world economic and political systems.

In Search of "Place"

The third broad background trend is the changing connection between place and community. Just as urban observers in the 1950s and early 1960s began to discuss "The Exploding Metropolis" (Editors of Fortune 1958), so rural social scientists in that era began to write about "The Expanding Rural Community" (Anderson 1961). Since the earliest studies of rural sociology (e.g., Galpin 1915), it has been obvious that rural communities are large, rather than small, if community is defined as the territory over which a local population moves as it meets its daily needs (Hawley 1950, 150). With changes in transportation and communications technologies, the community territory has continued to expand for rural people. It has expanded now to the point that students of the community are asking whether the territorial conception of community has any real utility in explaining how people live and the actions they take in public affairs in rural areas.

No one argues, of course, that this is strictly a rural trend. To the contrary, the spatial element in community definition is questioned for urban and rural areas alike. At issue are the implications of the tendency for most people to be involved simultaneously in several community-like networks, few if any of which coincide with local territorial boundaries. Does this mean people now have several communities? Does it mean the local community is dying out as it becomes merely a stage where outside networks impinge upon one another? What are the consequences for community development and social well-being? Key questions about the future of rural areas hinge on the projected consequences of this bifurcation between place and the organization of social life.

Assessing the Implications

Against these background patterns—the growing social cost of space, the growth of world systems, and the changing role of territory in community life—some specific trends and rural conditions in recent years can be appraised. Demographic and economic trends in particular have received much attention in recent literature on rural America.

The demographic trends are clear, at least in general terms. In the United States, the nonmetropolitan population grew more rapidly than the metropolitan population overall and in most states during the 1970s. But by the late 1970s, the "turnaround" had slowed down, and in the early 1980s it turned almost back around in most states—although there is no evidence of a return to the earlier pattern of massive rural to urban migration. Although the reasons for these trends are still under investigation in demography (Fuguitt 1985), it seems apparent that economic factors, such as the energy boom of the 1970s and the energy bust of the 1980s, were important contributors.

The 1980s began with a severe economic recession in the United States, and this ended a period of strong rural economic growth (Brown and Deavers 1987). The slowdown in the rural economy in the 1980s can be attributed to the convergence of a number of influences. At the international level, increased foreign competition, the strong dollar, and weak world markets had negative effects on manufacturing, agriculture, energy, and forest products industries. Rural community economies often depend on these—and often on a single one of them. The shift to services as the booming sector of the national economy since the early 1980s has been of relatively little benefit to rural areas because the kinds of services that have grown rapidly (e.g., business and computer services) and their markets tend to be concentrated in urban areas. Deregulation of banking and transportation industries, according to Henry, Drabenstott, and Gibson (1986), removed some of the protection rural areas once had from the high interest rates associated with the costs of urban banks and from the true market costs of transportation. Finally, structural changes in agriculture in the early 1980s and weather-related farming disasters have created severe economic pressures in many rural communities. Taken together, these trends paint a bleak picture of the situation in rural areas.

A major effect of the recent upheavals has been to exacerbate problems associated with prevailing rural patterns—with the growing social cost of rural space, the increasing importance of world dynamics affecting rural community life, and the changing role of territory in rural social organization. The result is a cluster of severe rural problems. Five problems in particular deserve attention as challenges for the future. These are: the income (or poverty) gap; the gap in services, infrastructure, and amenities; economic and social inequality; personal and social disruption, and a social crisis that might well be called a crisis of community.

The income gap between rural and urban populations apparently is not cyclical and it is not receding (Henry, Drabenstott, and Gibson 1986: 35); in fact, there is evidence of an increasing gap. For example, by the mid-1980s, the poverty rate in the United States for nonmetropolitan counties (see Brown and Deavers 1987: 1-6) was one-third higher than for metropolitan counties (18.3 per cent compared to 12.7 per cent). A gap is shown both in estimates of per capita income and in survey data on unemployment and underemployment (Joint Economic Committee 1986: 144-157). This is a matter of crucial importance given the obvious requirement that jobs and income must be the initial focus of any solution to rural problems. Rural development or rural revitalization simply cannot start if it does not start with jobs and income. Although there are exceptions, such as the Northeast where poverty tends to be at a higher rate in urban areas than in rural areas, the national picture, in the wake of trends mentioned earlier, is one of rural economic distress. In many rural areas, jobs simply are not available to meet local needs. Furthermore, the rural economy is highly unstable, as shown in the recent histories of two major rural industries, agriculture and manufacturing. At the heart of the problem is lack of diversity in local economies. Diversity is needed to give stability in the face of shifts caused by global economic and political forces.

Jobs and income, however, are not all. Services and amenities also are sadly lacking in rural areas, and the rural infrastructure for economic development—roads, bridges, communications facilities, and the like—is far from adequate to meet the current and future needs of people. Distance, density, and poverty have combined to deny adequate levels of health care, child care, education, and related services to many rural people. In the rural South, for example, rates of illiteracy and infant mortality are at Third World levels, and a big part of the reason is inadequate resources and services to meet human needs (Beaulieu 1988). Where services are lacking, deficits in human capital are profound, as shown by problems of attracting jobs and venture capital to areas such as the rural South. In all regions, distance from urban centers increases the cost of service delivery, and for many people, it decreases the likelihood that services will, in fact, be delivered. Rural communities therefore must struggle to provide police and fire protection, sewage treatment and disposal, and other municipal services. Increasing demand for services—an almost universal theme today—is rarely matched in rural communities by increased access to the resources necessary to provide services.

Inequality is another rural problem, one receiving far less attention than it deserves in analyses of rural social life. In modern society there are two major sources of inequality, one resulting from the distribution of resources in the economic order and another resulting from the circumstances of one's birth—i.e., race, ethnicity, sex, location, and so on. The former, indicated by measures of income inequality, tends to increase as the average income increases. Accordingly, in rural areas where the average income tends to be lower than in urban areas, inequality tends to be higher. Inequality of the other kind, that based on non-economic factors, can be particularly disruptive because it directly contradicts egalitarian ideals. As it happens, the most severe inequalities based on such factors as race and ethnicity tend to be in rural populations. Frequently, the consequences are hidden in the countryside—hidden physically by spatial isolation and masked also by the more visible concentrations of disadvantaged population in cities. The evidence for American minority groupings shows that the most severely depressed families live in rural areas (e.g., Durant and Knowlton 1978).

Recent studies also show strong patterns of rural social and personal disruption (Wilkinson 1984), in contrast to the idea that rural life is inherently peaceful, harmonious, and healthy. The weight of evidence, while far from conclusive in a causal sense, shows nearly the opposite of this idea, at least for some key indicators. Mental health is an example. The best evidence available shows higher incidence rates for the most severe psychological disorders in rural than in urban areas (Wagenfeld 1982). Recent research on county rates of suicide and homicide in the Northeast (Wilkinson 1984; Wilkinson and Israel 1984), shows that these rates also tend to increase with rurality. Moreover, there is good reason to think this may be only the beginning. Rural researchers have not given adequate attention to drug and alcohol abuse, incest, family violence, and other problems. But in the specialized literature on many social problems, theories and findings implicate the very conditions that abound in rural areas, namely poverty, isolation, inadequate services, and inequality.

These problems converge to produce a critical period for the future of the community in rural areas. The background factors discussed above—social cost of space, world systems, and loss of a clear territorial base for community life—set the stage for a discussion of this crisis. These problems clearly discredit the popular image of the rural community as a place where people identify with and help one another in times of need and where neighbors work together smoothly and effectively to face common problems. Moreover, the contemporary trends producing rural distress call for far more cohesion and self-help capacity than the distressed communities could be expected to possess. Findings, in fact, show a negative association between the extent of ruralness of local areas and the effectiveness of local mobilization for development (Wilkinson, Camasso, and Luloff 1984). The community clearly is in a state of flux in rural areas.

Community

How these trends affect the community is a most important question for the future because the community is a central factor in the well-being of people. The community is where people experience "society" directly in their daily lives. If the institutions of society are to be integrated in the individual's immediate experience and behavior, this must occur in the community. Community, in fact, is an essential human need and a natural human disposition—something people pursue and achieve naturally as an aspect of the quality of being human, unless this disposition is suppressed by extant social and economic barriers. The latter—suppression of the community by barriers to its natural occurrence—is the central threat to the future well-being of people in rural areas.

A troubled condition of the modern community is described by Roland Warren (1978) with his concept of "The Great Change." Technology has contributed to increased mobility and outside contact and to the development of specialized, formal, and rationally organized social relationships. Large organizations have developed, cutting across communities and linking parts of, but not whole, communities into greater national and world systems. Thus, the "horizontal axis" of the community—the local network that integrates specialized systems into a community system—has given way to the "vertical axis," which links parts of the community to the outside. As a result, says Warren, the locality has become mainly an arena where special-interest groups with outside ties pursue their own goals.

While Warren maintains that the local community persists in American society, albeit in a more turbulent, dynamic form than in the past, others, describing the same processes of change, argue that community now must be sought in nonlocal settings, such as networks that cut across localities (Bender 1978) or in relationships at the national level (Martindale 1963). For many observers, the local community as a coherent, integrating unit of social life is nearly a thing of the past.

Applications of this view to rural areas tend to emphasize the growing strength of outside ties, the domination of local affairs by outside government and outside firms, and the virtual collapse of the traditional close-knit community. Critics of this view, however, have pointed out that the demise of the small community is easily exaggerated (Richards 1978). The idea that a cohesive, pastoral community is being disrupted by urbanization and change is based on a romantic myth about community life in small towns and rural areas. The myth ignores the fact that ties to urban centers are the lifeline of the community in rural areas. Moreover, it ignores the stresses and strains experienced by farm families and other residents of rural areas throughout history. A more realistic appraisal of the current situation in rural areas is needed to understand the challenges to community development in the future.

One way to examine the present and future condition of the community in rural areas is to ask questions about the essential elements of the community as defined conventionally. By this approach, the community has three necessary elements. The first is territory—community exists in a place, although the connection to place, as noted above, is changing. Second, a community is a whole or a "gestalt" of social life. People have outside contacts, of course, but the community contains all of the basic institutions for meeting needs and expressing common interests of people. Third, a community has a bond of common identity or "solidarity." This means people share an interest in their common life and are able to act with solidarity when issues arise that stimulate the shared interest. Thus the community is a place of residence, a local society, and a field of collective actions expressing common identity.

How does the community in rural areas presently rate on these elements? While there is much variation among localities, the main pattern on the element of territory, as noted above, has been one of expansion. Rural residents travel over large territories to meet their needs and conduct their social relations. While they might express a kind of psychological identity with the immediate place of residence, the probability of an active solidarity appears to be low. Travel over a large territory is a typical rural pattern because the local society tends to be incomplete. It tends to lack one or more of the essential social institutions for meeting needs—work, for example, or educational services, or shopping opportunities, or several of these. Obviously this is a reciprocal relationship. The territory expands as people seek means of meeting needs, and this reduces the probability that the local area will contain a complete set of social institutions. It follows that community identity, or at least the kind of identity that creates the capacity for community action, is limited by dispersion of people in travel and by the gaps in local structure this dispersion entails.

Thus, although a small settlement might have something of an advantage over larger settlements in the potential for cohesion, this potential advantage in no way assures the emergence and maintenance of community in small settlements. To the contrary, the expanded territory over which needs are met, the gaps in local services and groups, and the constraints these place on local collective action represent serious problems of the community in rural areas today.

There are far more serious problems for the future well-being of residents of small towns and rural areas than the "demise of community" as described in literature on the passing of traditional or folk society. It is true, however, that these serious problems, unlike the passing of traditional society, can be addressed through positive actions in rural policy and at the local level in community development programs.

Community development is needed in the present to make it possible for people in small towns and rural areas in the future to live their lives together, to meet their essential daily needs in a truly local territory, to have a local society as a base for participating in institutions that extend beyond the local area, and to express the bond of community solidarity in collective actions.

Community Development

Turning from the discussion of problems to the search for solutions, a most important starting place is the recognition that opportunities exist for community development even in the turbulent environment of rural areas in the modern world. For example, residential preferences and widely shared values continue to venerate the small-town community, thus giving a base of positive sentiment on which to construct and promote rural development programs. Furthermore, new communications technologies—the space-shrinking technologies of the information society—can reduce the friction of rural space, making the resources of modern society available instantly to people in remote localities. Similarly, the shift from a manufacturing economy to an information and service economy means that human knowledge and skills, rather than location and natural resources, will be keys to local economic development in the future. In the small-town community of the future, ties to the outside need not be the nemesis of community. Instead, they can be channels of access to vital resources. In addition, small communities, by virtue of the "human-scale" of their local social organization, can have advantages over larger communities for building local solidarity, other things being equal. The availability of these opportunities and advantages, however, gives no assurance that communities in rural areas will be able to use them for their own development.

Given the trends of the times in rural areas, community development is not likely to happen on its own. If the potential for "community" is to bloom and have its own revitalizing effects on rural social well-being, at least four needs must be addressed. These are requisites for community development in rural areas. First, jobs and income—good jobs and steady income—must be secured for the residents of small towns and their surrounding rural areas. Second, services and facilities are needed to support a complete community in the small town settlement. A complete local society is needed to serve the needs of people but also to allow the natural disposition toward community to emerge in relationships among people. Third, inequality, a most formidable barrier to social interaction in many small communities, must be reduced to allow a true form of local solidarity to grow and to generate effective community actions. Fourth, informed and committed local leaders are needed to help accomplish development goals and cultivate the social relationships and shared identity that are the essence of community. An agenda can be built with these goals for the future development of communities in rural areas.

Without intervention, however, the forces that have contributed to pressing rural problems will continue to restrict progress in community development. Regional and local efforts are essential, but for these to be successful, they must be organized within a context of resolve and action at the national and international levels. One of the most obvious facts of rural life in an essentially urban world is that many problems have their roots not in local areas but in the structure and functioning of the larger society. Rural employment, for example, is intimately connected to national and international economic structures. Rural services are affected by organizations that operate in the larger society. Rural inequalities are rooted in worldwide inequalities. Although rural areas have special needs that require special efforts, many of those special needs require action at other levels.

Ultimately, however, the process of community development, whether in small towns and rural areas or in urban centers, is a local one. Actions and policies of outside agencies can set the stage, but community development itself is an "inside job," a process of community-building by community actors and groups. Community "develops" as people work together to try to improve their community. The goal of outside development agencies should be to set the stage for this process to occur within the community itself.

In this latter sense community development means increasing the capacity of a local population to pursue its own interests through effective collective actions. This should not be confused with developments in the community that do not develop the community as such. Economic development without community development, for example, tends to be exploitative and divisive. But when economic development is pursued as a strategy of community development, it can enhance social well-being. As many studies suggest, the local community, if able to act in a concerted fashion on matters of local interest, is the best possible defender and promoter of local welfare in negotiations with outside interest groups.

Case studies give vivid descriptions of instances in which economic development, particularly manufacturing growth, has failed to promote community development in rural areas (Summers 1986). A frequent case is one in which an elite segment of the local population, acting under the guise of a community-improvement program, conspires with outside firms and agencies to implement local development plans that will benefit the elite group and exploit others. Another is the case of actions by government authorities to attract employers with promises of concessions that ultimately will produce negative effects on local welfare, outweighing the positive effects of employment. Another common case is one in which economic development occurs without adequate planning for related developments in housing and services. The literature also describes situations in which exploitative practices of development firms in rural communities are marked, at least superficially, by investments in symbols of community solidarity such as teams, monuments, and fairs. Development for the future in rural areas must attract economic investments, but it must, at the same time, guard against the false forms of community development involved in community exploitation.

Community development also requires a more or less complete network of local groups and services for meeting the needs and expressing the interests of people. Otherwise, the population tends to travel to other sites for many of the routine activities of daily life, thus weakening the probability that the sense of community among local residents will grow and be translated into effective community actions. Moreover, community development requires equality, and as noted above, rural areas tend to be characterized by relatively high levels of inequality. These impediments to community development within rural areas are results, in large part, of the patterns of economic social change in society as a whole. Steps clearly are needed to address these problems so as to free the latent potential of rural communities to promote their own well-being.

The Community of the Future

Certainly the community of the future in rural areas will not be the isolated and dependent village or the open-country settlement of the past. Neither of these could support the kind of community required for social well-being in modern society. In fact, using the conventional definition of the community as place, comprehensive local society, and field of collective actions, there probably will be no such thing as a "rural community" in the future, if such a community exists now. Ecologically and socially, rural areas have become peripheral regions of larger rural-urban fields, not separate rural fields. The future of the community in rural areas rests on the future strength of rural-urban connections.

The contemporary trends that pose serious problems for rural social well-being also contain elements that could affect the future strength of rural-urban connections. New information technologies, of course, have the potential of linking people in rural areas directly into international networks, but whether this will strengthen or weaken social relationships in local areas is an open question (Dillman 1985). These technologies also apparently can contribute to urban growth in rural areas that are far removed from previously established growth centers, as noted in studies of the nonmetropolitan population turnaround of the 1970s (Fuguitt 1985). If this pattern of growth outside the old, central-place hierarchy should continue, newly developing centers in rural areas could contribute directly to strengthening the rural-urban connections that carry the prospects for the future of community development in the countryside. The long-term effects of the new technologies will depend, as Dillman argues, on how the technologies are deployed; however, the potential exists for the effects on rural-urban connections to be positive.

Development of economic resources and social infrastructure in small towns and rural areas to strengthen rural-urban relationships could contribute to a most attractive future alternative to the extreme forms of urban and rural living conditions found in many societies today. The ideal model of the rural-urban community of the future would retain the advantages of rurality but would also have the advantages of urbanity—a small center but one with sufficient scale and diversity to ensure ecological stability in the changing environment of the larger society. In the rural-urban community rural residents would have access locally to a full complement of services and groups to meet daily needs. Moreover, in this community, the painful and destructive polarization that sometimes occurs between rural and urban portions of small communities would be overcome by a high level of interaction among neighbors who, through new linkages to the outside world, would be able to meet their needs together in local social interactions. Such a setting could be the ideal grounds for local collective actions to promote community goals and to remove barriers to social well-being in rural areas. Although this ideal model of the rural-urban community denotes the actual situation in few local settlements today, it expresses a possibility for the future that might be cultivated from implicit elements of current trends.

Conclusion

This review has concentrated on a small portion of the complex matrix of forces shaping the future of the community in rural areas. Those trends mentioned, nonetheless, reveal serious problems and some opportunities for development of communities in rural areas. The prospects for the future can be stated briefly as follows:

(1) Many communities in rural areas are in a state of economic and social flux, a most unstable and distressing condition wrought by patterns and upheavals beyond the control of local residents, and this state of flux carries no assurance of better days to come.

(2) Indicators of economic and social well-being for rural areas, even for those in highly developed countries, give a sad report on present and future prospects. In the general case, rural settlements face economic deficiencies, limited access to essential services, debilitating inequalities, and, as a consequence, depressed ability to mobilize for effective community actions.

(3) There is some basis for optimism about the future, however, in the ubiquitous tendency for community to develop among people who live together when impediments to community interaction are removed. Also certain implicit tendencies in contemporary economic and social trends that could be cultivated so as to address some of the impediments to rural community development are encouraging.

(4) A grim scenario of the future seems far more plausible than a hopeful one for communities in rural areas, however, unless a commitment arises among leading actors in national and international arenas and generates sustained policies of rural development. Even with a strong commitment expressed in policy and practice, community development in rural areas faces at best an uncertain and troubled future.

In this turbulent environment of rural change and uncertainty about the future, theory, more than either ideology or short-term political and economic expediency, can offer a direction for action once a commitment to rural well-being has been established. From my own theoretical perspective, which sees community development as an essential but imperiled component of social well-being in rural and urban areas alike, three general propositions outline an appropriate course for efforts to stimulate rural development in the future. First, action is required at national and international levels, as well as at the local level, to address the rural economic and social problems which impede and suppress the natural tendency for community to develop in local social interaction. Second, efforts to meet rural needs for economic resources and improved services must have equality and community involvement as foci; otherwise developments in rural areas can disrupt and displace the potential for community development to emerge and contribute to social well-being. Third, the vision of the community of the future offering the greatest potential benefits is that embodied in the ideal model of the rural-urban community, a vision that unites the advantages of the rural with those of the urban and rejects the extreme forms of either. Development of the rural-urban community offers the best course of action for promoting rural well-being in the future.

References

Anderson, A.H. 1961. *The Expanding Rural Community.* Lincoln, NE: Nebraska Agricultural Experiment Station Bulletin 464, September.

Beaulieu, Lionel J. (ed.). 1988. *The Rural South in Crisis.* Boulder, CO: Westview Press.

Bender, Thomas. 1978. *Community and Social Change in America.* New Brunswick, NJ: Rutgers University Press.

Brown, David L. and Kenneth L. Deavers. 1987. "Rural Change and the Rural Policy Agenda for the 1980's." in *Rural Economic Development in the 1980s: Preparing for the Future.* Pp. 1/1-1/31. Washington, D.C.: Agriculture and Rural Economy Division, Economic Research Service, U.S. Department of Agriculture, July.

Bunce, Michael. 1982. *Rural Settlement in the Urban World.* London: Croom Helm.

Dillman, Don A. 1985. "The Social Impacts of Information Technologies in Rural North America." *Rural Sociology* 50: 1-26.

Durant, Thomas J., Jr. and Clark S. Knowlton. 1978. "Rural Ethnic Minorities: Adaptive Response to Inequality." in Thomas R. Ford (ed.). *Rural U.S.A.: Persistence and Change.* Pp. 145-67. Ames, IA: Iowa State University Press.

Editors of Fortune. 1958. *The Exploding Metropolis.* Garden City, NY: Doubleday.

Fuguitt, Glen V. 1985. "The Nonmetropolitan Population Turnaround." *Annual Review of Sociology* 11: 259-80.

Galpin, Charles J. 1915. *The Social Anatomy of an Agricultural Community.* Madison, WI: University of Wisconsin Agricultural Experiment Station Bulletin 34.

Hawley, Amos H. 1950. *Human Ecology: A Theory of Community Structure.* New York: Ronald Press.

Henry, Mark, Mark Drabenstott, and Lynn Gibson. 1986. "A Changing Rural America." *Economic Review.* July/August: 23-41.

Howes, Candance, and Ann R. Markusen. 1981. "Poverty: A Regional Political Economy Perspective." in Amos H. Hawley and Sara Mills Mazie (eds.) *Nonmetropolitan America in Transition.* Pp. 437-63. Chapel Hill, NC: University of North Carolina Press.

Joint Economic Committee (eds.). 1986. *New Dimensions in Rural Policy: Building Upon Our Heritage.* Washington, D.C.: Congress of the United States, June.

Kraenzel, Carl F. 1955. *The Great Plains in Transition.* Norman, OK: University of Oklahoma Press.

Martindale, Don. 1963. *Community, Character and Civilization.* New York: The Free Press.

Richards, Robert O. 1978. "Urbanization of Rural Areas." in David Street (ed.). *Handbook of Contemporary Urban Life.* Pp. 551-591. San Francisco: Jossey-Bass.

Summers, Gene F. 1986. "Rural Community Development." *Annual Review of Sociology.* 23: 341-71.

Wagenfeld, Morton O. 1982. "Psychopathology in Rural Areas: Issues and Evidence." in Peter A. Keller and J. Dennis Murray (eds.). *Handbook of Rural Community Mental Health.* Pp. 30-44. New York: Human Sciences Press.

Warner, W. Keith. 1974. "Rural Society in a Post-Industrial Age." *Rural Sociology.* 39: 306-18.

Warren, Roland L. 1978. *The Community in America.* Third Edition. Chicago: Rand McNally.

Wilkinson, Kenneth P. 1984. "Rurality and Patterns of Social Disruption." *Rural Sociology.* 49: 23-36.

Wilkinson, K.P., Michael J. Camasso and A.E. Luloff. 1984. "Nonmetropolitan Participation in Programs of the Great Society." *Social Science Quarterly.* 54: 1092-1103.

Wilkinson, K.P., and Glenn D. Israel. 1984. "Suicide and Rurality in Urban Society." *Suicide and Life-Threatening Behavior.* 14: 187-200.

6

Developing the Farm-Dependent Rural Economy: The Policy Choices[1]

Mark Drabenstott

Rural America is not a homogeneous economy. To the contrary, rural America has been a collection of economic winners and losers throughout the 1980s. Farm-dependent regions, a subset of the rural economy, suffered many of the rural economic losses in the past decade. Of the 2,441 nonmetropolitan counties in the nation, approximately 600 depend principally on agriculture for their income.[2] Being dependent on agriculture, these counties must view rural development quite differently than rural counties with other economic bases, such as retirement and manufacturing.

The 1980s have been especially turbulent for farm-dependent rural America. Following a prosperous decade in the 1970s, the farm economy went through a sharp downturn in the early and mid-1980s, and growth has been slow since then. Farm income has been strong the past four years, but the links between farm income and rural economic activity are weaker than they once were. The structure of agriculture changed so dramatically in the 1980s that a recovering agriculture does not lift all farm communities, perhaps not even most of them.

Following the difficult 1980s, rural communities dependent on agriculture look to the future with some caution. Most farm areas have had only limited success in diversifying their economies. Their fortunes remain distinctly tied to agriculture. Moreover, with U.S. agriculture now fully integrated into a world market, a complex set of forces beyond the control of local decision makers now affects their economic future. The prospect for rapid technological change, and attending structural change in U.S. agriculture, only adds to the uncertainty.

What can farm-dependent rural areas do to spur development and promote more stable economic growth? This chapter examines steps state and local policy makers can take to improve the rural economic outlook of farming regions. The first section of the chapter reviews economic changes that have occurred in farm-dependent rural areas. The second section describes the new rural economic reality that will constrain policymakers in the 1990s. The third section considers policy steps to boost rural economic growth where possible and to encourage adjustment where growth is not possible.

Trends in the Farm-Dependent Rural Economy

Before considering how policy makers can improve the rural economic outlook, it is useful to see where the economy has been. Two things describe the performance of the farm-dependent rural economy in the 1980s: sluggish growth and great structural change.

Sluggish Economic Performance

Overall, the economies of farm-dependent rural areas were sluggish in the 1980s, despite record farm income in recent years. In the 600-odd nonmetropolitan counties that depend principally on agriculture real personal income increased an average 0.8 percent between 1980 and 1987, the last year for which data are available. Growth peaked early in the decade, turned negative in the mid-1980s, and has increased slowly since then (Figure 6.1). The U.S. economy, meanwhile, enjoyed more steady income growth of 2.5 percent a year. Nonmetropolitan incomes increased an average 1.4 percent a year.

The Changing Structure of U.S. Agriculture

Dramatic change in the structure of agriculture for the past decade and more has weakened the link between farm income and local rural economies. Farm production is now concentrated in the hands of large

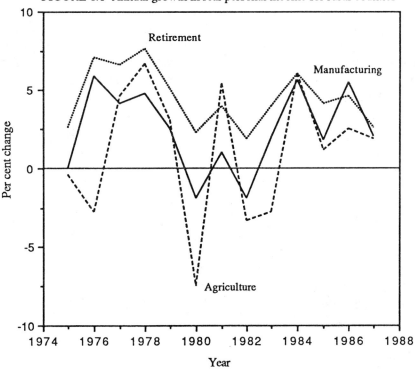

FIGURE 6.1 Annual growth in real personal income for rural counties

Source: U.S. Dept. of Commerce, Bureau of Economic Analysis, Washington, D.C.

farms that, while still controlled by families, operate much like similarly sized urban small businesses. The largest 307,000 U.S. farms now produce three-fourths of the nation's food and fiber (Table 6.1). In 1987, these farms had average assets of $1.2 million and average gross incomes of $355,000. These commercial farm businesses operate within much larger market regions than small family farms have in the past. They often purchase inputs directly from manufacturers and market their products directly with major processors. Financing needs often exceed the capacity of local lenders.

Meanwhile, the seventy-two percent of U.S. farms which are considered "small"—those with annual sales less than $40,000—receive only one percent of agriculture's net cash income. These farms depend on off-farm sources for nearly all of their family income, and thus tend to be located in areas that offer nonfarm employment opportunities.

determinant of income growth to these farms than either farm economic conditions or farm policies.

The decline in farm numbers means that farm production can be supported with less public and private infrastructure in rural places. Large farms tend to make business decisions based on a much larger market area. They may have direct marketing contracts, for example, with food processors some distance away. Or, they may arrange financing with major credit institutions in large cities. Thus, a concentration in farm production is being matched by a consolidation of agribusiness. In fact, consolidation in the farm input and grain industries has been a hallmark of the farm economy in the 1980s. With that consolidation comes fewer local agricultural businesses to sustain small farm communities. In short, fewer farms is leading to fewer viable farm communities and a general decline in public infrastructure in rural areas.

Farm prosperity, therefore, will not bring prosperity to all rural communities now located in farming regions. Rather, larger farms point toward fewer small rural communities in farm-dependent rural counties. Those communities large enough to serve as market centers for a large region will enjoy continued growth as agribusiness services are concentrated there.

Summary

Farm-dependent rural America's economic growth has been more variable and more sluggish, on average, in the 1980s than the nation as a whole. These counties, in the main, remain heavily dependent on agriculture and were relatively unsuccessful in diversifying their economies in the 1980s, the main explanation for economic problems through the decade. Economic upheaval in the 1980s spawned great structural change in farming and its supporting agribusiness services. The structural change points to fewer viable small communities in the future.

The New Rural Reality

Before discussing policy options for farm-dependent rural America, it is useful to first outline the parameters that will constrain the policy decision. Four factors, in particular, help to describe the new rural

TABLE 6.1 Size and structure of U.S. agriculture, average levels for 1983-87

Annual Sales	Number of farms (thousands)	Percent of all farms	Percent of direct government payments	Percent of gross U.S. farm sales	Percent of net cash income
Less than $40,000	1,635	72.0	15.0	10.1	1.0
$40,000 to $99,999	321	14.1	23.9	14.9	13.3
$100,000 to $249,999	218	9.6	32.9	24.1	25.6
$250,000 to $499,999	72	3.2	18.0	18.1	21.6
More than $500,000	27	1.2	10.1	32.8	38.5
Addenda: More than $100,000	317	14.0	61.0	75.0	85.7
All Farms	2,272	100.0	100.0	100.0	100.0

Source: *Economic Indicators of the Farm Sector, National Financial Summary, 1987.* Washington, D.C.: Economic Research Service, U.S. Department of Agriculture.

reality: uneven rural performance, limited federal policy, rural fiscal pressure, and efficient rural financial markets.

Rural Economic Growth Will Be Uneven

The rural economy will remain a collection of winners and losers in the 1990s. There is every indication that a quilt-like pattern of unevenness will continue, both in farm-dependent rural areas and elsewhere. Rural communities each have a unique set of economic assets and liabilities. With the U.S. and farm economies both now subject to a manifold and complex set of global forces, different parts of the rural economy will respond in very different ways.

Put another way, there appears to be no rural economic tidal wave coming that will lift all boats in the 1990s. Instead, there will be a continual ebb and flow, some rural communities prospering, some declining. Quite simply, not all of the rural communities in the 600-odd farm-dependent rural counties will survive. Populations in many farm communities peaked in the early 1900s. Although many of the communities have hung on the past fifty years, it appears unlikely that all will prosper into the next century. Such is the ongoing sequel of U.S. agriculture— developing technologically and becoming part of a world food market.

Limited Federal Rural Policy

Rural development policy will be mostly the province of state and local governments in the 1990s. That role will occur by default; no clearly defined federal rural policy appears likely. The United States has a farm policy; it has no rural policy (Drabenstott, Henry, and Gibson 1987). For more than fifty years, the nation has allowed farm policy to do the work of rural policy. As a result, farm policy has great inertia within Congress and U.S. agriculture. Rural policy, on the other hand, has little legislative momentum.

Farm policy reaches too few rural people to achieve broad rural policy objectives, even in many farm-dependent rural counties. For example, only one in 175 Americans lives on a commercial farm, that is, a farm with annual sales greater than $40,000 (U.S. Department of Commerce 1988). Only one in fifty rural residents lives on such a farm. Moreover, counties with predominantly small, part-time farms are more dependent on a broad mix of economic activity than farm income alone.[3] These counties may represent half the farming counties in the nation, but account for an even bigger share of the population in farm-dependent rural America.

Ironically, a broad reassessment of farm policy goals and programs could arise from an unexpected source—the Uruguay Round of General Agreement on Tariffs and Trade (GATT) negotiations. The Uruguay Round could result in a liberalization in agricultural trade rules. Such an accord would require that nations modify income support programs to eliminate price distortions on world markets. In essence, that would make farm income support programs more transparent and more like welfare payments. With such change, consumers may reconsider the validity of farm income support as a goal of public policy. Federal rural development initiatives, meanwhile, could gain support (Drabenstott, Barkema, and Henneberry 1989).

Considerable rural policy innovation is occurring at the state government level. States are considering and implementing programs ranging from rural job training to rural venture capital and technology transfer (John, Batie, and Norris 1988). Rural states appear to have concluded that federal budget austerity will prevent broad scale federal rural development programs (John 1987). Barring dramatic policy developments in the 1990s, that conclusion appears warranted.

Rural Fiscal Pressure

With a variable rural economy in prospect, it follows that some rural local governments will face persistent fiscal pressure. Strained budgets already are evident in many farm communities. Fiscal pressure will inevitably lead to change in the provision of rural public services. Change will come either through innovation or necessity, and in the long run the former will be cheaper to society. Such basic issues as county courthouses, and the need to consolidate services across county lines, will be part of the innovation or the necessity.

Efficient Rural Financial Markets

A fourth reality in rural America is that rural financial markets now work efficiently. That is a benefit to farm and rural businesses because capital is readily available, in sharp contrast to many periods through history when capital was scarce. Deregulation has integrated rural and national money markets, in the process giving rural financial institutions the tools to retain deposits. One seeming negative, however, is that rural borrowers now must pay market-based interest rates. The regulation of the past amounted to an indigenous interest rate subsidy. Now, viable rural businesses must be able to pay market rates. In short, rural America must now compete with urban America for capital.

Summary

Farm-dependent regions face a new rural reality. Economic growth will remain uneven, due to the uniqueness of local characteristics at a time when global events will affect all. Rural development policy probably will fall to state and local governments; it is unlikely that federal farm programs will be quickly redirected to rural initiatives. Farm communities are likely to face ongoing fiscal pressures. Finally, rural financial markets now operate quite efficiently, guaranteeing a steady supply of capital but at market interest rates.

Policy Choices for Farm-Dependent Rural Areas

How can farm states and farming communities influence their rural economic future? Rural policy makers face two fundamental choices: rural development policy and rural adjustment policy (Drabenstott, Henry, and Gibson 1987). The principal objective of rural development is to stimulate economic activity in rural places, even though market winds may be blowing in the other direction. The principal objective of rural adjustment policy is to ease the transition of rural people and resources to productive use elsewhere in the economy. Viewed this way, rural adjustment policy intrinsically focuses on people while rural development policy, while affecting people in profound ways, at root is related to place. With a rural growth that is likely to be uneven, rural policy should be a judicious mix of the two.

Rural Development Policy

Rural development policy often involves leaning against market winds. Economic activity has steadily migrated to urban places for the past century. Thus, it is prudent to keep rural development goals pragmatic, bearing in mind that rural development will not save all farm-dependent rural places.

To be successful, rural development initiatives must be tailored to the community involved. Still, four guidelines will be useful to all development initiatives: pool development efforts, target public spending, reassess rural institutions, and build on economic strengths.

1. *Pool development efforts.* Rural America must overcome some significant handicaps relative to the rest of the economy. It follows, then, that rural America must join forces if it wants to close the gap with the rest of the economy. There are simply not enough resources for every farm community and every farm state to succeed independently. Many heartland states are in the same economic boat, and yet each competes hard against its neighbors.

The problem is often worse within states. Iowa, for example, is a leading farm state with ninety-nine counties. Many of these counties have very similar economic make-ups. Economic development in Iowa must be seen not as a summation of ninety-nine individual economic development strategies. Instead, the state should pursue a strategy where gains and losses will naturally occur side by side, but where the gains will outweigh the losses. Such a strategy can be observed in some parts of Iowa where small towns have combined as "clusters." These communities pool efforts, recognizing that development successes will benefit the local area even if not every town shares fully in that success.

2. *Target public spending.* There will not be enough rural development to go around in the 1990s. Neither will there be enough state or federal dollars to go around. Farm-dependent rural areas will be left with the politically unpleasant task, therefore, of targeting rural development efforts where the chances of success are highest. Successful rural development will occur where policy makers build on existing strengths and admit that not every rural community will survive the new economic reality. The tendency to distribute funds to gain maximum political support for a program often means that investments are made where economic payoffs—in terms of business formation—are not the greatest.

Selecting appropriate indicators to differentiate winners and losers poses a real challenge. Research indicates that some characteristics do appear to separate rural winners and losers. For example, winning rural counties tend to be larger, they tend to be near metropolitan areas, and have low wages. They also tend to have a dense core of existing businesses. Losing counties, on the other hand, tend to be more remote, less populated, and have higher wages and transportation costs (Henry and Gibson 1988). Development efforts need to be targeted toward counties more likely to be winners while transition efforts need to be targeted toward counties more likely to be losers. While targeting development efforts may not be politically attractive, the alternative-spreading efforts too thin with only minimal success—is even less attractive.

3. *Reassess rural institutions.* Historically, rural America has given root to some enormously successful institutions. Two prominent examples are land grant universities and the Cooperative Extension Service. These institutions traditionally have been focused to a great extent on production agriculture. The question is, Can these institutions and their resident skills now be swung into play for rural development? That is already occurring to some extent, but not within a clearly defined rural policy.

Great resources can be applied to the rural economic problem. But historically, those resources have been solidly tied only to production agriculture. Is it time for states to reevaluate the focus of some traditional agricultural institutions, such as land grant universities and the extension service? That does not mean forsaking agriculture. It does mean transferring some of the skills we have developed in production agriculture to other parts of the rural economy.

4. *Build on economic strengths.* The key here is to thoroughly understand farm-dependent rural America's economic assets and liabilities. Agriculture remains the predominant economic base. Given that, chasing smokestacks makes little economic sense. Pursuing a strategy of adding value to farm products does. For agriculture, the only real rural development option will be food processing or biotechnology advances that lead to new product derivations. In either case, with very cheap labor in the third world, the key to a value-added approach will be state of the art technology. Without that, the rural location simply offers no payoff.

The strategy of adding value to farm production offers many benefits to farming communities in rural areas. The food industry is noncyclical, offering steady growth to rural communities. Dependence on government programs declines as macroeconomic conditions become relatively more important than farm policy benefits. Thus, rural communities can dampen the dramatic cycles in the farm economy that have been so damaging in the 1980s.

Rural Adjustment Policy

Rural development will not work for all farm-dependent rural America. Some places will continue to decline. What can be done for those places? There are two simple options: ease the transition for rural people and ease the transition for rural infrastructure. Job retraining is an obvious program to ease human adjustment, and many rural states have expanded such programs in recent years.

Rural infrastructure adjustment, on the other hand, is an area that continues to be overlooked. Many rural tax bases can no longer support the roads, court houses, hospitals, and schools they once did. The rural infrastructure problem is symptomatic of the new rural economic reality. Some rural places simply do not sustain sufficient economic activity to support their historical base of public services. The infrastructure problem persists because the rural economy adjusts more rapidly than the political economy. Many rural places are naturally reluctant to admit that they may need to consolidate their court house with the neighboring county.

What can be done to solve the problem? State policy makers could establish an objective of easing and encouraging adjustment in public infrastructure that reduces the long run costs to society. Some obvious programs to achieve such an objective would be incentives to consolidate the provision of public services—even including the consolidation of county seat services across county lines. The real policy challenge is to overcome existing vested interests who oppose change without giving rise to new vested interests who will then oppose any change in the future.

Conclusions

Farm-dependent rural areas look forward to a better economic decade in the 1990s following the difficult 1980s. Despite some attempts to diversify local economies, agriculture remains the dominant economic base for about a quarter of the nation's nonmetropolitan counties. Rural economic success will not be shared equally, and economic growth will not be strong enough to make all farm communities prosper.

102

In light of this outlook, farm states and communities do have rural policy choices. A judicious mix of rural development policy and rural adjustment policy is called for. To succeed, rural development efforts will have to be concentrated on viable communities. Traditional rural institutions may need to be re-evaluated. Finally, farm-dependent regions will have to explore ways of adding value to agricultural production; most communities will have few economic alternatives.

Notes

1. The views expressed here are strictly those of the author and do not necessarily represent those of the Federal Reserve Bank of Kansas City or the Federal Reserve System.

2. The definition of nonmetropolitan areas in this chapter is the same used in Henry, Drabenstott, and Gibson (1987). The county type framework was first developed by Lloyd Bender and others (1985).

3. Carlin and Green (1988) divided farming counties into three categories: large-farm, small-farm, and unclassified. They concluded that large-farm counties will rise or fall on U.S. agriculture's ability to compete internationally and the support farmers receive through government programs. Small-farm counties, on the other hand, offer a more diverse mix of economic activity, some of which--labor-intensive manufacturing, in particular--is also subject to international competitive pressures.

References

Bender, Lloyd, and others. 1985. "The Diverse Social and Economic Structure of Nonmetropolitan America," *Rural Development Research Report 49.* Washington: Economic Research Service, U.S. Department of Agriculture.
Carlin, Thomas A. and Bernal L. Green. 1988. "Local Farm Structure and Community Ties," *Rural Development Research Report 68.* Washington: Economic Research Service, U.S.D.A.

Drabenstott, Mark, Alan Barkema, and David Henneberry. 1989. "Agriculture and the GATT: The Link to U.S. Farm Policy." in *Economic Review*. May. Pp. 3-24. Kansas City, MO: Federal Reserve Bank of Kansas City.

Drabenstott, Mark, Mark Henry, and Lynn Gibson. 1987. "The Rural Economic Policy Choice."in *Economic Review*. January. Pp. 41-58. Kansas City, MO: Federal Reserve Bank of Kansas City.

Henry, Mark and Lynn Gibson. 1988. "Searching for Rural Success." in *Rural America in Transition*. Pp. 39-58. Kansas City, MO: Federal Reserve Bank of Kansas City.

John, DeWitt. 1987. *Shifting Responsibilities: Federalism in Economic Development*. Washington: National Governors' Association.

John, DeWitt, Sandra Batie, and Kim Norris. 1988. *A Brighter Future for Rural America? Strategies for Communities and States*. Washington: National Governor's Association.

U.S. Department of Commerce. 1988. *Statistical Abstract of the United States, 1988*, Washington.

7

The Role of Community in Rural Economic Development

Jerry L. Wade and Glen C. Pulver

High rates of general unemployment in the early 1980s, persistent pockets of unemployment in the late 1980s, a decade of decline in personal income in specific regions, and a widespread concern for sustained economic vitality have generated a great deal of political attention throughout the United States. Although jobless youth, the working poor, and the homeless can attest to the gravity of urban difficulties, nowhere are economic problems more evident today than in rural America. Conditions have turned seriously worse in rural areas. After years of slow but steady gain in the relative economic well-being of rural areas, a growing disparity now exists between people who live in these regions and their urban counterparts.

The rural economic crisis of the 1980s sharpened public awareness of the turn in the fortunes of rural America. Rural Americans now have lower incomes, fewer job opportunities, higher underemployment rates, and are more apt to live in poverty. And things are getting worse (Eberts 1986). Prior to 1973, per capita income grew faster in nonmetropolitan regions than in metropolitan regions. Some time in the mid 1970s metropolitan areas began to achieve greater income gains. In the 1979 to 1984 period, real per capita income rose 0.8 percent in metropolitan areas and only 0.3 percent in nonmetropolitan areas (Henry, et al. 1986).

Throughout most of the 1980s, the number of jobs in nonmetropolitan areas grew at a slower rate than in metropolitan areas. Although unemployment rates are only slightly higher in nonmetropolitan areas, underemployment is much higher. In nonmetropolitan areas 18.1 percent of working age people are considered underemployed, compared to 12.3 percent in metropolitan areas. Rural areas have a much higher incidence of working poor. The incidence of poverty in nonmetropolitan areas (18.3 percent) is one-third larger than that of metropolitan areas (13.8 percent) (Cordes 1987).

Some doomsayers believe few future economic opportunities exist in rural America, and thus communities located in these regions will die. Romanticists are convinced that rural America must be saved regardless of the cost. The positions of the doomsayers and the romanticists lead to different sets of policies and action programs, neither of which is likely to enable rural communities to find their place and develop their potential in the world of the 1990s.

The purpose of this chapter is to present a perspective on the economic environment in which rural development must take place, the nature of the rural economic conditions, and what communities can do to create their own "new future." Historic economic patterns and policies will be reviewed. This will be followed by a discussion of economic changes and their import for rural communities. The chapter will conclude with ways communities can achieve their potential in rural economic development and the kind of policy orientation necessary to support strong community economic development.

Historic Economic Policy and Patterns

Following World War II, the United States experienced a period of major economic expansion lasting approximately thirty years. The primary expansion occurred in the manufacturing sector of large industrial corporations. Dillman (1986), Hobbs (1987), and others have characterized these years as the era of the mass society—a period characterized by scientific management, efficiency and economics of scale.

These influences affected many aspects of economic and institutional life, including public and private decision making. Business focused almost exclusively on vertically integrated sectors; economic control shifted to concentrated and centralized corporate structures. National policy placed primary political control of economic development policy at the federal level. Because of the attention given to the national economy and macro systems, the community became less important as a locus of decision making. The perception that the community had little influence or control dominated. Coincidently, this view was reinforced by the social sciences, which focused attention on the predominance of the mass society and its preemption of the community.

During the 1950s, 60s, and 70s, economic development was a major political concern. U.S. population was increasing rapidly. The signs of new economic activity were everywhere. Two questions were paramount during those years of economic boom: (1) How is the industrial expansion to be distributed geographically throughout the country? and, (2) How can the "left out" groups get a piece of the action? The federal government was expected to answer both.

Employment was growing rapidly in the manufacturing and construction sectors. Products were needed to feed the rapidly increasing hunger for material wealth. Homes were needed for the burgeoning population. Less obvious was the even more rapid growth in the services-producing sector. In any event, historic applications of export base theory indicated the goods-producing industries were more important for community economic well-being. Because of the concentration of attention on manufacturing and construction, economic development became synonymous with industrial development.

Political control was maintained at the top, and the community was a limited participant. Economic development was detached, almost by default, from long-term community goals and the process of building strong communities. Reflective of the mass society paradigm, economic development efforts in most communities involved the homogeneous application of a set of common techniques attempting to achieve the same desired outcomes. Policy for economic/industrial development strived to increase the economic base of a community by "attracting" manufacturing plants. Most perceived that community leaders could do little to stimulate economic growth other than entice industrial locators of large firms.

The Changes

The world has changed significantly in the past two decades. Beginning in the 1970s, the basic production industries that had formed the backbone of the U.S. economy were struggling to maintain their international competitiveness. In fact, economic patterns and, subsequently, political relationships around the globe began undergoing major alterations. Throughout the U.S., basic and widespread changes in the structure of the economic system occurred. Characterizations of the present—the information age, the service economy, the communications era, the post-industrial society—all note the increasing globalization of the economic system. The world is experiencing a period of basic economic restructuring and reordering of economic patterns and techniques.

First, the structure of the economy is moving away from large, centralized manufacturing facilities that focus on standardized, high-volume production systems to systems that emphasize information, service, and decentralized production. Small firms and business start-ups have become the primary generators of employment growth.

Second, most of the new job growth in the developed world is occurring in the services-producing sector. Of the top forty industries projected to produce three-fourths of the net new jobs in the U.S. between 1984 and 1985, thirty-four are in the services-producing sector, five are in high-technology manufacturing, and one is in construction (Bureau of Labor Statistics 1986; Pulver 1986). Large segments of the services-producing sector, including industries such as insurance, data processing, computer software writing, mail-order catalogs, engineering consultants, and state and national government, can and do serve as basic employers. Clearly, industrial development focused on attracting manufacturing has a less important role.

Third, a major increase can be found in income controlled by the elderly. This is playing an increasingly important role in consumer and investment expenditures patterns, and thus the allocation of economic activity. The elderly are inclined to spend more on services such as health care, while the younger are more apt to spend on consumer goods such as automobiles. Younger individuals have less money for investment but are more likely to invest in longer-term, higher-risk opportunities.

Fourth, the focus on the nation-state as the controlling macroeconomic system is shifting to one of simultaneous globalization and localization of the economy. As a consequence, development policy is shifting from a community problem solving orientation and response to local felt needs to one of enabling communities to understand and respond to more global economic changes in building a future (Wade 1988). Today, the community is heavily dependent on international macropolitical and economic systems. Its future will be defined largely by its ability to respond appropriately to these complex conditions.

At the macroeconomic level, the dominance of the vertically integrated economies of the nation-state is being replaced by a dual economic system, global and local (community) economies. The global economy is dominated by large world-class corporations. The emphasis is on competition for increasing world market share. Large corporations are capital and knowledge intensive and focus on research and development, marketing and assembly. The actual work of producing things is often moved to companies producing for the world-class corporations under contract. Many large world-class corporations have experienced an actual decline in jobs because of their shift in economic function (Sunter 1986).

Global economic policy has begun to overshadow national policy. Capital moves relatively easily across national borders in response to shifts in exchange rates, interest rates, and political stability. Unfavorable international terms of trade can have a devastating effect on a country's industry. Although national policy remains extremely important, it must be chosen with a careful eye on the international scene.

At the same time, the actions of local policy makers, both public and private, have grown in importance. Independent companies or small branches of larger firms are supplying big corporations on a "just-in-time" basis. Other small firms emphasizing flexibility, quality, and service are frequently competitive in specialized niches in the international market. The rapidly growing services-producing industries are also composed primarily of small firms. Employment and income growth are less affected by plant location choices of huge national firms and more by the action of small establishments. Because of the size and ownership patterns of these establishments, community leaders are in a position to have a much more powerful influence on local economic conditions.

With these fundamental changes, the process of economic development shifts from reliance on a single or a few homogeneous strategies to multiple diverse strategies. Attraction strategies remain important as large regional or national firms continue to establish small branches in new communities. These strategies must, however, include services-producing industries as well as manufacturers. The major policy shift is caused by the growing significance of the small independent business in job generation. Community economic development policy now includes efforts aimed at the expansion of small existing firms and the creation of new businesses. Local leaders are increasingly sensitive to the importance of stopping the leakage of consumer dollars to larger markets and the importance of strategies that keep the economically powerful elderly population from migrating to other regions.

The quality of the local economic environment plays an important role in determining where new firms are started, where new branches are located, and where the growth of existing firms is stimulated. Limited access to capital, information, transportation, and communications retards rural economic development. These variables can be affected by policy manipulation. Community decision makers dominate both state and national leadership in the manipulation of policy, influencing access to most of these critical locational variables. Nonetheless, the policy tools local leaders have at hand (i.e., financing, regulating power, technical assistance) are strongly influenced by state and national legislation.

Rural Economic Conditions

Rural America has been profoundly affected by all of these general shifts in economic structure. For well over sixty years, rural America has gone through a gradual but major economic change. Rural areas, once heavily farm dependent, have become more and more like their urban counterparts. In 1920, three in ten Americans lived on farms and six out of ten rural residents did so. By 1980, less than three in 100 Americans and only one in ten rural residents lived on farms (Wimberley 1986).

Although agriculture remains a critical industry, the personal income generated by farming is of declining importance even in the most farm-dependent states (Schluter and Edmondson 1986). Farm earnings, which had hovered around six to eight per cent of total U.S. personal income from 1930 to the late 1940s when they reached ten per cent, dropped to less than two per cent in the 1980s. In 1979, a year of peak farm earnings in the United States, the people in the 702 most farm-dependent counties in the United States received only 19.8 per cent of their total personal income from farming. Dividends, interest, and rent accounted for 17.6 per cent, and transfer payments 14.5 per cent. Other nonfarm sources accounted for 48.1 per cent of personal income (Pulver and Rogers 1986).

In recent years, farm families have become much more closely tied to nearby communities. Large numbers of farm operators and their spouses are working off farm on a part- or full-time basis (Salant, et al. 1984). Currently over forty per cent of the farmers in nonmetropolitan counties work off the farm over 100 days. Nonfarm income from earnings and passive sources makes up about half the total family income of U.S. farm operator households (Jesse, et al. 1988). In many cases the nonfarm income sources sustain the farm family and the farm operation as well. Sixty per cent of farm households in the U.S. gross less than $25,000 in total household income. On average, these households experience a net loss from the farm business. The eighty-eight per cent of farm households with incomes less than $60,000 per year on average gain more income from nonfarm sources than from farming (Harrington and Carlin 1986).

Rural America has become a complex economy with diverse sources of income. One in five people working in nonmetropolitan counties is employed (including the self-employed) in manufacturing. About one in seven is in trade. About the same number are employed in government (BLS and USDA/ERS 1986). Twenty-one per cent of U.S. nonmetropolitan counties are identified as retirement centers. They are primarily dependent on income from dividends, interest, rent and social security payments (Bender, et al. 1985). About one dollar in three of total personal income in the U.S. is in the hands of the elderly.

In spite of the fact that the general level of economic well-being is declining in rural America, some specific rural communities are doing quite well. The regions most severely affected by income and employment reductions are those that are relatively remote and heavily dependent on farming, forestry, manufacturing, and mining. The high-priced dollar (in terms of foreign exchange) of the early 1980s which so severely affected the U.S. farm sector, had an equally devastating impact on rural employment and income from the goods-producing sectors. The rural communities most likely to be booming are those near urban centers with new branches of services-producing firms or high-tech manufacturers. Or, they may be at the center of an in-migration of retirees, near a growing suburb, close to the site of a mineral exploitation or some other expanding industry.

Like the rest of the United States, rural America's economic future remains closely tied to the success of the goods-producing sector. Government policies and individual decisions that affect the capacity of rural areas to be internationally competitive in farming, forestry, manufacturing, and mining are crucial. Some income growth may come from agriculture, forestry and mining but probably with reduced employment. Older firms in slower growing and declining manufacturing industries will continue to restructure production and distribution processes, creating new branch locations and/or expansions of some existing facilities. In addition, technological development will lead to entirely new products and business start-ups. Rural areas, too, must look to services-producing industries and high technology manufacturers for growth in employment.

The Opportunity

Changed economic conditions necessitate major modifications in the logic and process of economic development. Traditionally, economic policy in the U.S. has focused on maintaining and protecting industrial production. Policy has been based on the assumption that the industrial paradigm would continue to be the predominant means for organizing the U.S. economy, the belief that the U.S. would remain the dominant international economic power, and the premise that the future economic well-being of the economy would be through continued growth of the goods-producing sector. As such, the policy process, just like corporately controlled production systems, became largely centralized. Public policy was set by the federal government, and federal agencies developed the programs that implemented the various policies. Communities were funded, primarily through grants, to do as the federal government decreed. The role of the state was to expedite the process. Even in that role they were frequently by-passed as an increasing number of programs involved a direct federal-local connection. State initiatives were limited largely to industrial attraction strategies.

For a number of reasons, the industrial paradigm with its focus on stimulating large manufacturers and goods-producers no longer suffices. A significant shift in U.S. political perspectives has resulted in a sharp reduction of federal financial support to state and local governments. Most new employment is being generated by small firms. Services-producing industries will be the primary source of net job growth. International economic activity is increasingly preempting national policy. If the United States is to adjust to the new economic reality, it must abandon its historic preoccupation with national policy focused on the goods-producing sector and shift to one that is more comprehensive with greater local responsibility and opportunity.

In the contemporary world, each community must find and implement ways to increase efficiency and diversity, and identify opportunities for new productivity in a way that builds the kind of community people want. If the U.S. economy is to be successfully rebuilt into a dynamic, diverse, and healthy economy, policy will require more local input, with each community defining its long-term community goals and developing programs to achieve them. Communities must now play a more aggressive and important role in policy development. The federal and state governments are still active participants. No longer can the federal government dominate policy. But its social security expenditures, investments in the military, tax policy, and consequent dividends and interest and deregulation decisions affect the distribution of economic growth. With the reduction in direct federal assistance, states now play a more important role in providing financial and technical assistance. All must be cognizant of the overall power of the global economy. Economic development policy must be more complex, comprehensive, and politically integrated at all levels.

Communities wishing to be economically viable must combine a belief in themselves with a willingness to work hard and a commitment to sustained effort. On this foundation, they must build local economic development policy combining multiple strategies relevant to their unique goals and resources. These strategies must be well-informed to produce the greatest payoff.

Unfortunately, too often policy makers advocate relatively simple, single-purpose programs to generate more jobs and income. Little is accomplished by this approach. No single action or combination of actions will guarantee more jobs or income or a strengthened local economy. For example, some communities have invested in an industrial park with the necessary infrastructure, assuming that will result in a favorable location decision. The amount of vacant space in rural industrial parks demonstrates the inadequacy of industrial parks as single-purpose programs. Another community may decide it needs to spiff up its downtown and believes that is all that is necessary to increase business activity.

The need for comprehensive community economic development policy is especially acute in rural America. Rural economies are heavily dependent on small establishments and limited economic diversity. Their geographic separation from large urban centers makes access to critical variables, such as knowledge, capital, transportation, and telecommunications more difficult. Thus, rural community opportunities for economic growth are more limited. As a consequence, their policy choices must be more prudent. Therefore, to be effective, local economic development policy must be comprehensive, yet particularized by the community to its specific conditions.

Rural America's problems are compounded by a number of factors. First, their economic policy knowledge base is narrower. For example, bankers' lending experience may be limited to farming or agribusiness. Second, they are more distant from required external resources such as debt capital and technical assistance. Third, they have a narrower financial base in both the private and public sectors with which to acquire needed policy assistance. Urban taxpayers can support a substantial economic development department to provide economic analysis assistance. Rural communities can rarely afford to hire an equivalent level of professional expertise.

Perhaps the most important initiative that national and state governments could undertake to revitalize rural America would be to expand education and technical assistance in economic development provided to local government, business, and community groups. A great deal of energy is currently wasted in fruitless efforts simply because people are not well-informed about the community economic development methodologies available to them (John, et al. 1988).

More intelligent community economic policy also would prove helpful in framing state and national policy. State and national legislators would be better able to assess the effectiveness of existing legislation if community leaders were wiser in their decisions and actions. As it is, local decision makers all too often make policy choices based on the programs offered by broader governments rather than on well-defined local needs and opportunities. The results are usually less than desired. Clearly a place for national and state economic initiatives exists, but aggressive local economic policy development would be of great assistance in the formulation of more effective programs.

Summary

The responsibility for development and implementation of economic development policy and action is shifting from the federal level to the community level. This is the result of two changes. One is the shift in economic systems to the global/local economic structure. The second is the change of focus of federal policy from national to local.

Four implications of these changes are of vital importance to the future of rural well-being. First, community leadership is much more important and requires a far greater level of knowledge and understanding of the community economy and the changes occurring. Second, the role of the professional shifts from delivering predetermined programs to rural communities to being a resource available to rural communities to carry out locally defined policy. Third, policy education shifts from informing communities about policy to empowering communities to develop policy. Fourth, the policy emphasis of state and federal government shifts from policy that results in specific programs to policy designed to create an environment supportive of communities implementing their own policies.

During periods of economic transition, new possibilities and opportunities emerge for those who think in new ways and turn their ideas into action. The future of rural America will strongly be determined by the extent to which its people assume responsibility for their own economic well-being. The role of community in rural economic development is to be nothing less than the source of leadership in the development and implementation of local policy that begins to rebuild rural economies.

References

Bender, Lloyd D. and others. 1985. *The Diverse Social and Economic Structure of Nonmetropolitan America*. Washington, D.C.: United States Department of Agriculture, Economic Research Service.

Cordes, Sam M. 1987. "The Changing Rural Environment and the Relationship Between Health Services and Rural Development." Unpublished Manuscript. Laramie, Wyoming: University of Wyoming, College of Agriculture.

Dillman, Don. 1986. "Social Issues Impacting Agriculture and Rural Areas as We Approach the 21st Century." Joint Economic Committee of Congress. *New Dimensions in Rural Policy: Building Upon Our Heritage.* Pp. 19-31. Washington, D.C.: U.S. Government Printing Office.

Eberts, Paul. 1986. "Economic Development in Rural America: Situations, Prospects and Policies." Joint Economic Committee of Congress. *New Dimensions in Rural Policy: Building Upon Our Heritage.* Pp. 529-546. Washington, D.C.: U.S. Government Printing Office.

Harrington, David and Thomas Carlin. 1986. "The U.S. Farm Sector: How Is It Weathering the 1980s?" Washington, D.C.: United States Department of Agriculture, Economic Research Service, Agricultural Information Bulletin 506.

Henry, Mark, Mark Drabenstott, and Lynn Gibson. 1986. "A Changing Rural America." *Economic Review. 71: 23-41. Kansas City MO: The Federal Reserve Bank of Kansas City.*

Hobbs, Daryl. 1987. "Enterprise Development: Is It a Viable Goal for Rural Communities." Paper presented at National Rural Entrepreneurship Symposium. Knoxville, Tennessee.

Jesse, Edward V., William Saupe, Glen Pulver, Ron Shaffer, Brian Gould, and Susan Bentley. 1988. *"Status of Wisconsin Farming 1988." Madison, WI: University of Wisconsin, Department of Agricultural Economics.*

John, DeWitt, Sandra S. Batie, and Kim Norris. 1988. *A Brighter Future for Rural America?* Washington, D.C.: National Governors' Association.

Pulver, Glen C. 1986. "Economic Growth in Rural America." Joint Economic Committee of Congress. *New Dimensions In Rural Policy: Building Upon Our Heritage.* Pp. 491-508. Washington, D.C.: U.S. Government Printing Office.

Pulver, Glen C. and Glenn R. Rogers. 1986. "Changes in Income Sources in Rural America." *American Journal of Agricultural Economics.* 68: 1181-1187.

Salant, Priscilla, William Saupe, and John Belnap. 1984. "Highlights of the 1983 Wisconsin Family Farm Survey." Madison, WI: College of Agriculture and Life Sciences, Bulletin R3294.

Schluter, Gerald and William Edmundson. 1986. "How To Tell How Important Agriculture Is To Your State." *Rural Development Perspectives.* Pp. 32-34. Washington, D.C.: United States Department of Agriculture, Economic Research Service.

Sunter, Clem. 1986. *The World and South Africa in the 1990s.* Tafelberg, South Africa: Human and Rouseas.

U.S. Department of Labor, Bureau of Labor Statistics (BLS) and the U.S. Department of Agriculture, Statistical Reporting Service (USDA/ERS). 1986. "Employment in Rural America in the Mid-1980s." Joint Economic Committee of Congress. *New Dimensions in Rural Policy: Building Upon*

Our Heritage. Pp. 144-159. Washington, D.C.: U.S. Government Printing Office.

Wade, Jerry L. 1988. "Economic Development and the Small Community," Paper presented at the Eighth Conference on the Small City and Regional Community, Normal, IL.

Wimberley, Ronald C. 1986. "America's Three Agricultures." Joint Economic Committee of Congress. *New Dimensions in Rural Policy: Building Upon Our Heritage.* Pp. 192-199. Washington, D.C.: U.S. Government Printing Office.

8

Encouraging Economic Development in Rural America

William R. Gillis

Approximately three-quarters of the nation's communities are classified by the U.S. Census Bureau as rural.[1]

These communities are home to 56.6 million Americans. While some rural areas are doing well, the average rural American has a lower income level, a greater likelihood of being unemployed, and a greater chance of living in poverty than their urban neighbors (Weber,et al. 1988).

Figure 8.1 illustrates that while the current national economic recovery has benefitted both rural and urban communities, a widening gap exists between economic conditions in nonmetropolitan and metropolitan counties. Between 1980 and 1990, total metropolitan employment grew twenty per cent compared to only eight per cent in nonmetropolitan America. Average unemployment rates have remained at least 1.5 percentage points higher in rural areas than in urban communities throughout this decade.

Rural Disadvantages

The nation's nonmetropolitan communities have populations smaller in size and more widely dispersed than metropolitan areas. Nonmetropolitan counties have an average population of twenty people per square mile in the nonmetropolitan counties compared to 322 persons

FIGURE 8.1   Widening gap between metropolitan and
nonmetropolitan employment in the 1980s

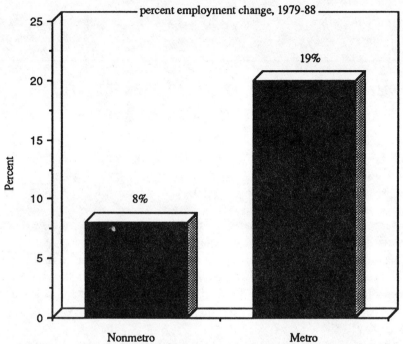

Source: Unpublished data; Economic Research Service, U.S. Dept. of Agriculture.

per square mile in metropolitan counties. This widely dispersed
population base places rural communities at a serious disadvantage to
urban centers in undertaking initiatives to improve economic conditions.
The following are among the most important of those disadvantages.

Lack of Realistic Opportunities

Although certainly not impossible, attracting new business and
industry to communities small in population size is considerably more
difficult than for places with a larger population base. In a study of
location decisions by more than 15,000 manufacturing firms throughout
the northeastern United States, Goode and Hastings (1987) document that
a community's chance of attracting a new manufacturing industry is

reduced substantially when the population base falls below 2,500 residents. Population size was found to be a key determinant in explaining manufacturing location decisions for each of the sixty-seven industries included in the study. Similarly, markets in smaller communities are often inadequate to support the development of more specialized retail and service businesses.

High Cost of Providing Key Public Facilities and Services

Public facilities and services, including roads, sewer and water systems, educational institutions, family services, and public transportation, each play a key role in supporting economic development. The "public" nature of these facilities and services means that the cost per taxpayer goes down as population increases. Consequently, small rural communities with their relatively small population base are generally at a disadvantage relative to urban centers in providing public facilities and services supporting economic development.

Fragmentation of Rural Economic Development Efforts

Rural people have more local governments to interact with than their urban counterparts. Rural areas, with 24 percent of the population, have 75 percent of the local government units in the United States (Weber, et al. 1988). Although it is difficult enough to coordinate economic development efforts of separate governmental units within an urban area, the task of coordination is complicated exponentially in rural areas. The result in many cases is fragmentation of efforts and ineffectiveness in rural economic development planning and implementation.

Need for Innovative Rural Economic Development Policies

Increasingly, policy analysts are challenging the traditional assumption that improved economic conditions in rural regions will follow naturally from improvement in the economic health of the state and nation as a whole (National Governors' Association 1988). Indeed, in every major region of the United States, employment has grown more slowly and unemployment has remained higher in nonmetropolitan places compared to metropolitan areas during the 1980s (Bluestone and Hession 1987).

Innovative programs and policies specifically designed for rural communities are needed if the growing gap between economic conditions in rural and urban America is to be closed. The vast majority of future job growth will occur in communities with populations in excess of 2,500. The economic reality is that smaller rural communities will not be successful in substantially expanding local job opportunities. Fortunately, within each of nation's rural counties, there is generally at least one and often several communities large enough to have substantial economic development potential.

The key to successful rural economic development is to focus job creation efforts in larger communities within predominantly rural regions, while linking residents of smaller rural communities to the newly created opportunities in these centers. Federal and state policies leading to the successful accomplishment of this goal fall into three distinct but interrelated categories:

- Policies focusing on rural people

- Policies focusing on rural communities

- Policies focusing on rural businesses

Each of these three policy options are highlighted below.

Policies Focusing on Rural People

The level of technical skills and education necessary to perform daily job tasks in business and industry is projected to increase at an exponential rate over the next decade (Reich 1987). Consequently, ensuring that rural workers have the skills and ability to participate effectively in an increasingly complex and technical economy is likely to be the number one factor determining the future economic fate of rural communities. With this fact in mind, the first priority for an effective initiative supporting rural economic development should be policies focusing on improving the productivity and employability of rural people. Examples of people-oriented economic development policies include improved access of rural residents to education, skill training, health care, and child care.

Education and Skill Training

Higher education and technical training will increasingly become a requisite for obtaining employment in tomorrow's economy. Half of all new jobs to be created over the next decade will require some level of education beyond high school. Frequent updating of technical skills is equally important as most workers entering the labor force today will retrain for entirely new careers at least three times over the course of their lifetimes (Hudson Institute 1987).

The availability of skilled labor is a critical factor influencing the ability of rural regions to attract and retain business and industry. For example, a Pennsylvania study indicates that even in areas with unemployment rates two to three percentage points higher than the national average, twenty-five percent of businesses surveyed reported problems recruiting skilled labor (Bell of Pennsylvania 1988). Data from this same study indicate that one-fifth of Pennsylvania's businesses are having difficulty recruiting workers with basic math, English, and communication skills. The long-term impact of labor recruitment problems is often the loss of existing employers and difficulty in attracting new firms to a region.

Rural residents on average have substantially less formal education than their urban counterparts. The gap in high school completion has persisted at about ten percentage points since 1960, and the gap in college education has actually increased over the past three decades. Low educational attainment and illiteracy are especially high in the rural South. While substantial differences exist among rural school districts, on average, rural schools have fewer resources, less adequate facilities, and less experienced teachers than urban counterparts (Ross and Rosenfeld 1987).

The problem of low educational attainment is compounded by a lack of effective skill training programs in rural areas (Bawden and Brown 1987). Factors such as geographic isolation, lack of professional support services, and funding constraints have led to an underutilization of existing training programs such as Joint Partnership Training Act and vocational education in rural areas (Hobbs, Heffernan, and Tweeten 1988).

A broader training issue, shared by both rural and urban areas, is that few states have developed effective systems to coordinate training programs with business needs (National Governors' Association 1988). This substantially reduces improvement of employment prospects of program graduates and limits the potential of training programs to solve the growing skilled labor shortages in rural areas. Improving both the utilization of existing training programs and the effectiveness of these programs in rural areas is critical to future economic development in rural America.

Health Care

A second rural economic development policy focusing on people as opposed to communities or businesses is health care. Health is a critical factor determining worker productivity and the ability of rural residents to earn an adequate living (Rosenblatt and Moscovice 1982).

Major differences in the organization and use of health care resources exist between rural and urban areas. In rural areas people tend to be older, poorer, and more geographically dispersed. Hospitals are smaller and not as well-equipped and flexible in dealing with change. Health care agencies in rural communities are fewer and often less able than their urban counterparts to compete economically and technologically for the health dollar (Jacques 1989).

As a result of these differences, rural areas generally have less access to health care resources than do urban residents. Cordes and Bruce (1989) identify a number of indicators that point to serious health resource needs in rural areas including: a smaller physician-to-population ratio in rural areas than in urban areas; the proportion of the poor who are covered by Medicaid is much lower in rural areas than in urban areas; and, a substantial proportion of the rural population is without a regular source of care. An additional and alarming health trend in recent years is the closing of rural hospitals. Often these hospitals serve as emergency centers and backup for local physicians. These closings represent a real loss to the communities they once served.

These disturbing trends in rural health care have broader implications than the physical well-being of rural Americans. The health fitness of the nation's rural work force is critical to its ability to participate effectively in available job opportunities and for business profitability.

Child Care

A third example of an economic development policy aimed at ensuring that rural residents are able to participate effectively in available job opportunities is child care. The entrance of women into the labor force is important to improving rural family incomes as well as in addressing the problem of growing labor shortages in rural areas (Center for Rural Pennsylvania 1988). Women will compose about three-fifths of the new entrants in the labor force between 1985 and 2000. Much of the increase in the numbers of women in the labor force has come from women with children (Hudson Institute 1987). The availability of child care is necessary for rural women with young children to participate in regular employment.

Organized child care is virtually nonexistent in many rural communities (Van Horn 1989). Innovative initiatives will be needed to strengthen the availability of child care and the ability of rural residents to participate in job opportunities within rural communities.

Policies Focusing on Rural Communities

Policies focusing on rural people can only be effective in improving rural economic conditions when combined with job creation efforts. Rural job creation strategies have traditionally focused on improving attractiveness of rural communities as a site for business and industry. State and federal financial assistance for improving highways, sewer and water systems, industrial parks, and business incubators are all examples of traditional initiatives designed to improve the attractiveness of rural locations for business and industry.

Rural policy analysts increasingly point to the need to broaden the focus of community-based economic development efforts to include initiatives to attract and retain new residents as well as new businesses (Pulver 1987). This recommendation is partly based on the realization that many smaller communities have only limited potential to attract new business and industry. However, the recommendation is also based on the recognition that adding new residents can often contribute as much to the economy of a small town as a new business.

New residents contribute to the economy of a small town in two ways. First, those residents who commute to surrounding employment centers for work bring their paychecks home. By spending these paychecks in local businesses and paying local taxes, new residents contribute to the long-run economic vitality of the community.

A second way new residents contribute to local economic vitality is by attracting new income into rural communities in the form of dividends and interest from personal investments and government payments such as social security income. Income from personal investments, social security, and other government payments represent the fastest growing income sources in rural America. Income from these sources grew at a rate more than five times as fast as income from manufacturing industries in nonmetropolitan areas between 1979 and 1986 (U.S. Department of Commerce 1988). Approximately one-third of total personal income in rural America comes from personal investments, social security, and government investments.

The tremendous growth of rural income from personal investments and social security in rural communities is partly attributable to persons of retirement age moving to smaller towns seeking a less expensive lifestyle. The retirement industry is big business. Research studies indicate that every dollar of retirement income coming into a rural community contributes two to three additional dollars to the local economy (Summers and Hirschl 1985). This is equivalent to the economic impact of a manufacturing firm.

Because of the growing importance of both retirees and rural commuters as income sources, it is critical that economic development policies focusing on rural communities be broadened to include initiatives aimed at attracting new residents as well as new businesses. Examples of key economic development opportunities focusing on rural communities include infrastructure improvements, community facilities and services, main street revitalization, and planning assistance.

Infrastructure Improvements

Investments in industrial sites, roads, bridges, and sewer and water facilities do not guarantee economic development will take place. Other essential ingredients, such as availability of key labor skills, access to markets and key inputs, must also be in place before development can occur. However, the lack of key infrastructure facilities can seriously hamper economic growth when other necessary ingredients are present.

As the fundamental nature of the rural economy has changed from an economy based on labor-intensive agriculture and natural resource based industries to today's more diversified and capital-intensive economy, the type of infrastructure needed to support economic activity in rural areas also has changed. For example, many of the roads and bridges constructed during the first part of this century were engineered for vehicles smaller than the large tractor-trailer trucks that carry products to and from rural communities today. Weight limited bridges and narrow roadways hinder business development in many areas.

Problems associated with sewer and water facilities have received special attention in the northeastern region of the United States. Because existing water and sewer systems are inadequate, an increasing number of rural communities are not permitted to construct new homes, restaurants, or factories.

In addition to the traditional focus on transportation and sewer and water facilities, infrastructure policy supporting rural economic development should be broadened to include housing and telecommunications. Ensuring an adequate availability of quality housing can aid rural communities in attracting new residents supporting the local economy. Telecommunications are becoming increasingly critical for the profitable operation of business and quality of life (Northeast-Midwest Institute 1988). Communities lacking telecommunications facilities will be at a substantial disadvantage in attracting both new businesses and new residents over the next decade.

Community Facilities and Services

Community facilities and services, including quality schools, recreation facilities, public transportation, health services, emergency services, and business support services, are important to attracting both business and people to rural communities. Attention to facilities and services is particularly important to smaller rural communities seeking to revitalize their local economy through attraction of new residents.

Improving the "livability" of a community is also an important inducement to attracting and retaining business and industry. In a recent statewide survey, the majority of Pennsylvania businesses identified the availability of quality community facilities and services as important to their decision to remain at their current location (Bell of Pennsylvania 1988). An analysis of site location decisions by sixty-seven manufacturing industries found that forty-five of those industries cited the availability of a diversified range of services as a significant factor in firm location decisions (Goode and Hastings 1987).

Main Street Revitalization

Maintaining a strong commercial and service sector is critical to maintaining a strong local economy. The downtown area is probably the single most visible indicator of economic conditions in a rural community. Places with deteriorating downtowns will have trouble attracting new investments because of their negative image. Conversely, places with healthy downtowns will be at an advantage in attracting investment.

The Main Street Model developed by the National Trust for Historic Preservation offers a proven approach for implementing this important element of rural economic development. The Main Street Model advocates a four-point approach to downtown vitalization including organization, design, economic restructuring, and promotion. This has been successfully implemented by hundreds of rural communities across the country.

Planning Assistance

In rural communities the planning and implementation of local economic development efforts is carried out largely by part-time professionals and volunteers. Daily, these individuals make vital resource decisions which affect the economies of their local communities. Often they have limited or no previous training or experience in making such decisions.

Technical assistance programs and training in economic development for rural leaders is generally lacking in most states. Although a number of university-based organizations as well as regional development groups and state agencies do provide economic development assistance to rural communities, these programs are generally very small relative to the need for assistance. In a policy agenda to improve employment and incomes in rural areas, it is vital to have programs to support efforts of rural leaders to implement and manage economic change.

Policies Focusing on Rural Businesses

A third focus for a statewide strategy to improve rural economies should be policies focusing on rural businesses or industries. Examples of business-specific initiatives include providing capital for starting or expanding rural businesses, supporting the development and adoption of competitive technologies, and international market development.

Rural businesses are less likely to take advantage of available, state and federal business assistance than their urban counterparts (Buss and Popovich 1988). Because of their relative isolation and the lack of professional planning assistance many rural businesses are often unaware of assistance available to them. Efforts to increase awareness of rural businesses of available assistance are needed to improve the effectiveness of both state and federal programs in supporting rural economic development.

Some states have addressed this problem directly through formation of rural enterprise zones which provide selected rural communities with priority access to state business assistance programs. Other states have designed special programs to target assistance to specific industries that are predominantly rural, such as agriculture or wood products industries.

Providing Financial Capital

Financial assistance to rural enterprises through loans, direct grants, and tax subsidies has been a traditional cornerstone of rural economic development policies. At the federal level, numerous financial assistance programs are administered by the Economic Development Administration and Small Business Administration. Most states have financial assistance programs aiding business people in acquiring land, constructing new buildings, site development, purchase of machinery and equipment, obtaining working capital, and venture and seed capital.

Federal and state policies designed to meet the financial needs of rural businesses should take into account the nature of the financial system serving these businesses. As public funds for economic development are limited, policy analysts are increasingly questioning the priority that government financial assistance to business should receive relative to other public assistance needed to support economic development (Vaughan, Pollard, and Dyer 1984).

Solid business ideas generally obtain financing. A survey of 134 new small firms in Wisconsin showed that the entrepreneurs' own money was the only source of financing for 74 percent of the sole proprietors, 60 percent of the partners, and 48 percent of the stockholders surveyed. In other instances, owners also used personal loans at banks or borrowed funds from the previous owner or relatives to increase equity in the business (Combs, Pulver, and Shaffer 1985). The point to be made is that a substantial number of private funding options exist for new and expanding businesses. Programs providing information on private funding options and helping budding entrepreneurs to package financial deals is often the most cost-effective means of ensuring that rural enterprises have access to necessary capital. Direct public financial assistance should be carefully targeted to sound business ideas for which private funding is not available.

Supporting Competitive Technologies

Historically, technological development has played a key role in the development of rural America. In particular, astounding technological advancements in agriculture enabled workers to leave the farm to support the rapid development of manufacturing within rural places. The growth in rural manufacturing was stimulated by advancements in transportation and communication technologies supporting the relocation of manufacturing from cities into rural regions. More recently robotics and other major labor-saving factory production innovations have led to the closing of obsolete plants and the layoff of hundreds of thousands of workers while stimulating new job opportunities in service-producing industries.

Recognizing the vital importance of competitive technologies, many states have established incentive programs to encourage major research institutions to focus attention on development of new technologies for business and industry (Vaughan, Pollard, and Dyer 1984). However, new technologies can only aid rural economic development if they are readily adopted by rural business and industry. As is the case for financial assistance programs, isolation and lack of information prevent many rural businesses from taking advantage of existing technology transfer programs. Overcoming these barriers is crucial to the future economic competitiveness of rural business and industry.

International Market Development

A third example of rural economic development policies focusing on specific businesses and industries is market development. Among the most significant economic forces reshaping the rural economy is the growing dominance of global markets. The value of the dollar, foreign policy decisions, export promotion programs, trade embargoes, domestic self-sufficiency goals in other countries, increased competition from foreign manufacturers, and the movement of rural manufacturing production facilities to other countries extend the influence of international forces into both the farm and nonfarm economies of rural areas. Assisting rural businesses and industries to compete effectively in the global marketplace is important to long-term economic prosperity in rural America.

Federal and state governments can undertake several actions to improve the effectiveness of rural business and industry in competing in international markets. Among the most important of these opportunities are policy initiatives designed to improve the economic competitiveness of rural enterprises discussed earlier in this paper, including efforts to improve the productivity of the rural workforce and the technical capability of rural firms. Without first assuring that rural firms are among the most competitive in the world, their expansion into international markets is doubtful. Only when rural businesses and industries are on a competitive par with both their domestic and international competitors can direct international export promotion programs play an effective role in rural economic development.

Priorities for Rural Economic Development Policy

This chapter has highlighted a diverse range of options available to federal and state government in support of rural economic development. Clearly, to implement all of these options on a comprehensive scale in all rural areas is not possible. The key to successful rural economic development policy is to identify and systematically implement those options likely to have the greatest positive impact on rural economies at the minimum cost to taxpayers. The following recommendations are put forward with this goal in mind.

1. *Policies focusing on rural people should be the top priority* for rural economic development policy. Ensuring the rural workforce has the productive skills and ability to participate effectively in an increasingly complex and technical economy is a necessity for future economic development in rural America. Unless this goal is attained, there is little hope of closing the widening gap between economic conditions in rural and urban areas. Priority should be given to improving the utilization and effectiveness of existing education and skill-training programs in rural areas.

2. *Regional employment hubs should be established in rural* regions. The economic reality is that a significant proportion of the nation's rural communities are not part of a population base large enough to effectively support job development efforts. Fortunately, residents residing in these smaller communities often live within reasonable commuting distance of communities that are large enough to realistically attract and retain business and industry.

At least one regional employment hub should be identified within predominantly rural counties. These communities should be given preference in state and federal job development programs. Regional employment hubs would typically be the largest communities within each county with the greatest job development potential. Concentrating job development efforts on those communities with the greatest economic development potential can substantially increase the return from tax dollars spent on rural job generation efforts.

3. *Residential-based economic development should be encouraged* in smaller rural communities building on economic growth in nearby employment centers. Even smaller communities with limited potential to attract new business and industry often have significant potential to attract new residents. New residents bring new income into the community in the form of paychecks earned in surrounding employment centers, investment income, and social security checks. These residents can have a substantial impact on the economy of a small town as they spend income in local businesses and contribute to the local tax base.

The goal of residential-based development in small towns is two-fold. The first goal is to improve the livability of the community through improved housing, family, and health services. Improving access to surrounding employment centers through better highways and public transportation systems will also contribute to this desirability of a small rural community as a residential location.

The second goal of residential-based development is to maximize the impact of residential development in small towns through systematic actions to capture a new income brought into the community by residents. Examples of local initiatives to capture more dollars locally is the development of main street businesses and holding regular community events such as festivals or community-wide sales. Many smaller communities have been successful in the development of home-based and craft businesses. Development of small business serving local needs combined with development of the area's residential base is an effective economic development strategy for many smaller rural communities.

4. *Increase technical assistance to rural communities and rural businesses.* In rural communities, the planning and implementation of local economic development efforts is carried out largely by part-time professionals and volunteers. In a policy agenda to improve employment and incomes in rural areas, it is vital to have programs to support rural leaders in efforts to implement and manage economic change.

Most states presently have in place a substantial network of university expertise, regional development groups, and state agency personnel. It is critical to the goal of improving economic conditions in rural areas that the resources of this network of professionals be tapped to provide economic development assistance to rural communities and rural industries.

Summary

Over the course of this past decade, the U.S. economy has continued to gain strength. Moreover the nation's unemployment rate is at its lowest level in twelve years. Indeed the U.S. economy appears to be poised for continued success into the next decade.

Unfortunately, many rural residents are being left behind and appear unable to participate in this future prosperity. Average unemployment levels remain substantially higher in rural compared to urban places. While some rural areas are doing well, the economic gap between average rural Americans and their urban neighbors continues to grow.

Innovative new policies are needed if rural residents are to emerge from the shadows of economic change to become coparticipants with their urban neighbors in the nation's future economic success story. A renewed commitment to rural economic development would represent

134

more than an investment in the future of rural America. Investment in rural economic development is an investment in America's heritage as a place of opportunity for all who wish to earn their livelihood and raise their families on the farms and in the tens of thousands of small communities that make up the nation.

Notes

1. The terms rural and nonmetropolitan are used interchangeably in this chapter.

References

Bawden, D. Lee and David L. Brown. 1987. "Human Resource Policies for Nonmetropolitan America." Paper presented at the National Public Policy Conference, Cincinnati, Ohio.

Bell of Pennsylvania. 1988. "The Pennsylvania Business Outreach Program: Statewide Progress Report." Document prepared by Theodore E. Fuller and William R. Gillis for the Bell Business Outreach Conference, Hershey, PA.

Bluestone, Herman and John Hession. 1987. "Patterns of Change in the Nonmetro and Metro Labor Force Since 1979." *New Dimensions in Rural Policy: Building Upon Our Heritage.* Pp. 121-133. Washington, D.C.: Joint Economic Committee, Congress of the United States.

Buss, Terry F. and Mark G. Popovich. 1988. "Growth From Within: New Businesses and Rural Economic Development in North Dakota." Washington, D.C.: Council of State Policy and Planning Agencies.

Center for Rural Pennsylvania. 1988. "Education, Skill Training and Rural Economic Competitiveness." Technical Paper 88-3, Harrisburg, PA.

Combs, Robert P., Glen C. Pulver, and Ron E. Shaffer. 1985. "Financing New Small Business Enterprises in Wisconsin." Research Report R3198. Madison, WI: University of Wisconsin, College of Agriculture and Life Sciences.

Cordes, Sam M. and Thomas A. Bruce. 1989. "Rural Health Policy." *Focus on the Future: Options in Developing a New National Rural Policy.* Pp. 156-163. College Station, Texas: Texas Agricultural Extension Service, Texas A&M University.

Goode, Frank and Stephen Hastings. 1987. *Northeast Economic Development Data Base.* University Park, Pennsylvania State University, College of Agriculture.

Hobbs, Daryl, William Heffernan, and Luther Tweeten. 1988. "Education, Retraining, and Relocation Policy." *Rural Development Policy Options.* College Station, Texas: Texas A & M University, College of Agriculture.

Hudson Institute. 1987. *Workforce 2000: Work and Workers for the 21st Century.* Indianapolis, IN.

Jacques, C.H.M.. 1989. "Health Care Needs Assessment for Rural Pennsylvania." Unpublished proposal to the Center for Rural Pennsylvania, Harrisburg, PA.

National Governors' Association. 1988. *New Alliances for Rural America.* Washington, D.C.

_____. 1988. *Making America Work: Productive People, Productive Policies.* National Governors' Association, Washington, D.C.

Northeast-Midwest Institute. 1988. "Telecommunications Infrastructure and Economic Development in the Northeast-Midwest Region." Washington, D.C.

Pulver, Glen C.. 1987. "Economic Growth in Rural America." *New Dimensions in Rural Policy: Building Upon Our Heritage.* Pp. 491-508. Washington, D.C.: Joint Economic Committee, Congress of the United States.

Reich, Robert. 1987. "The Changed World Economy: Implications for Rural Communities." *A New Agenda For Rural America.* Conference Proceedings. Pp. 11-20. St. Paul, MN.

Rosenblatt, R.A. and J.S. Moscovice. 1982. *Rural Health Care.* New York: John Wiley.

Ross, P.J., and S.A. Rosenfeld. 1987. "Human Resource Policies and Economic Development." *Rural Economic Development in the 1980s.* Pp. 15.1-15.20. Washington, D.C.: U.S. Department of Agriculture, Economic Research Service.

Summers, Gene F. and Thomas A. Hirschl. 1985. "Capturing Cash Transfer Payments and Community Economic Development." *Journal of the Community Development Society.* 16: 37-45.

United States Department of Commerce. 1988. "Local Area Personal Income Data, 1979 - 1986." Washington, D.C.

Van Horn, James. 1989. "Role of Child Care Availability on Rural Labor Force Participation and Competitiveness in Pennsylvania Among Small and Medium Sized Businesses." Unpublished proposal to the Center for Rural Pennsylvania, Harrisburg, PA.

Vaughan, Roger J., Robert Pollard and Barbara Dyer. 1984. *The Wealth of States: Policies for a Dynamic Economy.* Washington, D.C.: Council of State Planning Agencies.

Weber, Bruce, Ron Shaffer, Ron Knutson, and Bob Lovan. 1988. "Building A Vital Rural America." *Rural Development Policy Options.* College Station, Texas: Texas A & M University, College of Agriculture.

9

The Restructuring of the Global Economy and the Future of U.S. Agriculture

W. Richard Goe and Martin Kenney

One conclusion that can be reached from examining the various dimensions of the farm crisis is that U.S. agriculture is in an interregnum period of restructuring.[1] The economic future of many regions of rural America hinges upon the ways in which the agricultural system is restructured and realigned with the current transformations under way in the global economic system.

Several important points have been given little or no attention in most analyses of the agricultural crisis. First, the crisis in agriculture closely parallels the crisis of the entire U.S. economy. The agricultural crisis comes at a time when the preeminent position of the United States in the global economy is being undermined due to the growth of other nations' economies, particularly Japan. A new international division of labor is emerging, and global wealth is being redistributed (Kenney and Florida 1987). This period of restructuring in the global economy is forcing firms in many U.S. industries to devise new strategies to remain competitive.

A second important point is the extent to which present day agriculture is intertwined with the nonagricultural industries (Kenney et al. 1989). This occurred largely in the postwar era as agricultural development was shaped by the change in the U.S. political economy. Industries outside of agriculture became important sources of production and consumption patterns, as well as technological innovation in agricultural production.

This chapter contends that, due to these tight linkages with the larger industrial economy, the future of U.S. agriculture will be shaped by forces of change that are propelling the current restructuring of the global economy. The first section briefly examines ways in which U.S. agriculture was shaped by and integrated into the larger U.S. industrial economy in the postwar period. The second section outlines several important facets of global restructuring and how they are likely to influence the future of U.S. agriculture. Finally, the implications of these dimensions of change are discussed.

The Postwar Development of U.S. Agriculture

U.S. agriculture experienced a long-term expansion after World War II. Productivity surged as waves of new technologies were incorporated into agricultural production. The capital intensity of agricultural production increased, and farmers became much more dependent upon nonagricultural industries to produce and supply new technological inputs for farming. The implementation of these innovations ensured that the farmer became tightly integrated into the U.S. economy and created linkages between the farm sector and a widening range of nonagricultural manufacturing industries, such as the chemical and pharmaceutical industries (Kenney et al. 1989). Nonagricultural industries facilitated further productivity gains through technological innovations and technical improvements designed specifically for agricultural use, placing the farmer on a "technological treadmill."

The linkages between the farm sector and the larger industrial economy were also activated by the growth and industrialization of food processing. The favorable economic conditions of the 1950s and 1960s spurred food production innovations at the processor level. First, food additives, such as colorings, flavorings and preservatives, all linked the chemical industry with food processing. Second, U.S. citizens became willing to consume processed food products that had a long shelf life and were much more uniform in content and taste. The expansion of the processed food industry into new markets was facilitated by the proliferation of kitchen appliances and the industrialization of restaurant food production.

With the increasing integration of the farm sector into the industrial economy, the farmer became a consumer of processed foods and consumer durables such as automobiles and home appliances like other Americans. As a producer, the farmer became a supplier of raw materials for the mass production of processed food products by the food processing industry and, of course, the animal husbandry section of agriculture.

U.S. farms, both crop and livestock, became increasingly specialized. Crop farmers began to grow only a few crops, such as corn and soybeans in rotation, and crop diversity decreased. In many cases, dairy farmers withdrew from grain production and vice versa with grain producers. The uniformity of hybrid crops increased the efficiency of tractor-based mechanical cultivation and harvesting. Further, hybrids were bred to respond to radically increased amounts of chemicals for crop protection.

The development of the maize and soybean diet for cattle and poultry coupled with the increasing use of pharmaceutical and genetic breeding led to larger yields in dairy and meat production. In poultry or dairy farming which involved the use of a controlled indoor environment, production processes became highly automated, taking on the organizational characteristics of an assembly line. The economies of scale allowed by these technologies led to individual farms mass producing increasingly larger volumes of one or two crops.

Specialization greatly reduced flexibility in agricultural production. The economic fortunes of American farmers became tied to conditions in a narrower range of markets. Farmers became locked into a highly capital-intensive production system that required incurring debt and achieving economies of scale to expand and/or remain competitive. However, it was also a system that allowed the United States to become the global leader in agricultural production.

Due to this highly efficient production system, the United States was able to establish a hegemonic position in international agricultural markets. The U.S. diet, an integral part of the U.S. lifestyle, was initially exported to Europe, then (partially) Japan, and eventually, to some of the developing countries. U.S. wheat became the global standard, increasingly becoming the grain of choice for consumers in developing countries who shifted to bread consumption. As per capita incomes rose, beef and dairy consumption tended to increase among the middle classes. U.S. farmers were prepared to supply the maize and soybeans necessary to meet this demand. The success of agriculture in international trade was one facet of the hegemony of the United States in the global economy.

To recapitulate, the development of postwar agriculture in the United States was shaped through its integration into the industrial production system. As long as the industrial economy could continue to provide the incomes necessary to reproduce the American lifestyle, the agricultural system could expand and grow. The period from 1948 to 1972 was one in which agriculture experienced steady growth in yields, farm income remained relatively stable due to government subsidies (which could be accommodated due to a balanced federal budget), and the cost of food declined as a proportion of workers' incomes. However, in the mid-1970s, the industrial economy entered a period of instability and restructuring. This eventually destabilized agriculture as the crisis in the industrial economy became more severe in the 1980s.

Crisis in the U.S. Industrial Economy: Elements of Global Restructuring

Signs of instability in the U.S. industrial economy appeared in the late 1960s as the overheated Vietnam War economy began to lag. However, it was the 1974 oil crisis that completed the process (Florida and Feldman 1988). Throughout the remainder of the 1970s, the aggregate economy became increasingly unpredictable oscillating between periods of high inflation and recession. By the 1980s, many U.S. industries had become seriously uncompetitive and faced intensifying competition from foreign producers. The severe recession that gripped the nation's economy from roughly 1979 through 1983 exacerbated this situation. Many of the traditionally robust manufacturing industries that were the heart of the industrial economy, such as steel, automobiles, farm machinery, consumer electronics, and semiconductors, experienced severe decline.

To become more competitive U.S. firms began to reorganize and restructure. Firms scaled back the manufacturing labor force through employee terminations and layoffs, early retirement programs, further automation, and the shifting of production operations offshore. U.S. employment in manufacturing has declined absolutely since 1979, with some recovery since the end of the recession. Wages have come under steady and prolonged attack, and labor unions have been forced to accept concessions to retain jobs. Restructuring also has involved a wave of mergers and acquisitions. The position of the United States as the global industrial leader is being seriously challenged as the global economy undergoes restructuring.

This restructuring is a consequence of advancing industrial development in other nations which has produced a shift in the global economic order. Japan has grown into the world's second largest economy, while West Germany and several newly industrialized countries (NICs) such as South Korea and Taiwan have also enjoyed robust growth. These countries have become increasingly efficient in producing high-quality goods and have taken away market shares from U.S. firms in a wide range of industries.

The crisis in U.S. agriculture lagged behind that in the larger industrial economy. However, agriculture now faces similar problems of reorganization and restructuring in response to overproduction, a declining global demand for unprocessed U.S. agricultural products, and new competitors in the world market. Given agriculture's integration into the industrial economy the restructuring of the U.S. agricultural system will likely be shaped by processes underlying the current period of global restructuring. Attempting to outline all the of processes that characterize the global transformation is far beyond the scope of this chapter. However, several of these processes have significant implications for the future of U.S. agriculture and deserve attention.

Advanced Technology

Advanced technology is an important variable in the restructuring equation. New technologies can reinvigorate the competitiveness of declining industries and provide new opportunities for economic growth through the development of new industries and commercial products. While the United States has clearly held a dominant position in technological development for much of the postwar period, it is widely perceived that other countries, especially Japan, are rapidly closing the gap in their ability to harness technological advancements for economic growth and development. Thus, an important dimension of global restructuring is the increasing competition to capture the profit potential of newly developed commercial technologies and make production processes more efficient through technological application.

In a broad sense, an important facet of global restructuring is the development of a new, more efficient production system based on new applications of advanced technology and new ways of organizing production (Kenney and Florida 1987). Information technologies and biotechnology, are two broad areas of advanced technology significant for the present and future global economy. There is intense competition among the advanced industrial nations to develop commercial applications of these technologies and both are likely to be important areas of advanced technology for agriculture in the near future (Office of Technology Assessment 1986a: 4). Agricultural applications of information technology can be classified under three basic types: (a) monitoring and control technologies; (b) information management; and (c) telecommunications (Office of Technology Assessment 1986a: 32). Monitoring and control applications use remote sensing and microelectronics to automate specific aspects of agricultural production, such as machinery performance, livestock identification and feeding, irrigation, livestock environment and waste monitoring and control, and crop and feed storage control and processing (see Figure 9.1).

If these diverse applications were ultimately combined into a unified system through a local area network it would revolutionize information management aspects of agricultural production and permit continuous monitoring and control from a central location. Telecommunications can link to computerized information services that allows important information on conditions within the larger agricultural system (e.g., market prices) to be obtained more rapidly than from conventional media sources. At the heart of this system may be a central on-farm computer that will be used to organize, process, and store these diverse information flows, as well as perform stand-alone functions such as spreadsheet analysis. These applications of information technology promise to make agricultural production much more information intensive.

Information technology also permits farm management and production strategies to be adjusted more efficiently in response to changing conditions by allowing more effective information management. Productivity gains from information technology will be dependent upon the ability of farmers and farm managers to interpret information adjusting and coordinating management and production processes accordingly. In this sense, "knowledge work" will become a much more indispensable component of agricultural production.[2]

Biotechnology can be summarized as the ability to engineer living organisms at the cellular or molecular level to undertake desired activities. Over the last fifteen years scientists have developed the tools

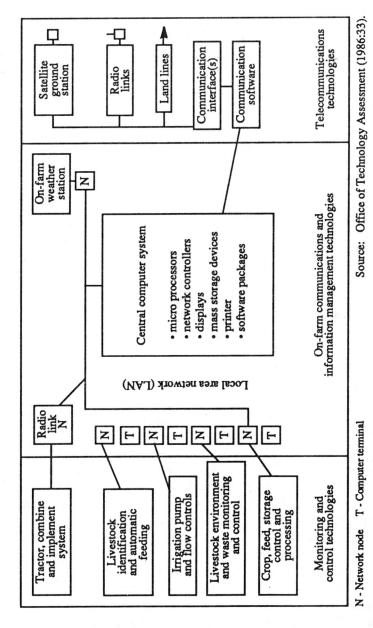

N - Network node   T - Computer terminal

Source: Office of Technology Assessment (1986:33).

FIGURE 9.1   Example of system architecture for an On-Farm Digitial Information Network

necessary to design life forms. Biotechnology will have significant impacts upon agriculture, chemicals, pharmaceuticals, food processing, and waste processing. Biotechnology research is under way in all facets of agricultural production. One example of the scientific advances made by biotechnology is the development of plants that are herbicide resistant, thus making it possible to apply greater quantities of herbicides. Biotechnology provides the means to integrate the genetic program of the seed and agricultural chemicals at the molecular level.

Another example of the new biotechnology products and the one that has received the most attention is the genetically engineered bovine growth hormone (BGH) for increasing milk production in dairy cows. Research by Kalter and associates (1986) and the Office of Technology Assessment (1986a) has indicated that adoption of BGH would lead to the elimination of over 25 percent of U.S. dairy farmers. Further, there would be a regional shift in production favoring the South and West thereby worsening the plight of the smaller Northern farmers. Thus, BGH technology portends a catastrophic effect on the more vulnerable small farmer.

Information technology and biotechnology have yet to become widely established technologies in agricultural production. Most biotechnology applications for agriculture remain largely in the research and development stage. Further, there has been considerable social resistance to their introduction due to the potential unknown dangers of releasing genetically modified organisms into the environment. Applications of information technology such as microcomputers, videotex systems, and computer automated feeding systems have become incrementally established. However, applications of information technology have yet to be implemented in agricultural production on the scale that has occurred in other industries.

It remains to be seen how quickly these advanced technologies will become established on a wide scale in U.S. agricultural production. Biotechnology applications will not become established until regulatory and safety issues are resolved. The further establishment of information technology applications will be influenced by the process by which the farm sector acquires the technical skills necessary to employ information technology effectively. Nevertheless information technology and biotechnology not only provide important potentials for further decreasing unit cost, but could also be used to create greater flexibility in agricultural production.

The Shift Toward Flexibility in Production

The crisis in the U.S. industrial economy has been attributed to a lack of flexibility in adjusting production to shifts in the composition of consumer demand (see section on shifts in consumer demand below). A production system based upon standard products made on semiautomatic assembly lines is by definition rigid because heavy capital investments in machinery can only be recouped through high volume production runs. Reconfiguring the system to produce other products is inefficient and can require workers with entirely different skills. Shifts in consumer demand that necessitate a wider variety of products cannot be effectively accommodated.

By the late 1970s it became obvious that rigid production systems were fundamentally unsuited for the changes under way in the world economy (Piore and Sabel 1984). The predictable response is toward a system capable of greater production flexibility and diversity. The development of programmable automation, an application of information technology to manufacturing, permits the possibility of small-batch production and greater product diversity at nearly the same cost as mass-produced items. Automated machines can easily be reprogrammed to perform other tasks and produce other products (Jaikumar, 1986). Firms using this type of system can adapt production to shifts in demand. Weak products can be discontinued and new products introduced more rapidly.

Biotechnology and information technology applications provides the possibility of greater flexibility and product diversity in agricultural production. New crops or animals with desirable genetic traits can be developed more rapidly. Information technology provides more flexibility in managing agricultural production through the automation of monitoring and control procedures. The use of resources can be controlled more efficiently. Changes in market conditions can be monitored more effectively. Problems in production, such as high insect infestation or low moisture levels, can be more quickly identified and ameliorated before they threaten yields. The unifying principle of information facilitates the management of diversity in agricultural production.

Flexibility may also involve the use of polycultures and a return to diversity in agricultural production. This could require the knowledge for cultivating a much wider range of crops including specialty crops that meet consumer demand in expanding niche markets. This strategy has already found some limited success. Some farm operators were able to withstand the effects of the recession through producing "alternative" commodities such as kiwi fruits, almonds, asparagus, wild flowers, and "hormone-free" beef. This may become even more important as consumers demand new products and more "natural" products.

It should be emphasized that flexible production in U.S. agriculture is only one possibility that may emerge as future applications of biotechnology and information technology are developed for agriculture. Another path would be to extend uniformity in production to secure the increased yields of mass-produced, low quality agricultural commodities via more heavily industrialized agriculture. However, with the shift toward flexible production in the larger industrial economy, increasing competition in global agricultural markets, and the fragmentation of consumer markets, a more "craftsmanlike," flexible agriculture could possibly emerge in the United States.

Shifts in Consumer Demand and the Fragmentation of Mass Markets

The success of the postwar U.S. industrial economy depends upon the acceptance and consumption of a relatively narrow variety of standard goods by the U.S. public. The development of mass markets for standard goods was supported by the growth of disposable income in America's burgeoning middle class. Mass-produced consumer goods became symbols of the American lifestyle and reflected postwar prosperity.

An important dimension of the restructuring of the global economy is that mass markets are becoming fragmented. Consumption patterns are changing in most advanced industrial societies. The U.S. middle class is now composed of numerous family types including single-parent families, married couples with no children, single professionals with middle-class incomes, and cohabiting couples rather than being monolithic. In many two-parent families, both parents are employed. This trend is increasingly desired by American women and is often necessary to maintain a middle-class level of consumption. These groups possess a diversity of goals, values, and motivations that is reflected by various patterns of consumption.

As these groups demand and consume diverse goods and services. The resulting market is disaggregated.[3] Further divisions are produced by the growth of ethnic groups and the tendency of many American consumers to purchase beyond their means in order to obtain goods that reflect current fads or are regarded as status symbols. The emergence of highly disaggregated markets is both facilitated by and contributes to the growth of flexible manufacturing systems that can quickly reorganize production to meet expanding market opportunities.

The fragmentation of mass markets clearly has implications for U.S. agriculture. It has already transformed demand for food products as seen in the growing array of innovative processed food products that are continuously being introduced into grocery stores and targeted toward different consumer groups, such as low-calorie "lite" products, microwave cuisine, and gourmet frozen dinners. It is further exhibited in the explosion of Thai, Chinese, Indian, Mexican, and other ethnic restaurants which require nontraditional foods as inputs. Many of these are imported, but are being increasingly grown in the United States.

In addition, the demand for food products in the United States has become much more diverse as the American diet has expanded far beyond the traditional meat and potatoes fare. This trend is highly interconnected with the health and environmental movements that continue to increase in strength and encourage rejection of canned goods, red meat, and other foods with chemical additives and high levels of cholesterol.

The incorporation of health consciousness into American food consumption decisions has led to the emergence of the low-salt, low-fat diet while the trend toward dieting and weight watching has created a demand for low-calorie food products in smaller portions. Fast-food restaurants have responded by creating salad bars and differentiating menus. Food processing companies have rushed to develop innovative products to meet these shifts in demand. Further disaggregation of markets for food products implies that agricultural producers must be aware of shifts in consumer demand and be flexible enough to shift production to high demand product areas.

The Necessity of Environmentally Sound Production Practices

The postwar expansion was achieved at the cost of large-scale environmental degradation which became the focus of organized public resistance in the late 1960s. Public opposition led to the passage of the National Environmental Protection Act in 1969 and the formation of the Environmental Protection Agency in 1970. Although having some effect, these and subsequent policy initiatives obviously have not eliminated environmental degradation in the United States.

The policies of the Reagan administration, along with the problems created by the crisis in the U.S. economy, have diminished the strength of the environmental movement at the federal level. However, indications that significant environmental concern remains at the grass-roots level exists in the ability to mobilize opposition to environmentally suspect projects, the opposition to the use of agricultural chemicals, and the growth of the "sustainable agriculture" movement.

The industrialization of agricultural production contributed significantly to the environmental problem. Productivity gains through chemical technology and monoculture have been made at the expense of environmental costs, health and safety concerns, and the erosion of genetic resources. The publication of Rachel Carson's *Silent Spring* in 1962, which identified numerous commonly used farm chemicals as carcinogenic and harmful to humans and the environment brought agricultural practices to public attention.

Monocultural mass production of crops requires vast quantities of chemical fertilizers, pesticides, and herbicides and leaves topsoil fully exposed to erosion. Agriculture's role in the pollution of streams, rivers, and underground water sources through erosion and chemical runoff has been amply documented. Environmentally sound solutions have not been readily forthcoming from agribusiness industries or the federal government. For example, minimum tillage, the agricultural chemical companies' solution to erosion, generally requires increased application of chemicals.

In animal agriculture, meat production can be increased by the use of growth-stimulating chemicals, subtherapeutic use of antibiotics, and chemical additives. Some of these chemicals have been linked to cancer (e.g., diethylstilbestrol and sodium nitrite) and antibiotic resistance in human pathogens. The concern over food safety, along with that over the relationship between cholesterol and heart disease, has further contributed to changes in dietary practices.

If the recent discovery of substantial levels of pollutants in Iowa's water table provides any indication, pollution resulting from industrialized agricultural production is reaching crisis levels (Board of

Agriculture, National Research Council 1990). At some future point, U.S. agriculture (and U.S. society) must face this situation. Solutions will be needed to ameliorate these problems and ensure that agricultural production is environmentally sound and addresses food safety concerns.

One possible solution currently emerging is "sustainable" or "alternative agriculture," which combines polyculture, organic farming techniques, and state-of-the-art hybridization to form a production system that is environmentally sound. At the moment, support for this form of agriculture is still relatively small. However, it is gaining some momentum through the efforts of such organizations as the Land Institute in Salina, Kansas, and the Institute for Alternative Agriculture in Greenbelt, Maryland, along with a small number of agricultural scientists within the land grant university system. This momentum will be reinforced by the increasing inability of U.S. farmers to pay for agricultural inputs.

Shifts in International Trade Patterns

Another important factor contributing to the crisis in the U.S. industrial economy is that, in aggregate, U.S. firms have lost previously held shares in international export markets and have failed to significantly penetrate expanding markets in other countries. A massive trade deficit attributed to inequitable trade arrangements and monetary exchange rates has resulted. Although given little emphasis by many analysts, agriculture's trade performance has also been sluggish due in part to the increased perception that U.S. agricultural products are not of top quality. Additionally, the global expansion of agricultural input companies is transferring significant technologies to many U.S. competitors.

Even though there have been recent signs that exports are increasing due to the falling value of the dollar, there is little indication of a short-term reversal of the trade deficit. The deficit increases with increasing American consumption of foreign goods. It is unlikely that shifts in exchange rates will provide a solution to the problem. Rather, deficit reduction will likely depend upon the particular restructuring strategies employed by U.S. firms and improvements in the quality of U.S. goods and support services.

A loss in export markets was also a primary factor contributing to the crisis in U.S. agriculture. Yet, while the industrial economy was weakening in the early 1970s, agriculture was undergoing a burgeoning expansion attributable primarily to a rapid increase in exports. Prices rose drastically, leading then U.S. Secretary of Agriculture Earl Butz to advise farmers to plant "fence row to fence row." Agricultural economists chimed in, predicting increased global food demand and advising farmers to expand their holdings.

Even as the situation looked bright for agriculture, the underlying conditions steadily worsened from the mid-1970s onward. Inflation rapidly escalated alongside production. Real net farm income plummeted from 1973 to 1977, underwent further cyclical decline from 1977 to 1981, and dropped precipitously again after 1981. Increased grain prices and the increased burden of oil imports brought intensified efforts by importing countries to reduce agricultural imports.

Simultaneously, political reasons forced the U.S. government to employ embargoes against Japan in 1974 and the Soviet Union in 1980, thereby calling into question the reliability of the U.S. as a supplier. The embargoes and high prices prompted additional countries to enter the world market as competitors (e.g., Brazil and Argentina). Competition in the marketplace for U.S. products increased severely due to European Economic Community subsidies, high U.S. target prices, and rising production by Lesser Developed Countries. The United States even became an importer of some products such as vegetables from Mexico and orange juice concentrate from Brazil.

The crisis in the larger economy also affected agriculture. The recession in the early 1980s increased real interest rates as high as 21 percent. Efforts to stem inflation by the Reagan administration boosted the value of the dollar in international markets and made U.S. exports uncompetitive. Finally, the United States increasingly became viewed as a supplier of last resort for low-quality, unprocessed agricultural commodities. This is illustrated by the increased number of foreign complaints about the quality of U.S. grain stocks over the past several years (Office of Technology Assessment 1986b: 5).

All of these factors undermined the hegemony of the U.S. in global agricultural markets. Even so, the agricultural sector has managed to maintain a positive trade balance. This was accomplished partly through government price subsidies that drastically lowered the price of U.S. grain exports. A return to the export volumes that fueled the 1970s expansion is not likely in the short term as competition for international markets is intensifying. And, agricultural improvements in the developing countries decreases reliance on the United States as a food supplier even allowing several of these countries to become competitors. Further, trade restrictions inhibit penetration into agricultural markets in the European community and Japan.

There are indications that some trade restrictions will be removed in steps meant to ensure the overall stability of the larger international economy providing opportunity for expanding agricultural exports. However, international trade policy must go beyond efforts to create competitive pricing to include strict quality standards. Agricultural products from the United States must establish the same international reputation for high quality as consumer electronics from Japan, automobiles from West Germany, or chocolate from Switzerland.

Discussion

The incorporation of advanced technology into production processes, the growth of flexible production, the fragmentation of consumer markets, the growing necessity of environmentally sound production, increasing competition, and shifts in international markets are all important dimensions of the current global restructuring. All of these processes act upon the U.S. agricultural system and will continue to shape it.

Greater access to information is a crucial factor for operating within the emerging framework of the global economy. The nature of agricultural production entails relatively long lead times. However, access to current information is critical for implementing flexible production and understanding the fragmentation of markets and shifts in international trade. Information technologies being used in other industries to create more efficient organizational linkages may also benefit U.S. agriculture.

Besides the benefits of information technology within business firms, future coordination of activities between firms and across different industries will be important. One such application is "electronic data interchange" (EDI), which uses computer networking to electronically link retail and wholesale firms, and manufacturers. By providing more efficient information flow at each stage of the production and distribution system, EDI allows both functions to be coordinated more efficiently. For example, instant access to updated product orders from wholesale firms means manufacturers can coordinate production runs on the basis of actual demand.

EDI would clearly be beneficial for farms operating in the emerging framework of the global economy. Computer linkages between farms, food processing industries, and distributors could allow agricultural producers to be better informed about changing patterns of domestic and international demand allowing more effective response. While EDI is being used to link retail food distributors with wholesale suppliers and food processors, agricultural producers have yet to be integrated into these networks.[4] Computerized information systems designed for the farm sector need to be expanded in scope to include linkages with all organizational elements in the food production and distribution system. The successful development of flexibility in agricultural production would be greatly aided by more complete information regarding the characteristics of consumer demand for food products provided by EDI.

The fragmentation of consumer markets coupled with the increasing competition in global agricultural markets suggests that the successful farmer in the future may likely be the one whose production process is flexible and able to adjust to market changes. Bulk commodity production may never again experience the profitability of the postwar period, barring natural disasters and food shortages in developed countries. This implies that large scale production of any commodity will be a low value-added business, always threatening to move to places with low land values and low labor costs. The more lucrative elements resulting from market fracturing can be best exploited by smaller, more flexible producers.

Ultimately, a successful flexible production system must allow farmers to exploit markets that are expanding, even as other markets in which they are engaged are contracting. As previously noted, flexibility in agricultural production could involve the use of polyculture, the return to diversity in production, and the use of genetically engineered plant and animal varieties along with further automation of production and management processes through information technology. This is not to argue that industrial agricultural production will be rapidly phased out. As long as a lack of environmental restrictions, market demand, and economies of scale permit an adequate rate of return for mass-produced commodities it will continue. However,the growing necessity of environmental controls for agriculture will, at some future point, necessitate radical changes in these production methods. Flexible production may hold the greatest promise for medium and small producers as it could allow them to participate in more lucrative niche markets while requiring less debt and capital investment.

Flexible production may also provide a solution to the loss of export markets. The dominant strategy in international trade for U.S. agriculture has simply been to export components of the U.S. diet to foreign countries. Given that other countries have become increasingly competitive in producing such commodities as corn, wheat, soybean, and red meat, these likely represent mature markets that provide little prospect for growth. An alternative strategy might be for U.S. producers to begin to produce commodities that are integral parts of diets in other countries and would directly appeal to foreign consumers. Provided such commodities are amenable to North American soils and climate and no trade restrictions exist, the production of specialty export commodities for foreign niche markets could provide an important dimension of a successful flexible production system.

Although outlines of change are appearing, specific ways in which the U.S. agricultural system will ultimately respond to and emerge from the current economic crisis remain unclear. This chapter has outlined several important dimensions of the socioeconomic framework emerging from the current restructuring of the global economy. The tight linkages of the U.S. agricultural system with the larger industrial economy means that agriculture has already been, and will continue to be, affected by these trends. It appears critical that future agricultural policy focus on facilitating the adjustment and adaptation of the farm sector to the emerging requirements of the global economy. This can contribute toward alleviating the crisis in regions of rural America dependent upon agriculture.

Notes

1. This restructuring has already manifested itself in a number of ways including the further shakeout of farm operators and the reorganization of the Farm Credit System.

2. Knowledge work in agriculture will be augmented by the further development of expert systems and applications of artificial intelligence for agricultural use. These software programs will assist in interpreting information and suggesting possible courses of action. Thus, to some degree, expert systems

will automate knowledge work, itself. Among the first expert systems for agriculture are PLANT/ds and PLANT/tn which were developed for the diagnoses of soybean disease and provision of turf-grass management, respectively (Goe and Kenney 1988).

3. This is reflected in the increasing produce diversity on the market. For example, Chrysler Corporation sold ten basic car models in 1965 while in 1987, its dealers stock twenty-five models. Coca-Cola has gone from a single product to a variety of permutations under its brand name aimed at different consumer groups. Levi Strauss and Company, which once produced one standard pair of dungarees, now sells over five thousand styles of apparel.

4. Safeway, Incorporated and Shop 'n Save are examples of retail grocery chains that are using EDI.

References

Board of Agriculture, National Research Council. 1990. *Regulating Pesticides: The Delany Paradox.* Washington, D.C.: National Academy Press.

Carson, R. 1962. *Silent Spring.* Greenwich, CT: Fawcett Publications.

Florida, R. and M. Feldman. 1988. "Housing in U.S. Fordism: The Class Accord and Postwar Spatial Organization." *International Journal of Urban and Regional Research.* 12: 187-210.

Goe, W.R. and M. Kenney. 1988. "The Political Economy of the Privitization of Agricultural Information: The Case of the United States." *Agricultural Administration and Extension. 28: 81-99.*

Jaikumar, R. 1986. "Postindustrial Manufacturing." Harvard Business Review. November/December: 69-76.

Kalter, R., R. Milligan, W. Lesser, W. Magrath, D. Bauman. 1986. "Biotechnology and the Dairy Industry." Ithaca, N.Y.: A.E. Research Report 84-22, Department of Agricultural Economics, Cornell University.

Kenney, M. 1986. *Biotechnology: The University-Industrial Complex.* New Haven, CT: Yale University Press.

Kenney, M. and R. Florida. 1987. "Beyond Mass Production: The Social Organization of Production and Innovation in Japan." *Politics and Society.* 16: 121-158.

Kenney, M., L. Labao, J. Curry and W.R. Goe. 1989. "Midwestern Agriculture in U.`S. Fordism: From the New Deal to Economic Restructuring." *Sociologica Ruralis.* XXIX: 131-148.

Office of Technology Assessment. 1986a. *Technology, Public Policy and the Changing Structure of American Agriculture.* Washington, D.C.: Government Printing Office.

_____. 1986b. *A Review of U.S. Competitiveness in Agricultural Trade - A Technical Memorandum.* Washington, D.C.: Government Printing Office.

Piore, M. and C. Sabel. 1984. *The Second Industrial Divide.* New York: Basic Books.

10

Families in the New Rural Community

Sonya Salamon

How rural families relate to their communities is important to the quality of life experienced by their members. Trends toward farm consolidations and increased numbers of part-time operators have reduced the number of full-time family farms and as a result structurally changed the critical family-community relationship. The population decline in remote rural areas now jeopardizes the tax base and consequently schools, businesses, and other institutions vital to community viability. A federal policy fostering the persistence of the most numbers of family farms or a massive infusion of funds to rural communities is highly unlikely (Deavers 1987).

This chapter examines how the transformation of the rural social fabric now in process challenges the maintenance of a viable family life in rural areas. Some local-level responses to the consequences of the vast social changes are presented that involve rethinking the bonds among rural households and the interdependent linkages between families and community. Local initiatives creating support to families are required if rural communities are to endure as a social context like that which formerly provided an attractive way of life. These initiatives, however, necessitate skillful guidance from policy makers and implementors who are able to provide the knowledgeable assistance that can help rural community residents redefine their lives and social supports. Such changes are difficult to conceptualize or originate internally because people may be locked into traditional solutions and cannot envision new alternatives.

Rural Communities and Families

The Traditional Farming Community

The hallmark of the traditional rural social organization was *gemeinschäft*; integration based on face-to-face interactions by those sharing a common set of values, beliefs, and way of life. People lived in relatively stable agriculturally based communities composed of families linked to land. As farmers, families strove for intergenerational continuity in the family and land relationship, sometimes in competition and sometimes in cooperation with each other (Rogers and Salamon 1983).

U.S. family life embedded in an established extended kin network evidenced structural features similar to those found in other agriculturally based societies. Extended kin rarely shared the same housing, but they were close by, and contact was typically daily and face-to-face. Because of this proximity, options existed for members of a kinship network to substitute for one another, particularly women whose domestically focused lives made them more flexible and care oriented. If someone died or was ill, female relatives in the network were available to supply child care or cook meals. Elderly relatives could call on a variety of family members for aid. The diffusion of support meant that no one person was burdened by meeting otherwise overwhelming demands.

Multiple households linked by kinship ties as an extended family permitted a specialized division of labor in the agricultural enterprise and the household. An example, drawn from a contemporary Illinois field study, is of a farm operation consisting of a father and two married sons in which the father is a specialist in drying grain, one son does the marketing, the other repairs equipment, a daughter-in-law keeps the books, and the mother tends a garden large enough to supply all three households. Traditionally, such an exchange system had social costs. Because most farmland came through the male line, a young in-marrying woman whose husband was indebted to his parents for a start in farming, needed to keep her mother-in-law and other patrilineal relatives happy. The trade-off was that the mother-in-law, aunts, and other relatives provided child care and advice. Thus, if the young mother wished to work as a partner with her husband in the family business, the flexible extended family could accommodate that option.

Households closely linked by strong kin and economic ties particularly characterized small farming communities, where generations of intermarriage assured that everyone was at least distantly related and shared common origins and values. Therefore, exchange relationships reached beyond the household unit, binding the community together in a dense web of economic and social obligations. Men were likely to furnish farm enterprise-related services, such as labor sharing; women exchanged domestic services. Churches, business people, and social networks served as the safety net that, when working according to community ideals, provided for the ill, financially dependent, or deviants excluded from kinship support. Women were called on by the church, community, or families to furnish crucial services otherwise difficult to obtain in rural areas. Traditionally rural women did not work outside the home and were therefore always available to be the oil that made a smooth-running, flexible social system work (Fink 1987).

Gemeinschaft meant that rural families considered their relationship to other households and their place in the community important. A critical link between families and the larger social structure was affiliation with a church, whose activities crosscut the community and provided a core aspect of identity. In the past, rural ministers who made a lifelong commitment to a community, led and counseled a congregation on the basis of extensive knowledge derived from lengthy personal associations. A lifetime tenure assured pastors an historic and broad perspective on families and an awareness of the support available to those lives disrupted by crisis or illness. The intimate knowledge about local families and how the community worked enabled pastors to marshal help when necessary, and this constituted a responsive, informal safety net.

Another aspect of traditional community identity was the village, a center of activity containing the church, shops, and schools. Local business people and teachers, similar to the long-tenured minister, were lifelong community members who dealt with the families on the basis of an established personal relationship evolved from frequent face-to-face interactions. Traditional communities were also crosscut by a network of informal and formal organizations, such as card groups, service clubs, or a volunteer fire department, binding families in social and instrumental interdependence. Over time, one family might be called upon to act for the welfare of another without any direct benefit. Kinship interests were thus held in abeyance so that community good could be realized (Rogers and Salamon 1983). Stable residence fostered unselfish behavior of community residents. Families knew that services or goods they gave to those in need might be wanted by them in some future time of need.

For some communities and families, the described structures still operate, and identification with stable and functioning institutions provides integration for their lives. For most rural residents, however, profound changes have taken place, altering how families connect to kin and community. The next section describes the transformations that have taken place in previously dependable rural institutions, changes caused both by family choices and factors beyond local control.

Transformation of the Rural Community and Family

As a consequence of the depressed farm economy, the extended family form described above, while still a reality for some, is substantively altered for many. Family life in rural communities has undergone fundamental changes, making questionable whether some households can provide basic support to their members. Families being forced to leave farming are frequently those operating the full-time, middle-range family farms who entered farming in the early 70s (Campbell 1985). The agricultural and family developmental phases in which these families are enmeshed mark them as the backbone of extended kin networks and also make them most involved in rural communities. In farm-dependent counties, nonfarm income sources to support a family are seldom available. As families in these counties are forced out of farming, they must out-migrate for employment, often leaving behind dependent kin and communities bereft of committed and able citizens. As a result, previously tightly integrated families and communities are becoming fragmented.

In response to these new social and economic environmental pressures, rural families have evolved a more nuclear focus, an outcome causing them to resemble more the dominant U.S. family form. Less-mobile extended family members are left behind as younger more marketable relatives out-migrate to work, or if family members remain community residents, they must commute great distances to jobs. Rural households thus altered can no longer maintain past levels of engagement in reciprocal relationships; families by necessity shift concentration toward the nuclear unit. While the nuclear family provides more privacy and autonomy, it is simultaneously more fragile than the extended family. A nuclear family has fewer options for task specialization or role substitution than does an extended family. Nuclear family members traveling the great distances to work are hard pressed to accommodate the needs of dependent kin. Families are functionally torn as members are pulled in different directions and by multiple work roles.

A decline in rural fertility, though more gradual than that for urban areas, has also contributed to the emergence of more nuclear rural families. Even a stable extended family is smaller than in the past when large families assured that many siblings living in proximity would form an extensive network of potential providers. The effect of smaller family size on support available to rural families was compounded by the entrance of almost half of nonmetro women into the labor force as early as 1979 (Bokemeier and Tickamyer 1985). A central Illinois community studied in 1985-86 managed to hold young families despite a general move out of farming in the 50s, due to solidarity shaped by a strong religious and ethnic identity. Yet not only young mothers in this community worked outside the home, but grandmothers were found employed as well. Thus, the traditional advantage of the stable, extended family as a source of alternative providers, as for example grandmother substituting for mother, was no longer operative. Even in this close-knit German community, women were unavailable for child care, nursing the ill, or care of dependent elderly on a predictable, daily basis. The community was forced to provide church-subsidized day care in its parochial school despite the existence of an ideology that dictates that a woman's place is in the home. Clearly, rural communities must fill the vacuum created by the loss of traditionally family-furnished services, but the process has many unintended disruptive consequences.

Formerly, religious leaders could be expected to monitor community families for problems and needs, but today churches operate under entirely different national principles. Members of a community where I conducted fieldwork from 1975 to 1977 frequently cited the forty-year tenure of a Lutheran pastor as the source of their solidarity. A century after settlement a strong identity is maintained through endogamy and German as a home language. Under such stable leadership, the community bought and operated a local telephone company, supported indigent community members, and maintained a German language school that sustained their cohesion (Corner 1928; Salamon and Keim 1979).

A lifelong ministerial career with one congregation is highly unlikely today due to national church policies. For example, since the retirement of the above minister forty years ago, the congregation has been led by eight different preachers. Most denominations place new or retired ministers in rural congregations. Thus, ministers new to the rural community either move after five years or enter the community late in life. Such relatively uncommitted transients are unlikely to provide the knowledgeable leadership furnished by predecessors who made one church a life's work. Some communities lose churches entirely as a consequence of consolidation or closing forced by declining memberships. Pastors complain that people come to them "when it is too late," as for example to announce an imminent divorce. However, congregation members do not view a relatively new minister as understanding either their history, or their situation well enough to help. Due to a traditional reluctance to use public, institutional services because of strong values for privacy and self-reliance, this change in religious personnel policy leaves rural populations with inadequate mental health resources.

Local businesses have either changed management or closed so that it is unlikely that rural families are dealt with according to the traditional criteria of personal reputation, community contribution, or background. Rural banks are an illustration. The financial failure of locally owned rural banks heavily dependent on agricultural loans has been widely reported. Takeovers by nonlocal institutions have occurred in states (unlike Illinois) where strict branch-banking laws do not limit the expansion of larger, typically urban banks. Farmers can no longer rely on a reputation of wise management or expect flexibility from a bank because it has done business with their family for generations. Similarly, small, locally owned businesses, such as restaurants and drugstores, have given way to national franchises and regional malls as rural residents choose lower prices or big-city ambience over personal, informal, and perhaps unsophisticated management. As a consequence, family maintenance tasks, such as shopping, health care, financial affairs, and dining out, are now experienced in the relative depersonalized manner typical for urban or suburban families.

Weak commodity prices and sharply reduced land values produce lower local government revenues (Brown and Deavers 1987) because farm financial difficulties have a ripple effect in rural communities. Public services such as schools are often the first victims of reduced revenues, making the rural locale less attractive to young families. Past district consolidation solutions do not bode well for the future local school as a source of identity and integration for rural families or communities. In Illinois, local leadership has sometimes sacrificed community aims to political demands. In one case, three consolidating school districts would not hammer out a compromise allowing one the high school, so the new facility was built in neutral territory, out in the countryside. Thus, all three communities were prevented from receiving the benefits of traffic and business that a school brings, and all were effectively diminished by the compromise. Further consolidations will be required of most rural areas as more families out-migrate, the tax base erodes, and state regulations require redistricting. This will amplify the problem of preserving community identity without a major integrative institution.

Homegrown Initiatives to Support Rural Families and Communities

The changes outlined make continued rural residence less viable for young people through loss of the very social benefits that tie them to agricultural communities. To retain the young families who represent the future, while also attending to dependent old and young residents, remote rural communities together must explore social support alternatives. Given the current climate of cutbacks at both state and national levels, such alternatives must be homegrown. Communities are particularly challenged to replace the vital services previously provided to family and social networks by women now in the labor market. The inability of the family-level unit to meet the demands of its members pushes the level of response up to the next social unit, the community.

The identity and solidarity based on stable residence, unique to rural communities, permits innovations unworkable in the transient, impersonal urban context. Outlined below are some community-level options for redefining integral components of everyday life—small businesses, churches, and schools. It is these institutions that help keep people living in rural areas and attached to the locale. Following this discussion is a description of an innovative solution, developed in Japan, to the issue of the services historically furnished by family members. The Japanese "labor bank" presents a plausible model for recreating the rural community as a fictive, large, extended family that provides support for all its members while avoiding exploitation of any one group.

One way that villages remain vital is when local businesses generate enough income to survive. Their survival not only assures an ambience of activity but in many cases provides jobs for residents. Downtown metropolitan centers have begun to revive with specialty businesses inappropriate for regional malls. Rural communities are less likely to survive with boutiques. However, recent reports (*New York Times* 1987a) cite an innovation tried in both North and South Dakota to help stimulate a return to patronage of local businesses. The program provided low-interest loans to families who agreed to do their Christmas shopping locally, rather than drive the customary 250 miles to the nearest mall. The loans were issued in scrip honored only by local banks, a solution also successfully adopted in Urbana, Illinois, during the Great Depression to save community businesses. The news report described the program's success in a remote farming and ranching town of about 1,500 people. This homegrown innovation simultaneously earned locally owned banks money and kept that cash in the community by boosting community retail sales.

Many career decisions of religious personnel are often outside the control of rural congregations. Churches appear to have moved to operating according to corporate practices and, in particular, giving few rewards for rural service. Rural communities have traditionally been a wellspring for religious vocations and might again fulfill that role if committed pastors interacted with congregations over a more extended period. Perhaps rural congregations should more actively protest those aspects of national religious institutional policy that run counter to ideological goals.

Rural communities that situate schools outside village limits must blame themselves for negative outcomes. Historic rivalry between neighboring communities tends to prevent the cooperation necessary when financial and demographic resources dwindle. Locating the high school in a community within a consolidated district might be more palatable when viewed in the context of a "neighboring" program that policy makers propose as a solution to rural financial stress (Deavers 1987). Under such a program communities would specialize as providers of a particular service; linked communities in proximity would furnish other, complementary services. If a formal exchange linkage existed, not leaving some communities feeling cheated by the consolidation, a better attitude about sharing a critical institution might develop. In the past, when the changes in the school system were handled apart from the arrangements for other local institutions, losing communities simple felt deprived. The linkage of neighboring communities as providers of other services might break down traditional antagonisms toward cooperation.

A redefining of schools to serve communities facing a child-care crisis created by women working outside the home is advocated by Dr. Edward F. Zigler of the Bush Center in Child Development and Social Policy at Yale University. Zigler proposes implementing a second educational system within existing elementary school buildings. The program would serve children ages three to twelve, both before and after regular school hours and during vacations. Three-and four-year-olds would receive child care in the building, not formal schooling (*New York Times* 1987b). For rural areas where obtaining quality child care is a nagging problem, such a program in the local school could revive a flagging institution and potentially revitalize the community economically. Child care in schools, rather than in scattered homesites, becomes a mechanism for reinforcing community solidarity and identity. Such a system provides employment for some people that otherwise might not maintain community residence.

One of the most serious issues facing rural families and communities is replacement of the family-centered services formerly supplied by women. In urban areas the transition to women entering the labor market has been made by families buying substitutes—house cleaners, errand runners, child care providers, nurses for the elderly—in the public marketplace. These solutions may not be viable for rural families—their numbers do not support the variety of services that a concentrated urban population does. Rural areas need an alternative model.

One model is represented by the German community mentioned previously where both young women and their mothers now work outside the home. When a community day care provider was overwhelmed by children, the local church stepped into the breach. The church elders, in spite of religious doctrine opposing women working outside the home, instituted day care in their parochial school in the face of much opposition. This same church financially supported a grocery store in danger of closing and organized vans to transport members to work in nearby metropolitan areas. The church thus is monitoring and meeting new needs among its members. Church-based leadership has, of course, the advantage of being an accepted organization, having both an established space and social structure. However, such a redefinition of a church is best suited to communities that contain only a single religious institution. In this situation group needs can be viewed as coming before that of the individual, and leadership demands can be made that are not possible in nonreligious contexts.

Communities with a weak church or with several competing congregations need a different organizing core to deal with the multiple burdens being experienced by rural families. For many situations a nonreligious model is more appropriate to meet new challenges. I found an innovative structure developed, interestingly enough, in the highly urban context of Osaka, Japan. It is a good example of how the non-Western Japanese develop an alternative solution to a social problem shared by both societies.

The Rural Community as an Extended Family

The "labor bank" is described by Takie Sugiyama Lebra (1980) as observed by her in Japan while involved in a field study. The concept was conceived by an Osaka housewife in the last days of World War II. If families struggling to survive pooled the domestic labor that housewives typically do separately, she thought, some women could be freed from child care or cleaning for other tasks. A group of women in her neighborhood organized themselves, but it was not until 1973 after her children married that the formal women's mutual-help organization was founded. When Lebra studied the bank in 1978, it had grown to 2,600 members, ranging from teenagers to old women in 160 local branches throughout Japan.

The key to understanding the concept of replacing each woman's domestic labor by interdomestic cooperation is a "rational accounting system" (Lebra 1980: 135) that differs from the traditional, informal mutual-aid characteristic of both the Japanese and American countryside. Labor is quantified and recorded in a book equivalent to a bank passbook upon which one can deposit or withdraw. An hour of ordinary labor receives a point while heavier labor is weighted higher. One cannot withdraw from the bank unless labor points have been "deposited." The bank allows cash payment to meet fluctuations in the supply and demand of labor. Like the traditional extended family with its less formal exchange system, the labor bank allows people to specialize in what they do well. For example, one can offer a service such as child care to many simultaneously. Rational centralized accounting even permits exchanges at some distance between banks and over an extended period of time.

The bank in Japan is female oriented, that is, women exchange labor mainly with other women. However, it is easy to see the system expanded to involve families as the depositors, rather than only a female household member. Families could bank or save labor during a period when a member or members are able to give and draw heavily from the bank at another point in their lives without going into debt. The bank concept effectively can span many generations and cut across many households. The founder of the bank is reported to assert that domestic labor is more difficult to obtain than other labor, something rural families have long realized. The labor bank concept demonstrates that work typically not given monetary value is actually a scarce resource worth a great deal.

Lebra argues that the labor bank provides a form of "human insurance" that links previously autonomous households in reciprocal exchanges. The concept translated to rural communities would provide a social net to families faced with a disappearance of domestic labor previously provided by women now working outside the home. A communally funded resident, with his or her job to coordinate a community or multicommunity labor bank, could fill this vacuum. The differences in work schedules, generations involved, and demands of a job conceivably could be accommodated if enough households were involved. Furthermore, having a local resident professionally committed to monitoring the community, as did the minister or kinship networks traditionally, would assure that needy individuals were not forgotten. In the Japanese labor bank a member must contribute several volunteer hours a month outside the usual exchange system to meet the bank's philosophical goal of cooperation. Such donated labor could be allotted to, for example, elderly residents who need more labor than they can contribute.

The labor bank concept formalizes those exchanges vital to family support, which were previously carried out informally, as a function of kinship or religious obligations. Rural communities can no longer depend on these traditional mechanisms to take up the social slack. Yet the same needs exist and are further complicated by the changes in rural life, particularly for rural women. The labor bank provides a systematic accounting and monitoring mechanism, assuring that community members are not so burdened by demands that families are destroyed. However, implementing a labor bank will require leadership and the commitment of an entire rural community, or linked communities, to work.

In 1985 a "service credit" program, similar in concept to the labor bank was begun as a mechanism for utilizing the labor of elderly people with time and energy to spare. The design involves volunteers who report hours spent helping those elderly in need of assistance and getting credits they can draw on later (Cahn 1988; Rowe and Waldam 1990). A computer record of volunteer work, as a sort of central bank, is kept under the auspices of a church, hospital or other organization. The system assumes one hour of work spent helping a needy individual is equal to any other hour of work given in service. Six funded programs were established experimentally in cities across the country, and Missouri and Michigan have extended the model in some rural areas. Cahn, who conceived the program, visualizes the service credit as a new kind of money not controlled by the government, used only to pay people to meet the needs of society. Volunteers do not replace professional services, but provide the vital and personal services family and community members did in the past.

Incorporating a labor bank or service credit system at the community level serves to formalize informal kinship and communal structures of the past. They are institutions that can translate community identification into action, uniting the entire community as an extended family concerned with its members' welfare. They are idealistic concepts, but perhaps the innovative approach families and communities must take to make their lives viable in a changed social environment.

Conclusion

Rural communities have historically provided a highly valued and desired life for people. Young families only reluctantly leave that setting when economic demands force out-migration. The challenge is for communities to fill the void created by the inability of family members to fulfill traditional kinship obligations. Local scrip, elementary schools as day-care centers, and a labor bank, are all ideas that, if adopted, would directly and indirectly integrate a community while meeting real family needs.

A commitment to act often is not enough for rural residents to accomplish changes in the basic social structure of their rural community.

Those embedded in a social structure seldom possess the objectivity, long view, or information required to transform it. It is here that policy makers have an important role to play. Knowledgeable professionals are a critical resource. Rural people must be presented a choice of options and alternative methods to achieve chosen ends best suited for their situation. A choice of options and processes are important ingredients to develop a local plan for change (Coughenour and Busch 1978). The suggestions presented above are not costly, but financial aid in the initial stages could be decisive for getting a labor bank or day-care system set up and started.

The very characteristics of the rural community that hold people are also those that are particularly adaptable to solving their problems. Solutions that support families show young people that life in their hometown is viable. However, for extended families unaccustomed to the level of nonkinship-based cooperation demanded in the new community form, major accommodations will be essential. The priority of individual household over group welfare emerging with the emphasis on the nuclear family in rural communities may have to undergo transformation in what should be a new phase of pioneering.

Rural development objectives are often limited to economic issues. The implication is that if decent jobs are provided to rural residents, quality of life will take care of itself. Economic solutions, though important to rural residents, do not meet the full spectrum of requirements for a satisfactory and manageable family and community life. The structural changes of women working in the labor force and the out-migration of the young, though helped by a sufficient income, mean that to maintain families in communities radical changes must be made. A return to the *gemeinschäft* ideal of community as family, though not in the image of our traditional ideal, seems essential. That is, a new interdependence is needed among rural families who have tended to turn inward, not outward, to deal with change. Traditionally interdependence was mainly kinship based or focused by religious affiliation, but the new interdependence is best served by linkages at the community level. Bellah, et al. (1985) in a book about America mores titled *Habits of the Heart*, expressed concerned with our shift to an individualism that turns people away from community. A more active involvement in public affairs is called for by the authors as a means of maintaining our democratic ideals and keeping our families and communities vital.

Solidarity, they argue, emerges from involvement—an attribute that would invigorate and breathe new life into rural communities.

References

Bellah, Robert N., Richard Madsen, William M. Sullivan, Ann Swidler, and Steven M. Tipton. 1985. *Habits of the Heart*. Berkeley: University of California Press.

Bokemeier, Janet L. and Ann R. Tickamyer. 1985. "Labor force experiences of nonmetropolitan women." *Rural Sociology*. 50: 51-73.

Brown, David L. and Kenneth L. Deavers. 1987. "Rural change and the rural economic policy agenda for the 1980s." *Rural Economic Development in the 1980s: Preparing for the Future*. Pp. 1.1-1.31. Agriculture and Rural Economy Division, Economic Research Service, U.S. Department of Agriculture. ERS Staff Report No. AGES870724.

Cahn, Edgar S. 1988. "Service credits: a market strategy for redefining elders as producers." Robert Morris and Scott A. Bass (eds.). *Retirement Reconsidered: Economic and Social Roles for Older People*. Pp. 232-249. New York: Springer Publishing Company.

Campbell, Rex R. 1985. "Some observations on the deflation of the farm assets in the Midwest." *Culture and Agriculture*. 3: 1-5.

Corner, Faye E. 1928. "A non-mobile, cooperative type of community: a study of the descendants of an East Frisian group." *University of Illinois Studies in the Social Sciences*. 16: 11-62.

Coughenour, C. Milton and Lawrence Busch. 1978. "Alternative futures for rural America: the cloudy crystal ball." Thomas R. Ford, (ed.). *Rural U.S.A.: Persistence and Change*. Pp. 211-227. Ames: Iowa State University Press.

Deavers, Kenneth L. 1987. "Choosing a rural policy for the 1980s and 1990s." *Rural Economic Development in the 1980s: Preparing for the Future*. Pp. 17.1-17.17. Agriculture and Rural Economy Division, Economic Research Service, U.S. Department of Agriculture. ERS Staff Report No. AGES870724.

Fink, Deborah. 1987. *Open Country, Iowa: Rural Women, Tradition and Change*. Buffalo: State University of New York Press.

Lebra, Takie Sugiyama. 1980. "Autonomy though interdependence: the housewives labor bank. *The Japanese Interpreter*. 13: 133-42.

New York Times. 1987a. "Christmas loans spur sales in small towns." December 25.

_____. 1987b. "Mapping future child care." October 25.

Rogers, Susan Carol and Sonya Salamon. 1983. "Inheritance and social organization among family farmers." *American Ethnologist*. 10: 529-550.

Rowe, Jonathan and Steven Waldam. 1990. "Beyond money: replacing the gold standard with the golden rule." *The Washington Monthly*. 22: 32-42.

Salamon, Sonya and Ann Mackey Keim. 1979. "Land ownership and women's power in a midwestern farming community." *Journal of Marriage and the Family*. 41: 109-119.

11

Individual and Social Problems in Rural Community Life

Lorraine Garkovich

The catalogue of "social problems" in the modern American community is seemingly endless. Teenage pregnancy, rising divorce rates, increasing poverty and homelessness, unemployment and hunger, nearly twenty-one million illiterate adults, achievement test scores that place American children far behind their European and Japanese counterparts, crime, drug abuse, and family violence only begin the list of social problems that represent flaws in the social fabric of the community. These problems and others fill our local newspapers and absorb a considerable amount of public attention, while public programs to "solve" these problems proliferate.

Is the social fabric of the community deteriorating or are we simply more aware of long-standing conditions? It will be argued that these conditions have always existed, but our definitions of them have changed. As a result, conditions or behaviors once defined as the result of individual choice and having only individual consequences have become "problems" requiring societal intervention. The key assumption underlying this discussion of individual and social problems in community life is that the definition of a situation or behavior determines our understanding of its source, its implications for the larger society, and appropriate responses. To understand how these new definitions may affect the relationship between individuals and institutions and, therefore, the nature of social policies, we must begin with an assessment of our traditional definitions of individual behavior and institutional life.

The Traditional View of Social Conditions in the Community

The social fabric of every society is woven together with the threads of the beliefs or myths that define the nature of the social world and give each society its characteristic hues and patterns. Burch (1971: 56) argues that belief systems or "social mythologies" are common sense notions "which tell us about the kind of people we wish to be and why we should hope to be that kind of people. They account for our regularized ways of doing things, our institutions. They deal with our collective origins that tell us what we are, where we are going, and why." Our dominant value system emerges from these beliefs as well as our definitions of the nature of human social life and our understanding of the purpose and functioning of the social structure. How we define social conditions is rooted in our beliefs and values, and these definitions determine if and how society responds to these conditions.

How is it that definitions of social conditions change or, in other words, that society begins to see a type of behavior as a "social problem" rather than as an isolated condition faced by an individual? There have always been poverty, family conflict, homelessness, and all the other "problems" noted earlier. However, in the past, society has defined the behavior or its consequences as essentially the concern of the individual and the result of individual actions and decisions. But for a variety of reasons, including the fact that the behavior or the condition becomes so widespread that it represents a challenge to our traditional understandings of social life, society eventually either redefines the behavior or redefines the essential character of our institutions. Typically, it is easier to redefine the social meaning of a behavior or situation than it is to restructure or realign the functions of an institution. As a result, as a society we have "discovered" and attached the label of "social problem" to a variety of conditions that previously were defined as individual problems. An example will illustrate this process.

Our beliefs and values have shaped our traditional views of the family as a social institution, defining its socially-desired form—the nuclear family of husband, wife, and children—and its socially desired processes—reproduction, socialization of children, and economic production. Deviations from these ideals are defined as problematic and demand intervention, but the solutions must be rooted in our sociocultural traditions. Therefore, actions oriented toward individuals that preserve the privacy of the family are most common. The linkage between events in the family as a social institution and conditions in the larger society and other institutions generally are ignored as are the implications of the changing family structure on the processes and functions of the family. These "blind spots" in our traditional views of the family as an institution hamper our understanding of the contemporary family and the changes it is experiencing.

This illustrates two important aspects of our traditional approach to understanding the purpose and functioning of social institutions. First, we tend to focus almost exclusively on individual resources, choices, perceptions, and modes of decision making. We assume that individuals act freely of their social environment, their choices are unlimited, and only individual inadequacies lead to problems and failures. Children fail in school because they choose to not study, young girls become mothers at an early age because they choose to not delay sexual gratification, people are poor because they choose to not work. Our cultural emphasis on individualism colors our understanding of the relationship between the individual and the society such that we fail to take into account the myriad of ways in which individual choices are shaped by their social context.

The second characteristic of our view of the social world is the tendency to treat our institutions and the problems that afflict them as discrete issues. We assume that the family functions independently of other social institutions. Yet, the numbers and types of job opportunities in a community determine whether families find employment, and whether the jobs they find provide sufficient wages to bring them out of poverty. To define problems and institutions as unconnected simplifies our attempt to make sense of the social world and extends our cultural emphasis on individualism into the social world. Yet, we cannot see that this view is inherently flawed, because our traditional beliefs color our understanding of social reality. What is needed is a revision of our collective view of the social world, one that takes into account its complex inter-connectedness.

The Community from a Social-Ecological Perspective

We conceptualize the physical environment as a set of interdependent and interacting systems and emphasize the functional relationships among organisms and between organisms and their physical environment. A social-ecological perspective applies this idea to understanding the nature of the social world. While we intuitively know that society, in general, and communities, in particular, are social systems, this view is at odds with our sociocultural emphasis on the individual. Yet, until we recognize the system dynamics of communities and societies, our efforts to understand and alleviate social problems are doomed to fail. A social-ecological perspective uses our knowledge of the workings of natural systems to understand the dynamics of human society. At a general level, a social-ecological perspective assumes that a particular community is one part of a larger social system called society which operates within a physical environment. The physical environment defines the resources available to the society for conversion to the energy, goods, and services that together are the basis for the survival of society and its members.

The community is a complex of subsystems called institutions that specialize in providing strategies for meeting needs such as, reproduction, production of goods and services, allocation of resources, or socialization. Each institution offers a range of appropriate actions for achieving the needs or goals associated with its purpose. Institutions emerge from the adaptive actions of individuals or groups of individuals as they seek means for satisfying their needs, achieving socially defined goals, or adjusting to changes in the socio-physical environment. Over time, institutions assume a modicum of stability, reflecting the cognitive, emotional, and economic investments of those who operate within their frameworks.

To illustrate, all societies must establish a mechanism for decision making with respect to the allocation of natural and social resources, a function fulfilled by the political institution. The particular configuration of the American political institution, its structure and processes, has emerged over two hundred years through the adaptive actions of individuals in search of the optimal ways of satisfying their needs. The concept of a "living constitution," reinterpreted to meet the needs and concerns of a changing society, exemplifies the adaptive nature of the political institution. On the other hand, the stability of its structure—the two-party system or the checks and balances among the branches of government—and the persistence of its processes—popular elections or the separation of war powers—exemplify the emergence of the vested interests that sustain an institution over time.

Individuals act to accomplish ends or produce changes in the "instrumental contexts of life" (Bennett 1976: 270). From an individual's point of view, each institution offers strategies for achieving desired ends within its functional areas. Individuals choose from among these based upon a wide variety of factors. Some of these factors are personal, such as the resources available to individuals, their perceptions or appraisals of their situation and the alternatives available to them, and their mode or style of decision making. However, some of the factors influencing their choices reflect the structure and functioning of the institutional subsystem such that particular resources may have less value in one institution, or certain strategies may not be available to all individuals. Thus, individual actions emerge from choices which are shaped by the alternatives and constraints that are the "texture of maps, rules, or diagrams" (Bennett 1976: 260) for action that comprise institutional systems.

Within the community, the institutional subsystems are inter-connected through overlapping functions, organizational components, members, and the dynamic character of systems. Some of the processes that link institutions include the following:

1. *Interdependence.* While each institution may be more or less complete in itself, each is also necessary to the functioning or operation of others. This interdependence can lead to synergistic effects. Synergism occurs when an interaction produces an effect that is greater than the sum of the parts.

2. *Feedback.* Changes in one institution lead to changes in others which produce still other changes among interconnected institutions. Feedback is the basis for the oft-stated rule of ecology—you can't do just one thing. In some cases, the feedback is expected or intended as when raising teachers' starting salaries leads to an increase in the number and quality of applicants. In other cases, the feedback is unexpected or unintended as when construction of an intracity highway hastens the succession process in a city neighborhood from middle to lower income families.

3. *Adaptation.* Institutions cope with changes in their external or internal environments so as to insure their continued operation. The adjustments or coping behaviors that constitute adaptation may aid in the maintenance of the status quo, or they may produce new structures or processes. Adaptations also may be adaptive for the institution but have negative consequences for its members. Finally, implicit in the concept of adaptation is "maladaptation."

4. *Inertia*. Institutions, and indeed all systems, tend to develop a vested interest in what they are. Inherent in the notion of inertia is the tendency for systems to make dynamic adjustments that enable them to maintain a structure, composition, or processes that represent vested interests. Inertia implies not a static stability but, rather, a tendency toward tension reduction.

In summary, a social-ecological perspective draws our attention to several important aspects of the human fabric of the community. First, human actions both shape and are constrained by institutions. If an institutional subsystem fails to offer the means for satisfying needs, adaptive actions by individuals may produce changes in the institution or, if institutional inertia is strong, individuals may be forced to seek alternatives outside the institution. During the 1960s, the establishment of alternative communities, grounded in a communal family structure, exemplifies the emergence of an alternative subsystem.

Second, both individual actions and institutional precedents for action have consequences or effects for other persons or institutional subsystems. In human systems, feedback can be altered, diverted, or circumvented by language, values or, more simply, human cognition. The suggestion that providing birth control information to teens provokes teens into sexual activity illustrates how values divert our attention from the influence of peer pressure on teenage sexuality.

Third, given the dynamic character of feedback, the self-regulatory nature so typical of mechanical and organic systems is often absent from human systems. As a result, individuals may pursue and, institutions may encourage, actions that, in the long run, may be detrimental to their survival. This is the meaning of "maladaptation," not that some actions are bad or wrong but that they reduce the long-term sustainability of the system, be it an institution or an individual. This tendency may be encouraged by vesting particular actions or strategies with special meanings (e.g., "we've always done it this way," or "we can't do that because someone won't like it").

Finally, the interdependence of institutions rests in part upon shared functional areas. Given this overlap, the only effective approach to addressing a problem in one of these functional areas is to take into account its interdependence with other institutions. Programs or policies directed at only one institution's manifestation of the problem affects only an isolated aspect of the problem.

Reinterpreting Human Social Problems in the Community

How can a social-ecological perspective help us to redefine human social problems in the community, and what would be the nature of programs designed to address these problems from this perspective? The keys to reinterpreting human social problems are acknowledging that institutions are irreducible social systems and recognizing the implications of the dynamic processes of social systems.

The Family

To view the family as a social system situated within and interacting with other social systems has important consequences for how we interpret the "problems" with the family (identified earlier). First, it means we must acknowledge that although the family is composed of individuals, it is more than the sum of these individuals. Family sociologists recognize that within the family, interpersonal relations produce an institution of durability and resiliency that exceeds what would be expected from its individual members. Second, despite our cultural belief in the family as a private, sacred institution, the family system is situated among and affected by many other institutions and groups. The structure and functions of the family reflect the influences of these outside forces. Yet, as a society we have tended to ignore the effects of public policies (such as tax codes) or programs (such as welfare assistance) on the family. Finally, and perhaps most importantly, given the central functions of the family within the larger society—reproduction, socialization, distribution of economic resources, and social affiliation—it can be argued that the health and vitality of the family is of pre-eminent concern to society. What happens within the family is not always a private affair; rather, it typically has consequences for other institutions and the society at large.

The assertion that contemporary changes in the family are maladaptive ignores the possibility that divorce, single parenthood, or latch-key children may be, from the perspective of the individuals involved, the best choice given their perceived alternatives. Stripped of our value-laden assumptions as to the "inevitability of the nuclear family," few people would argue that an individual should remain in a physically abusive or dangerous family relationship simply to achieve the goal of maintaining the nuclear family. Or, given the high mobility of

Americans, most families live away from their kin so working couples may have no option but to have children care for themselves after school. Individuals will seek alternative means for achieving their ends when traditional options, such as grandparents to care for children when parents work, are not available.

Similarly, although our cultural traditions idealize the nuclear family of breadwinning father, housewife mother, and children, financial pressures on contemporary families make two incomes almost essential for maintaining the equally idealized middle class standard of living. A recent report by the Economic Policy Institute indicates that working wives contribute over forty per cent of the average family income. Clearly, families can no longer count on a single breadwinner earning enough to provide for their needs. The alternative to a working wife may be poverty and welfare dependence. Indeed, The Center for Demographic Policy (CDP) reports that "if families had to do without women's wages, it is estimated that the poverty rate would go up by at least one-third" (CDP 1990: 2).

Furthermore, the definition of alternative family arrangements as maladaptive produces reactive social programs. Few community programs have been developed to assist individuals in alternative family arrangements in dealing with their situations as effectively as possible. For example, while American rates of teenage pregnancy are the highest among industrialized nations, few programs enable these young women to acquire their high school degrees or even provide basic information on child health and child-rearing practices. Rather, some school districts punish teenage mothers by denying them access to regular classes during their pregnancies or prohibiting them from participating in graduation ceremonies. While these punitive programs reflect an institutional tendency to maintain its vested interests in particular social forms, they do little to assist families in coping with changing social and personal conditions.

Since these problems have been treated as failures of the family, the effects of conditions or forces outside the family on the incidence of single-parent families, teenage pregnancy, and latch-key children have been overlooked or discounted. In other words, we have failed to ask, how have government policies or programs affected the family, and how have changes in other institutions, such as the economy, affected families? For example, dual career married couples for years endured an income tax "marriage penalty." That is, their tax rates on jointly filed income exceeded the rates they would have paid if they had filed as unmarried individuals. Also, in most states, families with a husband present are not eligible to participate in Aid to Families with Dependent Children, the primary maintenance welfare program. In both these situations, government policies may force families to make a choice between remaining intact and maintaining an adequate standard of living.

The health of the family mirrors the health of the economy. During the last two decades, American families have endured tremendous economic pressures from high unemployment, inflation depressing the buying power of real wages, high interest rates making home ownership an increasingly difficult goal to achieve, and significant numbers slipping into poverty despite having full time jobs. The feedback of these economic changes on the family alters the basis on which adaptive actions are chosen.

Finally, the interdependence of institutions and the possibility of synergistic effects should lead us to understand that the public/private dichotomy in thinking about the family cannot be in the best interest of the family or society. When families cannot provide economically for their children, when children are abused, or when teens have children, the consequences are felt outside the family. Family problems are social problems because they affect our educational, economic, and political institutions. The relationship between access to school meal programs and the educational achievement of low-income children demonstrates this interdependence, as does the relationship between child abuse and adult criminal behavior.

Our tendency to cling to the notion of the private family, a notion that is laden with cultural values, denies many families access to the social assistance that may be necessary for their survival. It is a short-sighted notion, albeit one that reflects the values of many groups with vested interests in the traditional family institution.

Education

Education is also a social system situated within and interacting with other social systems. The educational institution is much more complex than teachers, students, principals, and school boards. It also encompasses, at a minimum, publishers of textbooks; developers of competency tests; local, state, and federal legislative bodies that allocate financial resources; state and federal bureaucracies that have administrative power over educational standards (e.g., certification requirements for teachers, achievement standards for students); teachers unions; and parents. All of these groups make up the educational institution because they define the structure and processes of education. Thus, despite our cultural belief that teachers and students are the individual actors in education, the reality is that their choices and actions are clearly influenced by expectations and constraints impinging upon them from many other actors in the system.

Second, external events and conditions establish the cultural expectations that define the goals for education. When the educational system fails, as when students drop out or graduate from high school but are functionally illiterate, there are consequences for the larger society. The strength and health of the educational system are not just a concern for the students, teachers, and parents directly involved, but rather they are of consequence for all the other institutions in society.

The interdependence of the educational system with conditions in the rest of society can be illustrated through several feedback loops. In the late 1950s when Russia launched Sputnik, the national response was to join the space race. This effort required a major commitment to educating and training scientists. Within a few years, most school districts had increased their science and math requirements for graduation. Students who showed any aptitude in these areas were encouraged to pursue a college education, and the federal government increased its financial support of graduate studies in science and math. More recently, public concern over declining student achievement scores has led to legislatively mandated competency testing for both students and teachers. Student competency tests influence classroom content. Teachers direct their lessons toward those items covered in the tests; in this sense, the tests define the "bottom line" of knowledge students must achieve regardless of the opinions of their teachers. Teacher competency tests presume to objectify in some form what makes a "good" teacher and, if teachers fail the test, they are subject to dismissal despite their actual classroom performance. These feedback loops between the political and the educational institutions illustrate the constraints imposed on the content and form of teaching.

Another example of interdependence among institutions is the relationship between the family and education. With more couples working, some schools face pressures to provide child care after classes end until parents finish work. Because more children live with a single parent due to divorce or in "blended" families due to remarriage, children bring to school many emotional problems that affect their learning and behavior in classes. With more families moving due to divorce or job transfers, there are a significant number of children who have attended schools in several places, producing major dislocations in the content of their lessons. The once close involvement of parents in their children's education, in terms of oversight and active participation, is diminishing due to the myriad of forces acting upon the family. As a result, the schools are expected to perform their many functions increasingly isolated from parental support. On the other hand, many parents feel excluded from their children's education by the layers of administrators, regulators, and regulations that seem to impede their efforts to become actively involved. The partnership between the family and the schools that once provided support for children's educational endeavors is breaking down with negative consequences for both families and the schools.

A final example of interdependence among institutions is illustrated by access to educational opportunities which are, in part, a function of family income, since this determines residence and, hence, the quality of the schools children attend. Limited incomes are the result of unemployment, underemployment, or employment in low-wage firms. Limited incomes restrict residential mobility and, therefore, choice in schools. This is important because not all schools are alike. Some children attend schools that have several computers in each classroom while other children find only one computer per school. In the information age, access to computers at an early age is increasingly important. Those schools that cannot provide computers will graduate students who will not be competitive in the labor force.

On the other hand, a significant proportion of local school district funds are generated through taxes which reflect the wealth of a community. Communities with limited tax bases spend less per student than those with larger tax bases, and this affects the resources available to the school district. To illustrate this point, consider Kentucky where expenditures per student by local school districts range from $1,690 to $2,985 with a 1985-1986 state average of $2,139. A school district with a taxable property base averaging $39,000 per household (McCreary County) cannot generate the same level of economic resources for education as a school district with a taxable base of $123,000 (Fayette County). The feedback proceeds, as limited educational opportunities translate into limited work skills and, therefore, reduced competitiveness in the labor market. This feedback loop is likely to occur in rural school districts where economic opportunities for adults are limited and translate into limited family incomes.

These feedback loops demonstrate the interdependence of education and other institutions. The resources available to support educational activities are a function of the strength of the local economic institution. Alternatively, the skills of a local labor force, an important factor in determining the types of industry the community can support, reflect the quality of the graduates the schools produce. Communities with a high proportion of workers without a high school degree do not have the human resources to attract those industries with highly automated manufacturing processes or other types of skill work. The importance of this relationship has been demonstrated by Skees and Swanson (1988,) who found that the educational level of a community's labor force was the single best predictor of family income and the incidence of poverty. The interaction between education and the economy serves as a stepping stone to reinterpreting poverty from a social-ecological perspective.

Poverty

Poverty is a social problem that is rooted in the interaction among various institutional structures and processes. As such, poverty is a symptom of institutional failures or the unintended consequence of feedback loops among institutions. This calls for a reassessment of traditional definitions of poverty and important changes in how, as a society, we respond to the incidence and distribution of poverty.

Traditional explanations of poverty focus on individual motivations or choices, discounting the importance of the number and types of jobs available to potential workers in determining whether an individual's motivation to work or particular cluster of skills and experiences can lead to employment or a job that produces sufficient income to bring a family out of poverty. This may be illustrated with the following analogy. Imagine that you are standing in a crowd of people, each holding a number. Your number represents who you are in terms of your education, your work experiences, your family status, your age, your sex, and your race. Some of these factors you may influence, some you can not. The size of the crowd and the rate at which individuals leave for jobs depend upon the number of employment opportunities in the community. The type of job you can find when you leave the crowd, as well as its salary and benefit levels, depends upon the structure of labor market opportunity in the community. To a certain degree, any individual's opportunities to leave the crowd and to find an adequate job is contingent upon the opportunity structure in the local labor market area. For individuals with particular configurations of personal characteristics, few opportunities exist, or the opportunities are for jobs that provide less than a minimally necessary income. In the context of a social-ecological perspective, their personal resources do not provide access to the same number or type of opportunities as they possibly would in another economic (community) subsystem.

A comparison of the incidence of poverty in rural and urban areas demonstrates this interaction between labor market opportunities, unemployment, and wage levels. The poverty rate in rural areas (18%) was fifty per cent higher than it was in urban areas (12%) in 1986. The rate of poverty in rural areas persistently exceeds that in urban areas, and rural persons remain in poverty for longer periods of time than urban residents (O'Hare 1988). Poverty is especially a problem for young adults (18-44 years of age) with families. More than one out of every five young rural families was living below the poverty level in 1987. What is striking about the incidence of poverty among young rural adults is that sixty-two per cent were employed for at least part of the year. "The poverty rate for young rural families with one wage-earner was thirty-one per cent in 1986, compared to twenty per cent in urban areas, while the poverty rate for rural families with two or more wage-earners was more than double that of similar urban families" (O'Hare 1988: 11).

Individuals refusing to work does not explain the higher incidence of rural poverty among working-aged couples. Rather, the explanation lies in the availability and the kinds of jobs they can find. O'Hare (1988:11) notes a seventy per cent increase between 1979 and 1986 in the number of young rural adults in poverty working part time, while the number seeking employment rose from ten to twenty-three per cent. The most striking indictment of the opportunities offered by rural labor markets is the fact that "one-quarter of poor young adults in the rural labor force held two or more jobs in 1986." Clearly, work skills do not exist in isolation but, rather, fit into a marketplace. For rural people, limited job opportunities and a predominance of low-paying jobs produce a greater likelihood of poverty regardless of work skills or the desire to work.

This is exacerbated by the fact that since the rural poor are more likely than the urban poor to be employed and to own their homes, the rural poor are also more likely to pay federal, state, local property, and social security taxes. This means that for the rural poor, a smaller proportion of their incomes can be devoted to family maintenance.

Another factor that influences an individual's access to labor market opportunities is discrimination, or the systematic exclusion of categories of workers or the limitation of their job mobility due to assumptions about work habits or work skills. It has been argued that discrimination is maladaptive for employing firms since they exclude potentially qualified workers on the basis of presumed rather than actual abilities. But if all the firms in an area discriminate against a particular category of workers, then the practice does not have negative consequences for the firms since no one firm gains an advantage in employment. This also holds true for wage discrimination, the practice of systematically offering lower wages to particular workers. When all firms engage in this practice all benefit, since the firms have access to a pool of labor at artificially lowered wages. Discrimination, then, is maladaptive for firms only when a few engage in this practice, but the practice has serious negative consequences for the affected individuals. The tendency for institutions and their component organizations to maintain traditional or customary processes and structures can short-circuit the effects of individual actions at self-improvement.

Moreover, the effects of discrimination are reinforced as the consequences of limited economic opportunities and limited wages affect household members. In other words, "feedback between households and labor markets often creates new forces for discrimination" (England and Farkas 1986: 139). The interdependence of education and income levels in a community (discussed earlier) illustrates this point. In labor markets with limited opportunities for certain categories of workers, children come to realize that even the better educated and the more skilled find few jobs that offer families a comfortable standard of living. In other words, there are few role models who demonstrate that education improves one's life chances.

Finally, we must consider the economic value of public assistance vis-á-vis prevailing wage rates in a community. Economists argue that wages reflect the intersection of the supply of particular types of labor and the demand for that labor given a firm's market position for the goods or services they provide. In other words, firms producing for highly competitive markets will attempt to keep wages low since higher wages force the price of their products upward and reduce their competitiveness.

In general, there are industrial sectors (e.g., services, textiles, small electronic component manufacturing) that are highly competitive and labor-intensive, and there are geographic areas (e.g., rural communities, Southern communities) with a heavy dependence upon such industrial sectors. In communities with low wage rates, the income difference between wages and public assistance may be minimal. Indeed, when one takes into account the loss of in-kind benefits (such as Medicaid or subsidized housing or food stamps) that usually occurs when one becomes employed, and the tendency for jobs in highly competitive and labor-intensive industries to offer few benefits, then employment may actually lead to a net economic loss for a family. If the worker is a woman with dependent children, the additional costs of child care may also produce a negative balance. In these situations, continuing to utilize public assistance can be viewed as an adaptive action by individuals that insures their ability to continue providing support for their families. Moreover, many workers find themselves in jobs with few opportunities for advancement. These workers confront a job market wherein, regardless of their years of experience or the quality of their work, they see little opportunity to improve their economic status.

The feedback loop that links prevailing wage rates to the incidence of poverty becomes self-reinforcing. Low wage rates are associated with higher rates of poverty among working-age adults. A large pool of unemployed or underemployed adults increases the supply of labor which acts to maintain depressed wage levels. There is little incentive for individual firms to increase wages since this would have a negative effect on their competitive position, and the costs of poverty and support programs are spread throughout the community and the society at large. Hence, while low or depressed wage levels may be maladaptive for the economic institution as a whole, they may be an adaptive response for individual firms. Moreover, while the larger society may define utilization of public assistance as a maladaptive condition, for individuals it may be the most appropriate action given their situation.

Poverty, like the family, is not a private problem or a problem of individuals. Rather, it is a situation with causes and consequences that crosses institutional boundaries. Our traditional approaches to thinking about and acting toward poverty have suffered from linear thinking, which has limited our ability to understand that only by bridging the gaps within institutions and between institutions and organization levels (such as federal, state, and local governments) can we begin to effectively deal with this condition.

Policy Implications of a Social-Ecological Perspective

From a social-ecological perspective, the increasing complexity of social life means that no one individual, institution, or community is self-sufficient. Interdependence and feedback imply that simplistic solutions directed at a single aspect of any problem will inevitably founder upon the complex interconnectedness of social life. What is needed are policies and programs that recognize the interdependence among institutions. There are examples in both the public and private sectors of first steps toward this goal.

The rapid growth in the number of employed women, who now represent forty-four per cent of the labor force, and the fact that nearly sixty per cent of the women with children under the age of six are working, reflect fundamental changes in both the family and the economy. Together, these changes indicate a growing need to assess who will care for the children of this society. To date, we have addressed this problem with traditional thinking—children and child care are in the private domain of the family, and it is the family's responsibility to locate appropriate child care and to pay for it. But, a family's options are limited by forces beyond its control. Who cares for America's children, in what situations, and at what costs, reflect the intersection of answers to several other questions represented, at a minimum, by the following: How much can a family afford to pay for child care? Are spaces available in day care centers? Are relatives or friends available who are willing to offer child care services? How old are the children? and, If the children are in school, how do they get to child care after school? These questions demonstrate that family decision making regarding child care is not independent of events and conditions in the larger society (O'Connell and Bloom 1987).

What are some approaches to child care that involve these various institutions and actors? Some employers have come to recognize that employees perform better when not concerned with family problems and they have developed some innovative approaches to both work scheduling and benefit packages. Flex time (employees select their specific hours of work within identifiable limits), block scheduling (employees work extended hours and compress a 40 hour work week into three or four days), and job sharing (where couples share one full-time job) are three approaches to restructuring the work day that offer working parents greater flexibility in dealing with child care. The federal government experimented with flex time for 325,000 employees over a three-year period. A review of the program concluded that it "allows employees workable alternatives to enhance the quality of family relationships and child care" (O'Connell and Bloom 1987: 12). Flexible benefit packages offer employees the opportunity to select specific benefits from a menu of alternatives. Employees in dual career families can select those benefits that meet their family needs and a growing number of employers are offering child care assistance (e.g., monthly vouchers for expenses for on- or off-site child care), maternity leave (or in a few cases paternity leave), and the use of personal sick leave to care for an ill child or family member. O'Connell and Bloom (1987: 12) note that "most firms that operate or pay for child care facilities for employees' children report reduced rates of lateness, absenteeism and turnover, and improved employee satisfaction and productivity."

The problem of child care also requires intervention by political institutions at all levels. At a minimum, political actions that support and encourage private initiatives to assist employees in managing child care problems are required. But the private sector cannot afford to absorb the full costs of an adequate national child care program because private initiatives cannot reach all families who need assistance. This is because the majority of workers are employed by small firms that do not have flexible resources to absorb the costs of such programs. Therefore, a more proactive governmental approach is needed.

Tax credits for child care costs can provide relief to middle-income families whose weekly child care costs may range from $50 to $160 per child. But tax credits do little for low-income families who pay less taxes anyway. Low-income families need access to subsidized child care if couples are to gain maximum economic benefit from employment. This is especially critical since mothers are often the primary breadwinner in low-income families. State and local governments have responded to this crisis with various innovative programs. For example, short-term disability insurance in five states (California, Hawaii, New Jersey, New York, and Rhode Island) can be used for maternity leave.

In Massachusetts, companies providing on-site day care can receive up to a quarter of a million dollars in low interest loans to establish their programs. New York and California provide child care programs for state workers, while tax benefits are available to employers who offer child care assistance to employees in four states (Arizona, California, Connecticut, and Florida). Local governments have also been active. San Francisco has, since 1985, required developers of new downtown office buildings to contribute one dollar per square foot of office space for the construction of inner-city child care facilities. Fairfax County, Virginia, has established a center to assist employers in locating child care services for employees (O'Connell and Bloom 1987: 14). In other communities, local schools provide child care after hours for working parents or school buses transport children to private day care facilities.

However, as a society, we have thus far failed to acknowledge that it is in the national interest to insure that parents have access to safe, affordable, and convenient child care. A national child care policy accompanied by programs that enable couples to stay at home and care for newborns, ill children, aging or seriously ill relatives would alleviate many financial and emotional stresses on contemporary families. A 1982 Census Bureau survey of nonworking mothers with preschool children found that thirteen per cent of these women would look for work if child care were available, and twenty per cent of the women whose family incomes were less than $15,000 would likely enter the labor force.

The opportunity for mothers in low-income families to obtain employment is a key factor in improving these families' standard of living. In low-income families, wives' earnings can represent as much as sixty-five cents of every family income dollar, and so, the working wife makes a major contribution to lifting the family out of poverty. A recent study by the Economic Policy Institute concludes that working wives have been a key factor in helping families keep pace with the increasing cost of living. Indeed, without these working mothers more families would have slipped into poverty over the last decade.

Thus, simply from the perspective of assisting families in maintaining their standard of living, a national child care policy is in the best interest of both families and society. Finally, the experience of industries that have developed child care programs for their employees suggests that the costs of such programs may well be offset by their benefits. Child care options are good for business.

The crisis confronting American schools is one that can only be addressed through concerted efforts by families and by economic and political institutions. To a certain extent we have treated our schools as black boxes into which we place our children. But black boxes are not isolated from the rest of society—events impinge, resources ebb and flow, and expectations change. Schools that educate children without the involvement of families and other community institutions, without incentives for excelling, or without sufficient resources will fail. And schools that fail to accomplish their primary functions impede other institutions in the pursuit of their goals. There are a number of innovative approaches to improving education by capitalizing on the interaction among institutions.

Increasingly, businesses have recognized that their own future health is tied to the health of the educational institution. This is producing some innovative rearrangements in the traditional relationships between work, school, and home. In various cities around the county, firms grant employees temporary leaves of absence to teach junior and high school classes about modern business. Others offer students work-study opportunities providing the students with invaluable learning experiences. In other communities, businesses "adopt" a local school and employees donate time as tutors, funds for special school projects, or the purchase of new equipment. In Versailles, Kentucky, Texas Instruments has initiated a program offering basic literacy, high school equivalency, and other classes in the plant. The firm is working with the local school board to remodel a vacant elementary school building into an "adult education center." Plans are also underway to have local teachers "shadow" workers in various industries to develop a better understanding of the skills and knowledge required in modern industries. In Falmouth, Kentucky, the Fuller automobile engineering plant has donated classroom space, books, and the salary for a literacy teacher. This firm and others believe they have received a major return on their investments in education in terms of workers who are more motivated, ambitious, and productive. These programs reflect an awareness on the part of businesses that schools produce the employees of tomorrow and that their competitive position in national and international markets depend upon the quality of their labor force.

Other innovations focus on encouraging students to continue their education and to work to their greatest potential. In a few cities, such as Chicago and Philadelphia, individuals have guaranteed students, who graduate from high school with a B average, funds for college tuition. Increasingly more common, however, are programs to encourage academic excellence. Businesses and local governments in various communities have established pools of funds to reward students for achieving an A or B average on their report cards.

Another feedback loop receiving attention through innovative programs is that linking the family and the schools. In Kentucky and Missouri, parents receive special training to assist them in tutoring their children. For parents who themselves have not graduated from high school, the program focuses on parents and children learning together. Other programs focus on forging a partnership between parents and teachers to achieve a common goal—helping children to learn more and graduate from high school. "Forward in the Fifth," a program established in the Fifth Congressional district in Kentucky, expands this partnership to include schools, families, businesses, and nonprofit agencies in a coordinated effort at reducing dropout rates, increasing the number of adults achieving general education degrees or functional literacy, and encouraging academic excellence. Funding for the various parts of this program have been generated through grants from state government, private foundations, and fundraising in the local communities. Forward in the Fifth has, in a few years, dramatically reduced the high school dropout rate in an area that historically has been impoverished both educationally and economically.

But local school districts and the private sector cannot solve our educational problems alone. Nor should they. For the success of the nation's schools in achieving their institutional goals is a key component of national security. An educated citizenry is the heart of a democracy and the foundation of a nation's economic and military strength. The funding of education varies widely, with some schools attempting to accomplish the same educational goals as others with less than a third of the financial resources, in dilapidated and deteriorating buildings, and with limited supplies. Federal funding of education has declined twenty per cent since 1980, while taxpayer revolts have limited the ability of state and local governments to finance educational improvements. Further, even with unlimited taxing ability, a significant number of local school districts simply do not have the economic base to generate the resources necessary to support educational improvements. Only the national government has the ability to generate the resources to support a quality educational system by equalizing the resource bases of local school districts.

Conclusions

Alfred North Whitehead once stated: "The essence of dramatic tragedy is not unhappiness. It resides in the solemnity of the remorseless working of things." The tragedy of our traditional views of human social problems is that they assign responsibility and blame for events to individuals when, in fact, individuals generally confront conditions beyond their control. This is also true of institutions which are interconnected with many others within the larger society. In the last decade, there has been a tendency to decentralize federal responsibilities to state and local governments, which mirrors our traditional emphasis on individualism. It has been argued here that this approach has exacerbated existing social problems by reinforcing a false definition of the nature of these problems. The tragedy of human social problems will be adequately addressed only when we begin to reassess our traditional views, treat social life as a seamless whole, and recognize the interdependence among communities, institutions, and people.

References

Bennett, John W. 1976. *The Ecological Transition*. New York: Pergamon Press.

Burch, William R. 1971. *Daydreams and Nightmares*. New York: Harper and Row.

Center for Demographic Policy. 1990. "Child care: Who needs it?" *CDP Newsletter*. 1: 2.

England, Paula, and George Farkas. 1986. *Household, Employment, and Gender*. New York: Aldine Publishing Co.

O'Connell, Martin, and David E. Bloom. 1987. "Juggling jobs and babies: America's child care challenge." Washington, D.C.: Population Reference Bureau, No. 12.

O'Hare, William P. 1988. "The rise of poverty in rural America." Washington, D.C.: Population Reference Bureau.

Skees, Jerry R., and Louis E. Swanson. 1988. "Farm structure and local society well-being in the South." in Lionel J. Beaulieu (ed.). *The Rural South in Crisis: Challenges for the Future*. Pp. 141-15. Boulder, CO: Westview Press.

12

Civic Education, Rural Development, and the Land Grant Institutions

Donald W. Littrell and Doris P. Littrell

People with accurate, relevant knowledge, working through groups and coalitions to establish purposeful local public policy that enhances choice are the foundation of successful development action.

> It appears to us that a community which organizes its activity so that it maximizes the number of healthy, intelligent self-directing citizens, capable of viewing situations from perspectives other than their own, of weighing alternatives and making decisions, of defining new goals and inventing new ways of achieving them is in fact a democratic community and is producing members who can sustain it (Foote and Cottrell 1985: 60).

Rural development starts with people who reside in the villages, towns, barrios and counties that make up rural America. In hundreds of locations throughout this nation people organize, study their situations in regard to the larger environment, and form and implement decisions that improve the quality of living. Rural America is far too diverse, complex and vast to be planned or managed centrally. The starting point for the rural areas of America to develop in a manner that is pleasing or satisfactory is the people who live, work and govern in those areas. For the communities of rural America to mount successful, sustained rural development efforts, the people of rural America must have access to civic education that empowers them to form, implement and enforce local policy to shape the future purposefully. Access to civic education would provide the opportunity to learn the concepts, tools and procedures of effective local governance other than through trial and error. For present purposes, the concept of civic education has been expanded beyond conventional uses (related to learning the responsibilities of citizenship) to include learning which deals with the effective diffusion of power in civic life.

For the nation to have an effective rural development effort, people in the communities of the nation must be empowered to develop effective approaches to dealing with their particular situation using information that has utility for their environment. Effective rural development cannot be managed or controlled from Washington, D.C., and in most cases it cannot be successfully directed from the nation's state houses. Communities can be assisted by external resources if those resources properly or effectively match local conditions or aspirations and enhance the ability of communities to govern their own affairs, increasing control of their social and economic futures.

Civic Education and the Rural Scene

The present American educational system is teaching people the most about government that is most removed from them and is, to a great extent, immune to their direct intervention. A review of college courses, textbooks and high school texts conducted by the authors reveals that scant attention is given to anything "local." In addition, many traditional social sciences have largely abandoned the local scene as a field of inquiry, publication or teaching. Governing is presented as primarily a federal function with some recognition that states are important. Mass media focuses attention upon national and multi-national events and trends, and often does not show how the larger perspective affects or is connected to local situations and people.

Local citizens, whether of town, city, township, special district, county or a combination of all, are significant players in determining the quality of their lives. The local setting expands or limits the range of choices available to people. Even more importantly, the local setting helps define for each person one's individual image of what is possible for self and family (Bellah, et al. 1985).

Many community functions are influenced, managed or controlled by people through local structures that together make up a collective quality of life. A partial listing of such local functions helps to make the point: schools, land use regulations, housing codes, local political structures, water supply and sewer systems, trash disposal, fire and police protection, child care facilities, streets, roads, bridges, recreation, tax rates, employment, counseling services, health care, economic opportunity, environmental quality, financial services, and energy usage. It is also within the local setting that informal and formal social policy is formulated that determines which people have or do not have access to the community's collective resources. It is through social interaction that people learn who they are, their appropriate roles, and through which they develop attitudes and gain a sense of what is possible in both a collective and individual sense (Almond and Verba 1963: 13).[1]

It is important to realize that within each community there are sets of traditions, values, beliefs, customs that provide a social context or fabric. To be sure there are differences and even disagreements among citizens about these expressions, but in the collective sense they are a powerful force. Communities have a past, a set of experiences, a social history that often sets a reference or referral point to guide current thinking and decisions. Often communities have artifacts such as buildings or ethnic traditions that are extremely important, often far beyond their economic worth. All of these function to provide a local culture from which people of the community learn what is proper and improper behavior for themselves and others. It is through this veil of culture that people interpret the world and form judgments.

Why is this important? Rural communities are heterogeneous. While there are areas of sameness, there are also significant areas of difference. Communities exhibiting the same demographic, socio-economic characteristics may have arrived at their current situation through a very different social history and have differing values and beliefs.

It is people—their beliefs, traditions, structures and resources—that are the basic elements of rural development. It also should be understood that community people have terms for their requirements just as institutions have. Successful rural development involves the working out these terms. Overlooking this clarification too often results in each discounting the other's potential contribution to development.

Many people who fill positions in both the informal and formal structures of governance of rural American communities are volunteers. It is true that in larger towns, counties and in small cities, professional managers and technical specialists have been hired to do much of the day-to-day civic work. The fact remains that a majority of cities, towns, special districts and counties are managed or governed by volunteer boards, committees or councils (Ballard 1985: 167).[2] Outside the traditional formal structures of government there is an uncounted array of organizations such as economic development councils, chambers of commerce, civic organizations, community improvement associations, etc., which affect quality of life. These are directed to a great extent by volunteers. This is not to imply that governance by volunteers is inferior, but to point out that much of rural America is governed by people who often have little preparation for their role in government.

It follows then that citizens, leaders and elected officials often have little sustained, continuous opportunity to learn how "local" processes function; to share competence, resources and viewpoints; to forge a process of governance that provides a sound economic base, a just, fair and open political arena and a social setting that is stimulating to human potential.

For rural development to be successful, the process of governance must be creative, responsive, proactive, futuristic, progressive and efficient in literally hundreds, even thousands, of towns and counties across this land. For this to occur, citizens and officials—volunteers and professionals, elected and appointed, public and private—need ongoing opportunities to learn how the diverse local systems function, interact and affect each other. The local setting can and must be the training ground for purposeful, effective civic governance. The communities of rural America can be the classroom in which people learn to give direction to their own community's future.

Learning to understand each other and developing the capacity to work together is critical if rural America is to be made up of communities that provide an enriching quality of life.

Civic Education: Concepts for Governance

The empowerment of people to turn vision into reality is in fact the teaching of effective leadership. Bennis and Nanus (1985) note:

> . . . effective leadership can move organizations from current to future states, create visions of potential opportunities for organizations, instill within employees commitment to change and instill new cultures and

strategies in organizations that mobilize and focus energy and resources. (p. 17)

While Bennis and Nanus were referring primarily to formal organizations, the same can be said for community-based leadership. To use Bennis' term it is "transforming leadership." If people are to govern, to lead, they must be willing to deal with and exercise power. Rural development has at its core the purposeful exercise of power. This means that power is not exercised by one person or a small group of elites. Civic education strives to develop situations characterized by diffuse power. Civic education addresses much more than the responsibilities of citizenship, the civic or democratic rituals. It is teaching a broad base of people how to develop and use power, influence, authority and other tools of governance in an effective manner. In short, it changes power relationships with the community setting.

Power is not a constant within a given setting. The amount of power functioning within a given community is determined by the knowledge people have and their willingness to enter the governance arena, act on that knowledge through the exercise of power and influence (Freire 1968: 33).[3]

Communities are the central focus of civic education, for it is in this arena that people have the greatest potential to learn to function as citizens and see the results of their efforts. This learning might well be labeled *action learning* for such learning is not dealt with in the abstract but in relationship to one's interests and concerns.

The way a free society meets its problems depends not only on its economic and administrative resources but on its political imagination. Political vision thus plays an indispensable role in providing understanding of the present and of the possibilities of "change." (Bellah, et al. 1985: 271)

Anticipation is the capacity to face new, possibly unprecedented situations; it is the acid test for innovative learning processes. (Bolkia, et al. 1979: 25)

From these two statements one can understand why community is so central to both civic education and rural development. It is in the community arena that people learn to marshall collective resources by effectively using power to move toward a desired future. Through a process of envisioning a future and asking what work needs to be performed or action taken people can learn to anticipate the future and deal effectively with it.

In the community setting people have the greatest opportunity to experiment with developing a desired future. Experimentation is an important notion in both civic education and rural development, for both are starting points with uncertain outcomes. At the community level, however, people can learn to monitor the results and make timely and appropriate alterations in the process. Thus, the community is not only a place that furnishes the basic functions of life but it can also be a living experiment in the creation of a purposeful future.

To be most effective, civic education should deal with several basic elements of the political process as identified by Kingdon (1984): knowledge and information development, formation of public policy proposals, and developing political coalitions necessary to affect change.

It often has been stated that we currently function in an information age. While this is a largely accurate paradigm, the problem is accessing, having, developing, even knowing what information is critical to the successful engagement of community issues or policy formation. In a world in which there is a surfeit of information, the problem is often sorting out what is important to a given concern or policy question and forming integrated functional packages of understandable material. Thus, those interested in civic education need to be concerned with enabling people to develop new information that is accurate and trusted as well as to sort from the existing bodies of knowledge that which is relevant to their concerns.

People need information that is relevant to their particular situation if governance is to be effective. Most issues of rural development are complex and should be dealt with in an integrated manner, drawing upon knowledge from a variety of sources and disciplines.

The information necessary to deal with a community's specific concerns, interests and issues must have "trust validity." That is, the data should be site specific and generated in such a fashion that community people have a sense of ownership of both the information and the process through which it was developed. "From a practical point of view, the demand for valid, trusted information at the community level greatly outstrips the research community's capacity" (Littrell 1985: 191). Therefore, if people are to have high quality information which deals with a variety of community systems in an integrated manner they will likely have to develop it themselves.

Public policy at the local level can be considered from at least two perspectives. One is an overall community policy that gives direction to the future of a community. The other relates to more specific sectors within communities such as school board policy, environmental quality polices or economic development policy. But, for civic education, it is the policy formation, implementation and enforcement process and procedures that are critical. The policy formation process starts with the aspirations, beliefs and values of the collective citizenry which shapes the vision of what is desirable. With the knowledge of what people want to become, a planning process can be established that gives direction to the various community sectors. It is important to realize that ability to develop and enforce community policy is dependent to a great extent on the level of agreement and ownership of the citizens. To develop such ownership citizens must also be stakeholders, which demands significant involvement or opportunity for involvement in the formation of such policy. This process is analogous to that which has developed in today's leading companies (Kouzes and Posner 1987).

Within each community there are a variety of interests. Some people are not concerned about, affected to the same extent, or interested in the same issues or opportunities. This is a natural state of things.[4] What is unnatural are attempts to persuade diverse groups to agree on a thing to accomplish. Many a rural development effort has failed as the result of setting a top priority. What is important to civic educators and rural development specialists is they understand that it is possible to do different things together at the same time. People can cooperate while retaining their diversity by helping each other deal with different issues.

Through the formation of coalitions with similar or compatible concerns or interests, a critical mass of support can be generated for a variety of issues at the same time. Such a process takes time for people to learn and understand how their interests are linked and can be enhanced through ongoing coalitions or partnerships.

Elements of Civic Education

Civic education refers to people learning to become effective participants in the governance of their communities. Just as communities are connected to a network of factors outside their immediate environment so must be the process of local governance. To be effective in the arena of local governance it is necessary to function in a variety of settings, both internal and external. The issue or project at hand tends to define the decision making settings in which one must function. For example, a group of neighbors working with local law enforcement officials can establish an effective neighborhood watch program while at the same time be working with town, county, private concerns, state or national bodies on a local environmental situation. Local governance is not restricted to local decisions but functions wherever private or public decisions are made which impact the local site. The concepts, tools and procedures of civic education are taught/learned in such a manner that people can, if they so choose, be effective participants in the process of governance. This is an important difference from traditional teaching of history, government and civics, which is often presented in a passive vein. The differences are especially obvious when compared to the teaching of English, math, computer science, auto repair, etc., which are clearly intended to be used in day-to-day living. In today's and tomorrow's world it may be just as necessary to be effective in governance as it is in any other field, for public decisions influence an increasing range of our living.

Civic education, if it is to be effective in empowering people for self-governance, approaches the task from a holistic point-of-view. There are four basic elements that need to be taken into account in the development of civic education efforts. These are:

(1) *Awareness and understanding* of conditions, trends, situations, issues and the possible repercussions in both a communal and individual sense.

People not only need to be aware of local, state, national and international trends but also need to realize how their family, firm, job, community might be affected. For example, what does it mean to farm families or the rural community to know that many developing nations are planning to increase food imports? Or, what does it mean to local communities when entrance requirements at the state university are increased? In these cases new ways of managing may be demanded to deal with new trends or situations.

Such issues, trends and situations need to be understood from two points of view: a) how we are likely to be affected in both a private and public sense; and, b) how we can manage or deal with the situation so that the impact is dealt with in the most advantageous manner possible. Unless people realize how they are being affected by a given situation, it is difficult to form reasoned options about how to respond. For example, the response of a community might be very different to changes in University entrance requirements if ten per cent of its seniors attend than if forty-six per cent attend.

(2) *A sense of efficacy*-learning that they have the capacity to possess influence, to exercise power and influence in the public arena, as individuals or in a collective sense.

People may well be aware of trends and issues yet think they have no opportunity or ability to make a difference. What is often labeled apathy may well be a reasonable choice based on the logic of "why waste my time on a project or problem if I can't make a difference?" Helping people learn to be potent civic actors is as necessary as learning about a problem.

To be most effective, teaching and learning has to occur in the context of what people are interested in and concerned about. People want to know and understand up front how they can use this learning to make a difference. Educational experiences need to be developed through interaction with the intended students.

It should not be assumed that any one group has or does not have a sense of efficacy. For example, county commissioners may feel powerless to influence state transportation policy, a group of new mothers may not understand they could change community child care procedures, or a group of high schoolers might feel helpless in the face of school regulations. One's sense of efficacy is self-defined—based on life's experience and its interpretations (Kahn 1970: 48).[5]

Through their interactions people have learned or developed a self concept in regard to their capacity to influence decisions in a variety of settings. The county commissioners who feel powerless to influence state transportation policy may feel that they can have major influence in land use policy decisions. Usually one's sense of efficacy is developed as one learns how to exercise influence, directly or indirectly. Sometimes people choose to work through someone else rather than face the potential failure of direct influence attempts.

In the teaching/learning of efficacy the understanding of the social history of people and communities is important. People have often learned their "proper" roles in both attempting and not attempting to influence the outcomes of decisions. They learn to act accordingly.

(3) *Subject matter information*, including access to current usable, contextual and accurate data/information regarding specific issues, situations, interests or concerns.

Subject matter information is highly important when dealing with an issue. Subject matter data is often considered just technical information. Often, however, specific technical information is not enough. For example, when considering the establishment of water or sewer facilities it is not enough to know how to install the system. It is important also to know what effect it will have on housing development, traffic patterns and school attendance numbers. Thus, it is not enough to transfer specific technical subject matter information in regard to "how to do something" or "how to solve a problem." The implications of the transfer also demand careful attention.

An important facet of civic education in this area is the integration of that information into a relevant context. Often technical information has been developed to deal with as wide a range of situations as possible. Information or recommendations may need to be adjusted to be effective in a given context. When transferring information, careful attention should be given to the integration of that data with a specific site if it is going to have its greatest value.

(4) *Political and organizational development* concepts, procedures and skills in organizational management, political behavior, leadership and the process, structures and tools of governance.

These are critical to rural action and therefore to civic education. The will to govern and the knowledge to govern are both necessary, but are not the same. The ability to develop and manage organizations, structures and systems that produce intended results demands a wide array of knowledge and skill as well as endurance and energy.

Basic management concepts and procedures (e.g. budgets, time lines, personnel management, planning) that can be applied to local development efforts are central to effective civic action. Volunteer groups and official bodies need to be well managed from the point of view of their purpose or mission.

The process of effective governance demands a very broad collective knowledge base for the practical reason that communities are faced with a variety of related complex issues. Purposeful management also includes modern leadership concepts and group dynamics. Their use determines how all groups function to develop and implement a community agenda.

There currently exists an array of tools or procedures of governance that people can learn and use to deal with current situations and to give purposeful direction to create the future of rural areas. Some of those tools are: organizational development and management principles, taxes, land use, management information systems, regulations, contracts, building codes, volunteer management systems, monitoring national events and trends, special districts, budgeting, general planning, ordinances, school curriculum, human relations and group process skills and so on. These tools must be applied to specific situations and a context, and supplemented by information relevant to the issues at hand.

A powerful and important tool of local governance is a sustained process of citizen interaction that results in the articulation, implementation and enforcement of an overarching local public policy. This kind of policy gives direction to the development of a community, harnessing various community sectors so that they jointly contribute to the formation of an agreed-upon future. When such a policy has been openly hammered out, it provides the community with a political statement, a community platform from which to govern and manage. Such a policy framework not only gives direction to local decisions but also provides a frame of reference from which to interact with a variety of organizations, both public and private, from within and outside the community. By having such a policy, local communities need not be passive in relationships with external actors but can aggressively shape, influence, alter or reject proposals and deal with changing trends effectively.

Communities are not autonomous. "Communities exist in the larger society. That is obvious. They are linked to the nation and the world (Warren 1977: 205)." But America's rural communities have a greater capacity for self-governance and self-direction than is generally recognized. Sound civic education which supports rural development not only prepares people to be effective in the local arena but also equips or empowers them to deal effectively in larger arenas.

The Role of the Land Grants: A Call for Change

Land Grant institutions can play a major role in rural development, but to do so, they may have to change the way they work and relate to people. The purpose of the original Land Grant legislation was to enhance the quality of living in rural America. Much of the early legislation centered on agriculture and the farm family, a natural and necessary focus. The founders of the Land Grant system were interested in the economic and social liberation of rural Americans. Because the vast majority of rural families were farmers they chose agriculture, home economics and mechanization as tools of liberation.

A contemporary interpretation of the general goals of this legislation could be that, by liberating the majority (at that time) of rural residents from the physical and spiritual drudgery of farming, and the isolation of farm life, a more empowered rural citizenry would emerge. This citizenry could then collaboratively address its collective concerns. In other words, the general purpose of the Smith-Lever Act of 1914 might well have been civic education. If this is accepted, it can be argued that the purpose and mission of the Land Grant system is the empowerment of rural Americans to deal successfully with whatever issues they face through education that is accurate, relevant, and is understood by the diverse members who make up rural America.

Rural people are concerned about, interested in and are facing a great variety of issues which affect their well-being. Quality of education, health care, local government services, recreation, art, economic revitalization, environmental issues, farm and business profitability, tourism development, substance abuse, social justice, care for the elderly, counseling are but a few of the issues facing rural citizens.

For the Land Grants to reach their potential as major forces in rural development, several major changes will have to occur.

Scope of Land Grant Responsibility

The total University needs to be involved and responsible for the Land Grant mission. The leadership of the Land Grant university system needs to give indepth consideration to the basic question of what is their mission and conceptual base. Are they to be a people's university with a primary concern for increasing the access of citizens to university-based information and education?

Coalition Building

A key to the Land Grant's successful involvement in civic education and rural development is the willingness of presidents, governing boards, faculty, deans, extension workers to form vibrant, creative partnerships and coalitions.

This coalition building has the potential to originate networks which are increasingly effective in the delivery of education, resources and services but it also has the potential to develop a forceful voice in various political arenas in regard to rural development issues.

To create and maintain such relationships, ongoing dialogues must continue with the people and organizations who have as their mission the improvement of the quality of life. It is through such arrangements that the collective resources of the various stakeholders can be focused upon the issues facing rural Americans.

Research: Funding and Central Concerns

Who is going to pay for the research is increasingly the answer to who controls the research agenda (Busch and Lacy, 1983). For those interested in rural development this is a very troublesome question. If grants from foundations, contracts from private concerns, earmarked state and federal dollars are increasingly controlling the Land Grant systems' research agendas, and forming the research questions, where does that leave rural people? Where does it leave poor farmers, youth, small firms, small communities, rural school districts and the public interest in general?

The Land Grant research system needs to ask itself in clear honest terms for whom do we toil and who is reaping the benefits from our work?

A major contribution of the Land Grant research community to civic education and rural development might be the formation of co-equal partnerships, through which community residents learn to conduct action research and University people gain an understanding of issues facing rural citizens.

Rewards

Status, salary, tenure and other perks within the Land Grant system need to be reviewed and changed if civic education and rural development are to be successful. Teamwork, jointly authored articles, applied research, extension teaching are not as equally rewarded as the traditional "Lone Ranger Approach." If Land Grants are to be "people Universities," putting together teams of faculty that deal with issues articulated by citizens, then the administration is going to have to reward rather than punish such work.

Options for Civic Education

Land Grant universities can use the knowledge they and others have generated to design basic approaches to civic education. To be most successful in reaching people, several different delivery options need to be considered.

(1) Incorporation of the principles of civic education and rural development into on-campus courses in Rural Sociology, Agricultural Economics, Political Science, Public Administration, Sociology, Education and Community Development.

(2) Land Grant faculty and administrative leadership can form partnerships with state departments of education, school board associations, social science teachers' groups and others to start the process of building local civic education into elementary and secondary school curricula. It is possible that through such partnerships, local schools may start to view the local setting as a living classroom and seize the opportunity to contribute to rural development and civic education.

(3) Similar partnerships could be formed with a variety of volunteer youth-serving organizations such as Scouts, Boys and Girls Clubs, 4-H, and Campfire. Through such relationships, new opportunities would be available for thousands of adult leaders and youth to gain a basic understanding that people can make a difference, and at the same time they will develop skills about how to do so.

(4) Civic education workshops, conferences, seminars, etc., could become part of ongoing extension and continuing education efforts in the various states. Such offerings can be tailored through interactions with specialized groups such as teachers, agency staff, local teachers, local government officials and staff or a mix of people who are interested in or concerned about the future well being of their communities.

(5) Land Grant university extension staff have an unique opportunity to incorporate the principles, skills and procedures of civic education into their ongoing work. Extension faculty often work with people who are interested in one or more projects, or issues. Through the interaction of interested citizens and local extension faculty in the formation of options or approaches to dealing with given issues or concerns, considerable teaching/learning of civic governance can occur.

Succeeding in this role requires thoughtful change. The Cooperative Extension Service, in its public policy education efforts, tends to teach people about specific public policy issues rather than teaching people how to form, implement, and enforce general or local-based public policy. Richard Barrow's bulletin, *Public Policy Education*, gives the standard extension approach to such education: "Public policy education is an extension program that applies the knowledge of the University to public issues and educates them to make better informed policy choices" (n.d. 1). If people do not have the concepts, the tools of governance, or the realizations necessary to enforce or implement their choices, why should they choose?

Traditionally Land Grant institutions have shared the results of research but seldom have they extended to people the tools and concepts of research. How to conduct research or to develop valid community-based information has seldom been the subject of extension or continuing education programming. How can people in communities generate their own information that has both political and trust validity if they do not have an opportunity to learn the necessary concepts and tools to do so? It is possible that the Land Grants and others have developed an unintended dependency relationship (Littrell and Pigg 1989). In such a relationship, the institutions keep for themselves powerful tools of rural development—the concepts and procedures of generating accurate information. The relationship between the Land Grants and the people of the nation's rural communities may well need to be redefined. Traditionally, it has been the role of extension staff and citizens to identify problems, and the role of university staff to conduct research and report the results, usually in discreet packages. This approach has continuing, but limited, utility. To be sure, some research can best be conducted in campus-based laboratories; but the vast majority of issues facing rural communities can be addressed through a partnership approach to information development. This potential partnership of University and community people can develop information that has trust/political validity and scientific validity.

Thus a major role of Land Grant faculty both on and off the campus may well be helping people learn basic research skills and concepts, not in the abstract, but through the actual process of developing information for use within the community. Community people willing to use this information in forming and implementing decisions is the litmus test of trust/political validity.

The examples of civic education outlined above do not exhaust the range of possibilities. Land Grant faculty and the citizens of various communities are not limited in their design and creative approaches to civic education, especially if they bring to such undertakings a sense of adventure and experimentation. However, administrative leadership must be willing to invest significant resources in civic education if it is to be available to the citizens of America.

Summary

Throughout rural America, people are dealing with diverse issues, concerns and interests as they strive to manage, develop, revitalize, maintain, and change their communities, towns and counties. People are learning that there are not 100%, 50% or 25% solutions. There are a host of 1% or 2% and, sometimes, a 5% solution to their collective challenges. The issues facing rural communities are complex and interdependent and the vast majority defy simple explanations or solutions. There are seldom, if ever, ready-made answers waiting to be applied to easily solve the dilemmas of America's rural communities. It is in this context that civic education, rural development, Land Grant universities, people and community systems must function.

People and their Land Grant universities can form dynamic partnerships through which faculty and citizen become willing to teach/learn from each other so that the collective knowledge of university and community people can be brought to bear on the process of rural development and revitalization. By mounting purposeful research and extension efforts dealing with the issues facing local communities and by implementing widely accessible, sustained civic education efforts the Land Grant system will remain a people's university system. This system can empower ordinary people to carry out the functions of governance so that communities can accomplish their aspirations.

Notes

1. Almond and Verba point out "we can relate specific adult political attitudes and behavioral propensities to the manifest and latent political socialization experiences of childhood" (p.13).

2. John Ballard notes that the traditional requirement for most public offices was "the twenty-five dollar filing fee and lots of friends" (p. 167).

3. Paulo Freire states: "The pedagogy of the oppressed is an instrument for their critical discovery that both they and their oppressors are manifestations of dehumanization. Liberation is thus a childbirth and a painful one. The man who emerges is a new man" (p. 33).

4. For example, local community development surveys often demonstrate a wide array of interest and concern, just as did the state-wide surveys entitled "Through Our Eyes" conducted by the North Carolina Agriculture Extension Service in 1974, or the "Issues Facing Kentucky" study carried out by the Department of Sociology of the University of Kentucky and published in June, 1976.

212

5. Si Kahn points out that "If the members of the organization are not given the opportunity to participate in the decision making process, they will be less likely to understand and involve themselves in the exercise of power" (p. 48).

References

Almond, Gabriel A. and Sidney Verba. 1963. *The Civic Culture*. Boston, MA: Little Brown and Co.

Ballard, John. 1985. "County Government in Missouri." *Missouri Government and Politics* by Richard Hardy and Richard R. Dohm (eds.). Pp. 162-172. Columbia, MO: University of Missouri Press.

Barrows, Richard. n.d. *Public policy education*. Madison, WI: North Central Regional Public Policy Education. Publication Number 03.

Bellah, R.N., R. Madsen, W.M. Sullivan, A. Swidler, and S. Tipton. 1985. *Habits of the Heart*. New York: Harper and Row.

Bennis, W. and B. Nanus. 1985. *Leaders: The Strategies for Taking Charge*. New York: Harper and Row.

Bolkia, J.W., M. Elmandjra, and M. Malitza. 1979. *No Limits to Learning*. New York: Pergamon Press.

Busch, Lawrence and William B. Lacy. 1983. *Science, Agriculture, and the Politics of Research*. Boulder, CO: Westview Press.

Foote, N.N. and L.S. Cottrell, Jr. 1985. *Identity and Interpersonal Competence*. Chicago: University of Chicago Press.

Freire, Paulo. 1968. *Pedagogy of the Oppressed*. New York: The Seaburg Press.

Kahn, Si. 1970. *How People Get Power*. New York: McGraw Hill, Inc.

Kingdon, John W. 1984. *Agenda, Alternatives, and Public Policies*. Boston: Little, Brown and Co.

Kouzes, James M. and Barry Z. Posner. 1987. *The Leadership Challenge*. San Francisco: Jossey-Bass Publishers.

Littrell, D.W. 1985. "An introduction to action research." in Fear, F. and Schwarzwellar, H. (eds.). *Community Development Research in Rural Sociology and Development*. Pp. 187-195. Greenwich: JAI Press.

Littrell, D.W. and K.E. Pigg. 1989. "EXCEL: Collaborative Research in Action." Paper presented at the Annual Meeting of the Society for Applied Anthropology, Sante Fe, N.M., April 5-8.

Warren, Roland L. 1977. *Social Change and Human Purpose: Toward Understanding and Action*. Chicago, IL: Rand McNally College Publishing Co.

13

Governing the Countryside: Linking Politics and Administrative Resources

Jim Seroka and Seshan Subramaniam

Discussions about problems in rural areas in America rarely demonstrate how the policy dreams are expected to become political realities or how policy decisions on the part of other governments and community groups become reality. The starting point of this essay is that the success or failure of rural administration will contribute substantially to the success or failure of America's rural policy goals. Contemporary rural American communities are facing a crisis in their political and administrative institutions. These bodies need assistance, and often they need considerable reform. Any rural policy agenda is doomed to failure without corresponding strengthening of the rural administrative infrastructure. In this chapter, we explain the nature of the problem and propose a program for action.

Reconciling Image with Reality

A major common theme of the contributors to this volume is that rural economies, societies, and cultures are not static, homogeneous entities. Rural American communities are full of diversity, differentiation, antagonisms, and conflicts. Just as a serious scholar would be reluctant to claim that much has been explained by defining individuals by their urban origins, we should be reluctant to pay much serious attention to a standardized rural image.

Some rural areas, like their urban counterparts, are experiencing economic growth and revitalization; some have hopelessly deteriorating economies. Some rural areas are attracting new migrants; others are experiencing a population drain. Rural communities in some areas may fulfill the Norman Rockwell image of the good and simple life, but residents in other rural communities may share little with their neighbors other than their geographical proximity.

In short, if we are to discuss the politics and administration of rural communities, we must remember that the sole fundamental similarity among these communities is that the population density of these communities is relatively low. Other commonalities across rural America, both political and social, ultimately must be linked in both theory and practice to this basic unifier. Thus, we must avoid the temptation to classify all rural residents as poorly fed or housed, committed to grass roots democracy, dominated by rural elites, parochial and conservative in value orientations, or well-adjusted and emotionally satisfied by their community social life.

In addition, and perhaps more importantly from an administrative perspective, it is necessary to stress that local rural communities do not share identical or even similar socio-economic and political agenda and values with other rural communities. The policy needs, values, and administrative capabilities of rural governmental entities vary dramatically.

Rural Administrative and Political Variation

Even if rural American societies had standardized political needs and demands, the political system, institutions, and environments are not the same, or often even similar to one another. Rural administrative institutions vary according to their purpose, organization and function, quality of services, level of autonomy, administrative capacity, and political environment.

First, rural political and administrative institutions vary as widely as the American rural landscapes. In many states in the Midwest and Great Lakes regions, townships can be an important political institution and provide vital services to rural areas. In the South and West, many of the functions of the township are provided by the county or even the state.

In the rural areas of some states, such as Illinois, there are numerous special governmental districts with independent boards and autonomous taxing authority to administer limited public functions, such as flood control, parks and recreation, education, airports, fire protection, water and sewage, and even mosquito control. In other states, rural public administration can be much more centralized and dominated by the county.

Second, the services available to a rural resident can also vary enormously across governmental units, often within the same region, state, district, or county. Some governmental units may provide relatively effective health and welfare services, while in others, such benefits may be lacking. The level, type, and quality of public services vary dramatically across rural America.

Third, even a relatively standard institution, such as the county, will mean something substantively different across the face of rural America. The rural counties of states, such as Georgia, are relatively powerful and semi-autonomous political institutions. Counties in some other states, such as Massachusetts, are less important and tend to serve more as administrative conveniences of the state.

Fourth, within states and regions, there can be substantial variation in the performance and capacity of rural political institutions. A rural county, or even township, may employ professional managers or administrators to assist the policymakers in the day-to-day administration of the government. Some may use the most complex and modern public administrative techniques and be equipped with some of the most sophisticated technological devices. Others may be resistant to such "paraphernalia" and "new-fangled" techniques and prefer to conduct their business in the time-honored, personalized methods of the past (Seroka 1984).

Finally, the political environment of rural governmental units also covers the complete spectrum of possibilities. Many rural governments are hostile to intergovernmental cooperation; others are sympathetic. Some rural political bodies wish to expand their range of services; others wish to eliminate or reduce governmental operations in their communities. Some rural administrators and policymakers view their political environments as hopelessly conflictual, paralyzed by indecisiveness, resistant to change, or overwhelmed by competing interests. Others have characterized politics in their communities as stagnant or conflict free (Seroka 1986).

Thus, as was the case for rural economies and societies, little can be generalized as universally true about politics and public administration in rural areas. We can safely argue, however, that rural politics and administration differ from most urban models and that the scale of operations seems to be somewhat smaller than is the case for the urban political environments.

Competitive Definitions of Rural Standardization

Although there is little question that rural politics are dynamic and extremely diverse, the policymaking process in which rural communities may participate rarely recognizes that diversity, and it almost never makes allowances for it. Politicians, state and federal departments of agriculture, quasi-public organizations such as the Farm Bureau, and even the national media all have a strong interest in portraying rural America as relatively homogeneous, and rural interests and needs as relatively standard. There is a strong incentive for these groups to impose their particular viewpoints upon the policy process in order to exercise control over the policy agenda and define the parameters for policy formulation.

An illustration of this tendency is the criticism that presidential candidates encounter if they are not able to advocate a rural policy agenda that can be summarized in several short paragraphs. Governors and U.S. presidents are often expected to submit legislation that will solve all the problems of rural areas without radical changes or major outlays of funds. Perversely, few in government or the national media recognize that it may not be possible to conceive of a single rural policy.

Within the policymaking establishment, there are several competing viewpoints of American rural politics that tend to be most successful in competing for support and recognition from rural-based interest groups and organizations. One is equating rural with the business of agriculture; a second is the nostalgic desire to save America's family farmers from the ravages of modern society, and a third projects an image of rural poverty and stagnation that mirrors that of some sectors of urban societies. One can well wonder if this latter approach is not simply an attempt to claim a greater share of the nation's social welfare expenditures from urban units or to support local political machines (Perry 1972).

None of the three stereotypes portrays an accurate picture of the totality of America's rural experiences. Also, each of these viewpoints has generated policy proposals in which implementation may be dysfunctional to much of rural America and its communities.

The equation of rural with agriculture is an extreme misrepresentation of rural life in the United States today. Currently, fewer than three per cent of American households derive their income from agriculture, while approximately thirty per cent of Americans live in rural areas. Thus, in all rural areas combined, no more than ten per cent of the households live off the income from their land and derive most of their household income from agriculture (Deavers and Brown 1985). Through simple arithmetic, it becomes obvious that, on average, ninety per cent of rural residents earn much of their livelihood from transfer payments, rent, services, manufacturing, extraction of raw materials, and other activities not related to agriculture.

Although it can be claimed that a significant share of the service sector in rural areas is dependent on agricultural earnings, the relative size of that share varies dramatically across the country, and generally that dependency is diminishing over time. Few economists or regional scientists in the United States today would argue that a resurgence in farm commodity prices would do much to revitalize most of America's deteriorating small rural towns and communities. Rural America today is not agricultural America, and an agricultural-based rural policy may do surprisingly little to alter the realities in America's hinterlands, except for a small minority of its residents (Chicoine, Deller and Gunn 1988).

The second view that equates rural America with Jefferson's yeoman farmer gives even less credence to the objective realities than the "rural is agriculture" view. The widely admired family farmer of American folklore, although accounting for more than two-thirds of the farms in America, generates much less than one-third of total farm income and a correspondingly small share of agricultural production. The successful family farmer of today is more likely to own more than a million dollars in capital, own or lease more than five hundred acres of land, and be incorporated rather than resemble the popular image of the American family farmer.

It is not surprising, therefore, that public policies advertised to help the struggling family farm do little to benefit the small family farms, or do so with extreme inefficiency (Drabenstott, Henry, and Gibson 1987). Small landowners often lack the skills, resources, and information to participate effectively in these programs, and participation in these programs often disproportionately includes the more advantaged farmer.

Thus, one unintended result is that many major agricultural subsidies and other programs actually contribute to widening the income gap within the agricultural sector and a deterioration of the quality of life for the remaining small and poorer family farmers.

The third view of American rural life projects an image of unremitting poverty and hopelessness. It is, in many ways, a mirror image of a prevalent view of big-city society, only on a smaller scale and with more lonely and isolate overtones. Although rural poverty does exist and is deplorable, it is no more representative of rural life than the view that poverty is equivalent to urban life. In addition, even though mean incomes of rural residents are lower than income levels in cities, rural American income distributions (with certain well-known exceptions) tend to have lower indices of inequality than is the case in cities (West 1978). Finally, much of the remaining rural poverty is concentrated among the elderly who live in rural areas in disproportionately large numbers (Morrissey 1985).

Many public policies that have been proposed to address the needs of a decaying and desperately poor rural environment have tended to become small-scale replicas of urban policies. Unquestionably, some rural development policies have accomplished considerable good, and a few, such as rural electrification, have even revolutionized the rural communities they have touched. Overall, however, a national rural agenda that pays attention only to the less-productive segments of a subsociety will inevitably find that incentives for growth will decline and the political infrastructures of rural communities will continue to whither. As a result, the current nonrepresentative image of a universally poor rural society will, in time, become a self-fulfilling prophecy, and inequalities among rural communities will grow, rather than diminish.

In summary, the public policy agenda imposed by higher level governments, articulated and simplified by a centralized communications media, and aggregated and homogenized by large interest groups tends not to coincide with the politics and administration of rural America. Also, the policies often tend to weaken further the rural political and administrative institutions.

The Current Political Realities of Rural Public Administration

A major contributing factor responsible for the incongruity between rural needs and public policies implemented in rural areas is the mismatch between the general policy process and the political realities of public administration in rural areas. The essence of the problem is not so much that intergovernmental relations (IGR) in rural areas are less developed than in urban areas. Instead the problem is that IGR have followed a different path in rural America. Rural political communities tend to have a wide variation in administrative capacity, engage in competitive, not cooperative, inter-rural community relations, often possess a personality-based political style, find it difficult to benefit from economies of scale, encounter unrealistically high citizen expectations, and are affected differentially by the new administrative technologies than is true in urban communities (Seroka 1983).

It is difficult to predict the level of administrative capacity in a particular rural community. Studies have indicated that neither size nor socioeconomic development is a good indicator for the level of administrative capacity in rural areas (Seroka 1985). Some rural communities will possess the administrative infrastructure to apply successfully for state and federal funding for particular public projects. Other communities of similar size and similar socio-economic structure will lack that capacity. Some rural communities will employ or train the necessary manpower to develop and enhance the delivery of public services, ranging from schools to water and sewers, while others will helplessly watch these services deteriorate.

The current system of pluralist intergovernmental funding tends to assume that rural communities have an equal administrative capacity to compete for intergovernmental resources, projects, and assistance. Nothing, however, can be further from the truth. Rural communities that were initially successful in attracting IGR assistance develop the administrative infrastructure to become relatively more successful in the future and to eventually dominate the IGR programs in a particular region, regardless of that community's objective needs (Reid 1982; Seroka 1987). The history of the Community Development Block Grant program and similar assistance programs reinforces this viewpoint.

An alternative method of IGR support--direct grant programs such as Revenue Sharing--also ignores the problem of inequality in administrative capacity. These assistance programs assume a relatively equal capacity among rural communities to use these funds effectively. Simple observation of rural communities during the lifespan of this program conclusively demonstrates that assumption to be false (Seroka 1988).

The second political reality that must be considered in developing a rural policy agenda is that rural communities tend to interact with each other competitively, rather than cooperatively. Although American urban governments are also competitive, the necessity of joint survival induced by spatial proximity and the dominating strength of the central city encourages urban communities to cooperate on a wide range of programs, policies, and services. Even the highly competitive field of economic development is moderated in urban areas by the acknowledgement that there are inevitable spillover effects into neighboring urban communities.

The competitive instincts of rural governments, however, are rarely curtailed by pressures for the need to cooperate. Rural communities, by definition, have small populations, and are diverse, numerous, and are geographically separate. Furthermore, the external communications, trade, and commerce of rural communities are preponderantly directed toward urban trade centers, rather than toward one another. When combined, these circumstances create a competitive environment among rural communities.

Some of the consequences of this unrestricted intra-rural competition are the duplication of resources and infrastructure in the delivery of public services. This can often lead to less-efficient and less-effective service delivery; exploitation of rural areas by firms, state governments, and other entities; and failure to provide services that demand relatively high start-up costs and large population bases (Stocker 1977). In policy areas such as education, where state governments have encouraged voluntary consolidation of rural school districts, the negative consequences have been largely avoided. In areas with less intergovernmental assistance and support, such as health care, the situation in many rural areas has severely deteriorated.

A third reality in rural areas today is the failure of rural communities to accommodate themselves to the restructuring of modern politics following the redistricting and one-man, one-vote decisions of the Supreme Court. Nearly every rural community has its own folklore about a time in the past when its state legislator was able to deliver public projects and shape state policy to fit the needs of the rural constituency.

Today, the political system has changed, but many rural constituents still cling to the old patterns. Contemporary politics and administration value the accumulation of votes and other political resources, but rural areas provide fewer such resources than in the past. In addition, the personality-based and fragmented politics of many rural areas appear to many state legislators and administrators to be an anachronism that is perceived to be confusing, inefficient, and occasionally corrupt (Stocker and Wilson 1986). One negative consequence is that many rural communities, instead of undertaking concerted efforts on their own behalf, wait in vain for state and federal bailouts. In other words, the politics of many states have become much more modernized and bureaucratized, But many rural communities have not or cannot adjust to these changes.

The fourth incongruity between the modern national, urban-centered policy process and rural American administration is the trend toward policy specialization and centralization. In urban areas, it is the natural and prevailing response to meet a public need through the development of a need-specific agency and need-specific program that will alleviate that need by concentrating all the related functions and specialized skills in that particular agency. The centralized and specialized approach makes sense in densely populated urban and metropolitan areas. In rural areas, on the other hand, this pattern cannot be effectively duplicated.

Rural communities face an administrative dilemma when they attempt to specialize and centralize public programs according to the urban pattern. As a rural region specializes its public functions, it must also centralize them and make them less accessible and available to its public. State and federal mandates, for example, may require in rural areas that particular services, such as mental health and special education, be provided through favored administrative channels, such as multicounty districts. In rural areas, however, there are serious problems in providing services over a wide territorial expanse, and this problem is compounded by the relative scarcity of administrative assistance and the appropriate administrative apparatus necessary for specialization. State and federal mandates, in other words, seem to have forced rural communities to opt for specialized but less publicly accessible and controllable services over more generalized but more widely available and locally-based services.

Compounding the impact of the other problems mentioned above is the dual effect that the national communication network has upon heightening policy expectations among the rural population and, thereby, increasing their isolation and frustration. Through the national communication network, the rural public is constantly bombarded with information about events and circumstances in the urban environment, and it becomes immediately aware of policies and services available in the more relatively privileged urban areas. Rural administrators, however, lack the skills, resources, and often, the rationale to provide specialized services in their communities. This dissonance between rural and urban entities could reduce the self-esteem of the rural community. It could also heighten conflict and factionalize the community.

Rural America is no longer isolated from the national pool of information. This information, however, is almost exclusively urban-centered. A rural community today is not well informed and aware of conditions and situations in other rural areas, and it is, perhaps, less well informed today about its neighbors than it was in the past. Like the spokes of a wheel, rural communities are tied into the communication pattern of metropolitan areas, but there is little communication from the extremity of one spoke to the extremity of another. The flow of communications, in short, is biased and unidirectional. As a result, the system of communications can foster a spirit of isolation among rural communities and further weaken the administrative and political potential of rural America.

The final relevant factor is the significant impact that technology has had on increasing the differentiation in the rural environment. Technological innovations, ranging from personal computers to helicopter health transport systems, can do much to reduce the disparity between urban and rural America. As well, these innovations can contribute to a homogenization of the rural culture though the application of technology in the public policies of rural areas. However, it has tended to have the opposite impact.

Differences in the ability among rural areas to provide public services are growing. Fortunate rural communities are enhancing their relative positions, often at the expense of other areas. Unlike the adoption of innovations, such as rural free delivery (RFD), which was implemented simultaneously throughout the nation and did much to improve the quality of rural life, today's self-contained and often private diffusion of innovations and technology serve to exacerbate the inequities found in rural America and further fractionalize the political power and administrative capabilities of this sector of the American commonwealth (Brown 1980; HUD 1979; Lewis 1986). The enormous variation in the quality and availability of rural health care services is one highly visible and troubling sign of this disparity.

In summary, the political and administrative realities of rural America have changed radically from the situation that prevailed in the past. Also, the political and administrative realities of rural America are qualitatively and substantively different from the urban and metropolitan environment that dominates the policymaking process. Thus, in order to improve the development and administration of public policies in rural America and address ourselves more effectively to these concerns, we must adapt the policy process to accommodate itself to these new realities in the rural environment.

The Rural Administrative Reality

The major thrust of our criticism of the current national approach to rural policy making rests on the need to change the policy process to conform to rural American realities. This implies fundamental changes in the process of agenda setting, policy formulation, policy implementation, and policy evaluation in rural areas. It is our thesis that the application of American rural realities to the policy formulation process would do much to help alleviate many of the weaknesses that we see today in the implementation of rural policy, and it would also help to revitalize America's rural political institutions.

At a minimum, rural policymakers should endeavor to support five objectives that are most germane to the administration of America's rural communities. They are to:

(1) Enhance and encourage the widespread development of autonomous administrative capacity in rural areas;

(2) Depoliticize intergovernmental relations and apply economic criteria more stringently to intergovernmental funding decisions;

(3) Create incentives for locally-based intercommunity cooperation in rural areas;

(4) Permit noncentralist-specialist policy solutions in rural areas; and

(5) Develop further locally-based, inter-rural regional institutions and improve inter-rural communication.

Each of these objectives was selected to meet the specific needs of rural American communities as identified in the previous section.

Enhance Rural Administrative Capacity

One of the major weaknesses in the current administration of public policy in rural areas is the misleading and ill-founded assumption that rural communities possess the administrative infrastructure and skills to implement effectively and efficiently their public policies and services within their communities (Reid 1986). Although some rural communities, through planning or luck may have the manpower skills, resources, and technology to administer increasingly complex and sophisticated public programs, the majority of these governments do not.

Rural administrators tend to be amateurs, volunteers, or both. Also, they are rarely trained in contemporary public personnel practices, public accounting, budgeting, risk management, and so forth. Turnover among rural administrators is often high, and salaries are relatively low (Nix, Dressel and Bates 1977). In addition, the personal risk of failure in the rural public arena tends to be disproportionately high, while the personal political rewards and satisfaction from success are relatively low (Sokolow 1982). Record keeping is generally primitive and variable over time. Purchasing and contract decisions are often made and administered in a cavalier fashion, and there are often substantial personal political considerations imposed on many administrative activities, particularly contracting and hiring (Snavely 1986).

In rural areas, the costs of developing an administrative infrastructure to correct these potential problems are often unrealistically high and excessively time-consuming. The simple lack of economies of scale imply that professional administration would absorb a sizable and perhaps excessive percentage of total public expenditures (Fox 1981). Those communities that are not fortunate enough to have privately subsidized arrangements (i.e., capable volunteers, retired businesspersons with managerial skills, retired military officers, graduate student interns, etc.) will often do without any professional administration in an increasingly professionalized administrative environment.

Administrative capacity in rural areas can be enhanced through several mechanisms. First, the national government can reinstitute its now-defunct program of subsidizing circuit-riding town and village administrators. Programs such as this, can permit small rural communities to benefit from the expertise of public administrative professionals, develop administrative infrastructure, improve budgeting, train and develop local public personnel, and engage in other professional public administrative practices. The net effects are that rural communities could experience and appreciate the concrete benefits from the enhancement of administrative capacity and could be able to compete more effectively in the intergovernmental arena.

A second mechanism to strengthen rural administrative capacity is through the further development of state training and certificate programs. More states could follow the example of North Carolina where the Institute of Government is actively involved in the training and certification of public personnel in small and rural communities. Such programs need to include finance officers, public safety officers, personnel officers, and the like. It is important to note that the training needs of rural officials must have a strong practical orientation and avoid the temptation to become a simple listing of legal requirements. Training must also be conducted in rural areas, and incentives must be provided by the state to encourage widespread participation. Such statewide training programs would also encourage the more rapid diffusion of innovation, greater standardization of administrative practices, and additional one-to-one inter-rural communication and cooperation.

Third, public professional organizations, including the International City Management Association, National Association of Counties, National Association of Townships, American Society for Public Administration, and State level municipal clerk associations, could encourage the creation and development of rural sections in their organizations and the development of interorganizational cooperation on rural issues and problems. A comprehensive training curriculum and information clearing house relating to rural administration could also be developed by these organizations, as well as some financial support for administrative professional development in rural areas.

Land grant universities, other colleges and universities, and public administration programs could assist in the rural capacity building effort in many ways. The Cooperative Extension Service also has extensive local ties in rural areas which could be harnessed for these efforts. Land grant universities employ the expert personnel that can provide advice and counsel to rural communities, and the nation's master of public administration programs can offer their services in the form of subsidized interns to perform the actual developmental work.

Depoliticization of IGR

The depoliticization of intergovernmental relations in rural areas is an essential component in the program to improve the administration of public policies in rural areas. Currently, considerable political capital is expended by rural communities to receive federal or state funding for state-federal projects that differ little from traditional pork barrel. Many of these programs inefficiently serve community needs, reluctantly have little lasting value, and often do not contribute to a general regional plan for community development (Beaton and Cox 1977). Economic-rational criteria could be used more effectively in the distribution of intergovernmental funds, and public choice criteria could be used more extensively in the determination of the end use of these monies.

While traditional IGR funding is less than fully effective and efficient in rural areas, the ill effects from overpoliticization are compounded in rural areas. This is largely true because those rural communities that have objectively the greatest need for program funding will have the least administrative capacity to carry it out and the weakest political base to ensure favorable consideration by higher governmental decision makers.

Depoliticization of IGR is not synonymous with budget reductions or with the withdrawal of government from its traditional areas of responsibilities. A strong, professional presence is essential to ensure fair treatment for all rural areas and reasonably constant application of criteria for the determination of the type and location of projects and service delivery systems.

It would be incorrect to argue that depoliticization of IGR is simple revenue sharing. Government must establish some national goals and consistent policy objectives for its citizens. It must also strive to create a reasonably equitable environment for intercommunity competition. Without such criteria, public funds at one level of government will simply displace those of another, and qualitative change among rural communities would not occur.

Finally, depoliticization is useless without a strong program to enhance the rural administrative infrastructure within rural communities. Because much of the inequality in rural administrative infrastructure can be the result of the past exercise of political power, depoliticization without capacity building would only perpetuate and reinforce past trends and differences (Marando and Thomas 1977). Rural governments must recognize and adapt their behavior to the reality that policy decisions and resource allocations in state capitals and in Washington, D.C., are increasingly conducted in a bureaucratized and professional manner.

Incentives for Locally Based Intercommunity Cooperation

The third necessary step to transform rural policy processes is to create incentives for intercommunity cooperation. Unrestricted competition among rural communities has fostered a climate in which public services are duplicated, with accompanying losses of economies of scale, dilution of available expertise, and higher unit costs. It can also encourage a situation where public services are not provided at all. The current overly competitive environment among rural communities encourages communities to seek benefits without assuming any costs (i.e., the free-rider syndrome), eventually weakening the public good. It also encourages jealousy and potentially destructive behavior by some rural communities toward their neighbors who provide certain scarce public services.

As mentioned earlier, the negative consequences from intercommunity competition in urban areas are restricted by the realization among urban communities of the benefits from spillover effects resulting from close geographical proximity. In rural areas, state and regional governments must provide the balancing, cooperative mechanisms through the provision of externalities and enforcement mechanisms. The strengthening of locally based, rural regional governments, decentralization of public services, the devolution of some public local authority to regional authorities, state and even federal encouragement for cost sharing among relatively small governmental units, state subsidization or favored status for cooperative arrangements among rural communities, and some restrictions on local freedom of choice are some of the mechanisms that can be employed to encourage the provision of the collective good in rural areas and discourage counterproductive inter-rural communal competition.

Encouragement of Noncentralized-Specialized Administrative Models

An extremely significant and necessary mechanism for enhancing the administration of public policies in rural communities is to abandon the requirements for centralized-specialized policy solutions that are often mandated by state and federal governments under pressure from professional associations. As discussed earlier, centralized-specialized administrative approaches in rural areas often generate counterproductive responses in rural areas. The abandonment of such mandates would represent a revolution in the governmental conceptualization of the policy process.

Abandonment of the centralized-specialized model does not imply the abandonment of state and federal concern for rural communities. Governments can and should be involved in establishing incentives for cooperation and even uniform policy priorities and goals for their citizens. It is not necessary, however, that these governments regulate in minute detail how and in what sequence these policies are to be implemented (Martinez-Brawley 1984). Nor is it desirable that the powers of the state be used to impose a particular administrative solution to the problem or to enforce the private membership goals of professional associations that are seeking a skill monopoly.

Rejection of the professionalization-specialization model in rural areas would permit a rural community to combine services and consolidate functions, use scarce professional and administrative resources more appropriately, and innovate in the delivery of services and the implementation of policy. Multicounty, specialized agencies could be replaced by more localized but generalized service providers. This could also encourage more voluntary and intensive intercommunity cooperation on a narrower geographical base and provide an incentive for developing local public support for the public policy agenda.

Institutional and Communication Reform

Effective administration of public policies in rural areas is also adversely affected by the relative scarcity of local-based rural institutional and communication linkages that serve to bind rural communities together without the mediation of the urban centers. Advancement of the other four mechanisms would simultaneously improve local-based rural institutionalization and communication. Nevertheless, particular and detailed attention needs to be given to this aspect of the problem.

The strengthening of locally-inspired rural regional governments, cooperative service agreements, and regional professional and functional organizations would contribute a considerable amount to more effective locally-based institutionalization in rural areas. The personal interchanges that occur in these organizations and cooperative arrangements would also contribute to the problem sharing and exchange of ideas necessary for more effective inter-rural communication.

There are numerous benefits from the expansion of communications. Such a trend could heighten the political power of rural communities and help to restore some of the political power lost following the redistricting decisions of the 1960s. It could also lead to significant policy sharing, more effective use of administrative capacity, and more rapid diffusion of administrative skills and capacity. Finally, enhanced communication and voluntary local institutionalization could weaken substantially the power of narrow interest groups and associations (e.g., Farm Bureau) that presently argue that their interests are identical to the community's interest. These groups also argue that their present monopoly of political power can effectively determine the national rural agenda.

Conclusion

Rural areas in America are facing considerable problems and many challenges. These problems are often serious and may threaten the basic survival of many rural communities in the United States today. Continued neglect of the problem or continued forced application of urban administrative solutions in the rural countryside, however, should be avoided. Attempts should also be made to recognize the inherent differences between urban and rural public administration and to accommodate rural public administration to its political realities.

Public administration in rural areas can be enhanced through the encouragement of particular trends and practices within and among rural governments, states and the federal government. In particular, rural public administrators need to develop their administrative capacity, intercommunity regional ties, and communication patterns. States and the federal government should encourage these activities and simultaneously depoliticize their intergovernmental relations with other rural governmental units, create incentives for inter-rural cooperation, and permit more flexible administrative and policy solutions.

Although this program does not promise a complete resolution of the problems of government and administration in rural America, it is a first in a necessary series of steps. Above all, the process of public policy making in rural areas must be adapted to modern political realities in order for these rural governmental units to have any chance of success in altering the present crisis situation that now confronts America's rural communities.

References

Beaton, W. Patrick and James L. Cox. 1977. "Toward an Accidental National Urbanization Policy." *American Institute of Planner Journal*. 43: 54-61.

Brown, Anthony. 1980. "Technical Assistance to Rural Communities: Stopgap on Capacity Building?" *Public Administration Review* 40: 13-23.

Chicoine, David, Steven Deller and Steven Gun. 1988. "Impact of Changes in Rural Economies on Small Town Mainstreet." Paper presented at the 8th Conference on the Small City and Regional Community, Bloomington, IL.

Deavers, Kenneth L. and David L. Brown. 1985. "Natural Resource Dependence, Rural Development, and Rural Poverty." USDA, Economic Research Service, Rural Development Research Report. 48.

Drabenstott, Mark, Mark Henry and Lynn Gibson. 1987. "The Rural Economic Policy Choice." *The Federal Reserve Bank of Kansas City Economic Review*. Pp: 41-58.

Fox, William F. 1981. "Can There Be Size Economics in Providing Government Service?" *Rural Development Perspectives*. 4: 33-36.

Lewis, Edward B. 1986. "Urban Verses Rural Management: The Case of County-Administrator Counties in the United States." in Jim Seroka (ed.), *Rural Public Administration: Problems and Prospects*. Pp. 77-94 . New York: Greenwood.

Marando, Vincent and Robert Thomas. 1977. *The Forgotten Governments: County Commissioners as Policy Makers*. Gainesville: University Press of Florida.

Martinez-Brawley, Emilia. 1984. "Working with the Local Community." *Small Town*. 14: 14-21.

Morrissey, Elizabeth S. 1985. "Characteristics of Poverty in Nonmetro Counties." USDA Economic Research Service, Rural Development Research Report. 52.

Nix, Harold, Paula Dressel and Frederick Bates. 1977. "Changing Leaders and Leadership Structure: A Longitudinal Study." *Rural Sociology*. 42: 22-41.

Perry, Hugh. 1972. *They'll Cut Off Your Project*. New York: Praeger.

Reid, J. Norman. 1982. "Distinguishing Among Rural Communities: The Differences Really Matter." *Municipal Management*. 5: 83-89.

_____ . 1986. "Building Capacity in Rural Places: Local Views on Needs." Beth Walter Honadle and Arnold M. Howitt (eds.), *Perspectives on Management Capacity Building*. Pp. 66-83. Albany: State University of New York Press.

Seroka, Jim. 1983. "Rural Administrators and Policy-Makers: Cooperative Management in a New Environment." *Administration and Policy Journal*. 2: 105-127.

_____ . 1984. "Receptivity to Change and Modernization in Rural County Administration." *Journal of the Community Development Society.* 15: 1-15.

_____ . 1985. "The Impact of Growth, Type of Government and Governmental Positions on Rural County Political Processes." *Public Administration Quarterly.* 9: 342-353.

_____ . 1986. "Attitudes of Rural County Leaders in the United States Towards Intergovernmental Cooperation." *Journal of the Community Development Society.* 17: 55-72.

_____ . 1987. "Rural Community Growth Patterns and Policy-maker Attitudes Towards Administrative Innovation." *Community Development Journal.* 22: 127-130.

_____ . 1988. "Community Growth and Administrative Capacity." *National Civic Review.* 77: 42-46.

Snavely, Keith. 1986. "Personnel Management in Rural Municipal and County Governments: A Comparative Analysis." *Rural Public Administration: Problems and Prospects.* Jim Seroka (ed.). Pp. 95-112. New York: Greenwood.

Sokolow, Alvin. 1982. "To Manage or Not to Manage: City Council Styles in Small Communities." Paper presented at the Midwest Political Science Association, Milwaukee, WI.

Stocker, Frederick. 1977. *Fiscal Needs and Resources of Non-Metropolitan Communities.* Washington, D.C.: GPO, U.S. Senate Committee on Agriculture, Nutrition, and Forestry.

Stocker, Jerry and David Wilson. 1986. *Intra-Organizational Politics in Local Authorities: Towards A New Approach.* 14: 285-302.

United States Department of Housing and Urban Development. 1979. *Developmental Needs of Small Cities,* Washington, D.C.: HUD.

West, Jerry. 1978. "Consequences of Rural Industrialization in Terms of Income Distribution." *Growth and Change.* 9: 15-21.

14

Regenerating Rural America

Robert Rodale and Karen Lehman

Rural America. Somehow the words still conjure an image of peace, security, and quiet, the natural production of the stuff of life—milk, eggs, butter and cream, corn, tomatoes, wheat and barley. But in recent years, a question mark seems to hover behind this label that once embraced the majority of the land and citizenry of the United States. Can rural America survive its overwhelming farm debt, mass migration off the land, and daily destruction of the fabric of community life?

Some experts give up on agriculture and claim that rural communities will survive through an economic transition to industry and to services for tourists and retired people. This approach ignores rural Americans' capacity to tend their land in ways that will keep people and profit in the countryside. Others propose to save agriculture through farm subsidy programs or the introduction of biotechnologies. But these are simply extensions of the ideas that made modern farming practices unsustainable.

There *is* real hope for rural America, and that hope lies in the application of a concept both rich in tradition and modern relevance. That concept is regeneration.[1]

When regenerative practices are employed in the resolution of agricultural and community problems, success is possible where other approaches have failed.

Regeneration is the process by which nature, people, and communities heal after disturbance and increase their vitality. All of us have witnessed regeneration, perhaps without being aware of it. We can understand regeneration best by seeing how it works in nature. Visualize an area of fertile land in a temperate region of good rainfall that supports a forest of large, climax species, like oaks or maples. An old, dead tree in that forest is struck by lightning in a dry season, starting a fire that destroys the whole stand. How can the embodied energy in those trees—which was collected from the sun over many years—be restored?

Oaks and maples do not simply spring from the scorched earth. Rather, nature lays the groundwork for their re-emergence, and that of other climax species decades later through a process called succession. Species sprout and grow in waves, each of which creates a more favorable and supportive environment for the next. Just as the climax forest is the place for flora and fauna of specific types to live together, regenerating land also contains a community of numerous life forms, including animals, microorganisms, insects, and a special class of vegetation called pioneer plants.

Pioneer plants are the first wave in succession. They have four specific qualities. First, they grow easily in disturbed soil. Second, they like light. Third, they produce a great deal of seed. And finally, the seed of pioneer plants is mobile, moving easily in the wind.[2]

These pioneer plants grow quickly, covering and protecting the bare ground, and beginning its process of restoration. One of their main functions is to replace the soil's organic matter and humus that was burned in the forest fire. Another is to provide shade and other protection for the intermediate species which soon begin to grow.[3]

Only after the growth of a succession of pioneer and intermediate plants, does the restoration of the climax community of plants itself take place.

Regenerative Agriculture

The same process that rebuilds a stricken forest can regenerate the nation's farmland. Agriculture is the product of human intervention in nature—the intentional manipulation of plant communities. Sometimes we are so caught up with our own techniques and innovations that we devalue the contribution that nature is making. A regenerative approach to agriculture taps into nature's power to regenerate itself instead of working against it. When handled regeneratively, almost all agricultural lands have significant capacity for self-renewal.

The set of practices used by regenerative farmers encourages a process similar to that which occurs when degraded agricultural land is taken out of production and allowed to rest. When left alone, regenerating farm land has the following seven characteristics:

(1) There is a quick increase in the diversity of plant species, often including some legumes.

(2) A greater mass of plant and other life exists in the soil when biocide use—particularly herbicides—is discontinued.

(3) More plant cover is present on the surface of the soil throughout the year. That greatly diminishes or ends erosion.

(4) More perennials, and other plants with vigorous root systems, begin to grow.

(5) Past patterns of weed and pest interference with growing systems are disrupted.

(6) Nutrients tend to either move upward in the soil profile, or to accumulate near the surface, thereby becoming more available for use by plants.

(7) Soil structure begins to improve, increasing water-retention capacity.

These regenerative tendencies that rely on nature's healing capacity are powerful forces for improvement of the plant/soil environment. Regenerative farmers tap into nature's regenerative capacity through the systematic substitution of their farm's abundant internal resources for some of the purchased inputs that they have been told are essential for increased production.

The internal resources of agriculture are the things and qualities that are always present on a farm, and which are usually (but not always) abundant. Nearly all of them are things nature provides. The sun and land itself are internal resources of agriculture. So are rain, nitrogen in the air, locked up minerals in the soil, animals, the seed of farm-grown plants, the management expertise of the farm family, and the relationships among all those factors or elements.

Table 14.1 is helpful for visualizing the differences between internal and external resources. The line separating the two resource systems can move either to the left or to the right. Throughout the ten-thousand-year history of agriculture—with the exception of the last one hundred years—farmers the world over operated and produced using only their internal resources. The line was all the way to the right side. There were no external inputs into farm productions systems until late in the 19th century.

Where is the line today in the United States? There is no way to say with certainty, but the line is probably a short way from the left side of the page. Following the trend toward industrialization common to other modes of production, farmers have rushed in recent decades to make their farms sites for the conversion of purchased inputs into food. That fundamental change has increased their yields, but has so increased their costs of production that industrial farming world-wide is now in what appears to be an almost terminal state of depression.

Those of us working on regenerative agricultural methods are encouraging farmers to move their personal lines to the right. We are not asking them to avoid the use of all external inputs. But we point out that the way such inputs have been introduced into agricultural production during the past century has often unnecessarily diminished the vitality of internal agricultural resources.

For example, the air is seventy-eight per cent nitrogen. Some plants and very efficient microorganisms can take that nitrogen from the air and *fix* it in the soil for us. But when nitrogen fertilizer is applied to the soil, those internal nitrogen-fixing mechanisms are signalled to stop functioning. That is especially true of the nitrogen-collecting microbes in the soil, which begin working only in an environment where fixed nitrogen is not abundant. The same effect occurs when almost all the other internal resources of agriculture are replaced by external inputs, or by management based on the belief that high input levels mean high yields and therefore high profits. The first two points follow one after the other, but increasingly the third point—profit—has become elusive. The inputs simply cost too much.

Regenerative farmers use their internal resources intensively in ways that actually strengthen and purify the soil while improving the bottom line. Some management methods are old and well known, like crop rotations and integration of animals into the system where possible or desired. We know that when converting a farm from conventional to

TABLE 14.1 Resource systems for agricultural production

Internal	*External*
SOIL	HYDROPONIC MEDIUM

SUN
  main source of energy
	SUN
	  energy used as catalyst for
	  conversion of fossil energy

WATER
  mainly rain and small irrigation schemes
	WATER
	  increased use of large dams and
	  centralized water distribution systems

NITROGEN
  collected from air and recycled
	NITROGEN
	  primarily from synthetic fertilizer

MINERALS
  released from soil reserves and recycled
	MINERALS
	  mined, processed, and imported

WEED & PEST CONTROL
  biological and mechanical
	WEED & PEST CONTROL
	  with herbicides and pesticides

ENERGY
  some generated and collected on farm
	ENERGY
	  dependence on fossil fuel

SEED
  some produced on farm
	SEED
	  all purchased

MANAGEMENT DECISIONS
  by farmer and community
	MANAGEMENT DECISIONS
	  some provided by suppliers of inputs

ANIMALS
  produced synergistically on farm
	ANIMALS
	  feed lot production at separate location

CROPPING SYSTEM
  rotations and diversity enhance value of
  all of above components
	CROPPING SYSTEM
	  monocropping

VARIETIES OF PLANTS
  thrive with lower moisture and fertility
	VARIETIES OF PLANTS
	  need high input levels to thrive

LABOR
  most work done by family
	LABOR
	  most work done by hired labor

CAPITAL
  initial source is family or community;
  any accumulation of wealth is reinvested
  locally
	CAPITAL
	  initial source is external
	  indebtedness or equity, and any
	  accumulation flows mainly to outside
	  systems

regenerative agricultural practices, the farm economy must descend into a trough of lower yields before the soil environment builds its regenerative capacity. Studies at the Rodale Research Center have shown that if the farmer grows certain plants and avoids others, the trough of conversion will be shallower, and will last for a shorter time. This is actually a form of managed succession.

Some regenerative methods are either new or have not been widely adapted for use in American agriculture. Allelopathic interactions are extremely promising for use in regenerative weed control systems.[4] Interplanting is of course an old technique, but new ways are being developed to use it for grain production on American farms. Overseeding with legumes, often using aerial application methods, shows promise. Integrated pest management also has the potential to be a practical regenerative method. High standards of observation of farm conditions, combined with generally efficient management, are essential to the successful use of any of these methods.

In addition to improving the land, regenerative techniques increase the level of management sophistication, improve the interrelationships between the farmer and the plant/animal environment and build a base for the improvement of the psychological and physical health of the farm family.

The potential for improvement should be recognized. It should be incorporated into strategic planning for agricultural research. And eventually the idea that the American land can be improved in quality while it is being used productively should supplant the present goals of production or protection. The result will be a revitalized rural America that maintains its roots in the soil.

Regeneration in Communities

So far we have discussed regeneration in nature and the regenerative ways people can work with nature through agriculture.

Can human communities use similar methods to restore weakened or damaged parts? Is it possible for our society and even our government to draw inspiration from the regeneration metaphor, and tap the healing capacity of nature?

Moving from the farm economy into the general regional economy, we must move from the known and tested into the area of pure speculation. We are dealing with what *could be* rather than what *is*. But in the future, if we are able to look back on the successful use of regenerative principles in regional economic development, we will be able to see that a process of succession has occurred.[5]

Many communities have faced kinds of disasters that, to them, are tantamount to a lightning strike. Local industries such as coal mines, timber, or heavy manufacturing have gone bust, or the price of corn has plummeted. Suddenly, the energy that represents years of work and investment goes up in smoke. Unfortunately, whereas people know they can't recreate a climax forest simply by replanting its dominant species, they often try to recreate what amounts to climax economies by transplanting smokestacks from other states. These factories often spell doom for a struggling economy because they don't rebuild the economy from the ground up.[6]

Once again, regeneration is the better approach. And once again, the concept of pioneers, this time pioneer enterprises, is useful. Just as pioneer plants create an environment that allows other plants to gain a foothold on damaged land, pioneer enterprises create new local economic conditions more hospitable to other enterprises.

Pioneer enterprises such as farmers' markets—even tailgate markets—can be the first wave of economic succession, providing income, employment, and goods and services to local residents. By beginning with a study of the potential for local production of necessities like food, shelter, energy, and transportation, communities can rebuild a damaged economy from within. And again, many of the resources they will need to generate these pioneer businesses are the community's internal resources.

The economy is not the only dimension of community life for which the application of regenerative principles is important. Communities may be confronted with dilemmas in the more intangible elements of community life which comprise community spirit. Residents of towns with overdeveloped tourism industries may feel that they are living their lives for strangers. A town that suddenly booms economically may have to wrestle with its identity as it assimilates newcomers. Too often, community residents don't know how to talk about the importance of these dimensions of life and they are submerged under purely economic considerations.

A regenerative approach to both economic and social problems in communities depends on the clear understanding of a community's internal resources. Just as farmers can decide to depend more or less on their internal resources, communities are presented similar options. The following table (Table 14.2) compares internal resources with external inputs commonly relied on for community development:

Every community has to answer for itself where the line in the chart is right now—far to the left in its dependence on external resources, or to the right with reliance on its own capacities.

To move the line farther to the right, we suggest the five following steps:

(1) *Take an inventory of community capacity.* Most conventional development projects begin with a needs assessment which is nothing more than a *systematic search for incapacity* in a community. After a long list of deficiencies has been compiled, a corresponding list of outside experts who are supposed to be able to "solve the problems" is matched up with it.

But regeneration starts from a different assumption—that communities, if they recognize their internal capacity, can generate good ideas, finance businesses, handle waste effectively, and create forms of recreation that are uniquely theirs. They can begin by having each individual make an inventory of his or her skills.

This can be followed by making a list of the community's voluntary associations and sponsoring a community congress in which these associations come together with public agencies and private businesses to unite their abilities for community regeneration.

(2) *Plug the leaks in the local economy.* For every ten thousand people, American communities spend an average of $90 million each year on food, energy, health care, home repair, housing, recreation, and transportation.

Most of a community's gross income, however, is spent outside the community. In effect, the economic buckets of most American communities are leaky. Economic development experts usually try to tell communities how to pour more "water" into the top—despite the fact that the "water" in the form of subsidies and investment capital is becoming extremely difficult to find. Many communities are discovering that an essential step in strengthening their economy is to plug those leaks in the bucket and invest in themselves.

TABLE 14.2 Resource systems in communities

Internal	External
IDEAS come from the members of the community who will implement them	**IDEAS** come from corporate or public planners who have no direct stake in the community
SKILLS work draws on capacities of local residents	**SKILLS** professional and other workers move in from outside often creating a "boom town" phenomenon
GOVERNANCE local residents are active citizens and determine the quality of civic life	**GOVERNANCE** local residents are clients for public services and have little involvement in community affairs
RECREATION people entertain themselves and beautify their places with what they have at hand	**RECREATION** people consume mass media entertainment and prepackaged "beauty"
MARKETS industries and businesses, to the degree possible supply other local businesses and consumers	**MARKETS** the community's economy is based on exports
CONSUMPTION people buy many of the things they use in their local area; there are many diverse local enterprises	**CONSUMPTION** people leave town to shop and buy items produced elsewhere; the economy is dominated by one or two major industries
WASTE waste is used as raw materials for other productive processes	**WASTE** creates environmental and economic problems for the community or has to be shipped out -- often to someone else's backyard
ENERGY the community has identified ways to use locally available sources of energy	**ENERGY** energy is brought into the community as electricity or petroleum products
FINANCING local financial institutions and savings invest in community businesses	**FINANCING** community businesses seek capital from outside sources

Every dollar spent within a community will have the impact of $1.25 to $3 worth of economic activity. This does not mean that communities should try to produce all the goods and services they use or that they should try to cut themselves off from the outside world. It does mean, however, that if communities spend more on local resources they will see more of the benefit of their investment.

Almost every community in rural America could save millions of dollars by cutting back on what is spent outside the community for food and energy alone. In 1980, for example, a typical community spent more that twenty per cent of its gross income on energy, and ninety per cent of these energy dollars immediately left the local area. For a town of ten thousand people, that amounts to more than $40 million. If that money has been paid to a municipally-owned electric facility (such as that in Osage, Iowa, or Brownsville, Tennessee), it would have been recirculated through the economy and generated more that $100 million worth of business activity.

(3) *Invest in new and expanding local businesses.* An ability to plug the leaks in the local economy depends on the local capacity to produce. The formation and expansion of firms employing fewer than twenty people has generated nearly all of America's net employment gains since 1981.

Especially important are businesses that produce goods or services that replace current imports.

To increase the ripple effect of regeneration, invest in businesses that add value to local products (e.g., to foodstuffs through processing or packaging).

(4) *Try to recruit those industries that fit the community's vision of its future.* Development efforts that try to attract outside industry with investment inducements are attempting to purchase expensive external resources, and these associated inducements almost never do what they are intended to accomplish. Even when they entail no direct costs, they are enormously expensive in foregone tax revenue. There are tens of thousands of towns in the United States vying for a much smaller number of new factory starts each year. Rural towns simply cannot compete effectively in attracting these large external inputs.

The exceptions are those industries that offer a community more than the few hundred jobs they bring because they are in some way compatible with other community goals. Communities can emphasize these shared goals to attract the most desirable businesses.

(5) *Look for gold in the local dump.* Many of the things we currently throw away are the raw materials for fledgling industries—and this is just as true of rural communities as it is in urban centers. As rural townships face increasing difficulties with solid waste disposal, recycling waste can not only generate new business, but can reduce public expenditures as well.

By trying to keep these five steps in mind, communities may come to rely more and more on their internal capacity and learn new ways to tap it for greater self-reliance.

Experiences in Success

The principles of regeneration are being applied in communities from coast to coast, but there are some communities that seem to embody all of the elements of the regenerative process. One of these is located right in the middle of the country.

Greenfield, Iowa

Greenfield and other towns in Adair County were like a lot of other small midwestern towns that have suffered the ripple effect of the crisis in chemically-based export agriculture. Storefronts were emptying out, and people were leaving. But a few people in Adair County decided they didn't want their towns to disappear. They decided to do something about it. They invited the Regeneration Project at Rodale Press to come to Greenfield to help residents discover their regenerative potential. We shared our basic ideas about regenerative processes in communities and asked the eighty people who showed up to make a list of the things Greenfield and Adair County had going for it.

And what a list it was! "Very friendly helpful people." "Good soil." "Antique airplane display." "Good spirit of volunteerism." And on down through one hundred six more assets, including "near the birthplace of John Wayne and Johnny Carson."

An organization called the Regeneration Connection was born out of that group of eighty people and has been working steadily since February, 1987. Theirs is an intriguing list of pioneer projects and enterprises:

People Pages—*a directory of Adair County residents' talent and services, from genealogical research to tarp making;*
Thursday night events in the town square—*music and ice cream socials;*
Farmers' market;
Planting marigolds in the town square;
Grocery bags—*printed with the Regeneration Connection logo, inviting Adair County residents to create or participate in projects to build on the county's assets;*
Oral history—*projects in which kids interviewed their elders;*
Kids' Dreams—*what young people of Greenfield wanted to create in the town, resulting in such facilities as a park slab for skateboarding;*
Sensory museum centered on nature and local heritage;
Walking club;
Frisbee golf course;
Tourist book of assets—*to be made available in all rest stops throughout Iowa;*
Bed and breakfast establishments;
Community Center;
Yards of the week;
Public antique airplane museum.

At first glance, with a few exceptions, these activities wouldn't seem to be important to the economy of Greenfield and Adair County. But take another look at Table 14.2. County residents are using their own ideas, beautifying their landscape, developing their own recreation, supporting local businesses and farmers, and in general, putting their own stamp on community life.

The first projects they undertook were the small steps they thought most important—the little things that build community spirit. Economic benefit can follow when people who believe in themselves and their town gain confidence in their abilities as citizens, farmers, workers, and entrepreneurs.

The Regeneration Connection is a community-wide regeneration effort. But individuals and public or private institutions can also set the example that can trigger further regenerative efforts.

Waverly, New York

Some of the most creative ideas have come from food processors who have found gold in their garbage dumps. Consider Leprino Foods in Waverly, New York, which used to be cited as an environmental polluter. At one point the mozzarella cheese plant was given fifteen weeks to stop discharging high strength wastewater and storing nonrecoverable milk whey in a lagoon. Happily, the management hired an engineering firm with a regenerative orientation. Leprino Foods now treats its wastewater by separating out leftover milk proteins and microorganisms created during biological oxidation. Every day about eighteen thousand gallons of this protein-rich sludge is applied to three hundred fifty acres of company-owned farmland within ten miles of the cheese factory—land selected for its natural drainage and topsoil depth. Those nitrogen-laden "wastes" are fertilizing the tallest, greenest corn around—grown without benefit of commercial fertilizer. And fourteen wells monitoring ground-water are verifying that the nitrogen is taken up by crops and does not contribute to nitrate buildup.

Leprino's milky lagoon is also a thing of the past; the waste whey once mucking it up is a nutrient-rich blend of water and six per cent milk protein and water, and is now being used as a wet feed. Increasingly sought after by local farmers, an average of seventy-five hundred gallons a day of the whey feed is being hauled to nearby farms. There it is stored and piped to one thousand hogs and fifteen hundred cattle, which guzzle the nutritious brew at the rate of twelve to twenty gallons per head per day.

Stockton, California

The Stockton branch of the Sun-Diamond growers' coop processes one hundred thousand tons of walnuts each year. That results in a mountainous buildup of leftover walnut shells.

Until recently, the waste mounds of shells were sold off at marginal prices for use as turkey litter, sandblasting, and ground cover. The shells moved slowly and didn't bring in much money. The mountains of shells have shrunk considerably now that Sun-Diamond has built a cogeneration system that converts the clean-burning wastes into a respectable thirty-two million kilowatt hours of electricity per year and an enormous amount of low pressure steam used to refrigerate six million cubic feet of nuts, and to meet heating, hot water and air conditioning needs.

The cooperative's goal of adding value to the growers' product has also been given a boost. The value of the shells has jumped one hundred per cent since the plant was inaugurated. All told, those walnut shells are replacing purchased electricity sufficient to heat fifty-five hundred homes and natural gas sufficient to fuel nine hundred fifty homes. Furthermore, Sun-Diamond makes a profit by selling about one million dollars worth of extra electricity annually to the Pacific Gas and Electric Company for use in its northern California power grid. There are numerous other such examples of projects in which manufacturers are converting what seemed to be useless or even harmful by-products into valuable commodities.

Leprino Foods and Sun-Diamond are examples of industries that could be well-suited to rural locations; they add value to food products, and supply other local needs, in these cases, cattle feed and electricity. How can rural communities develop the capacity to finance such businesses locally?

Southern Arkansas

If they are like the community of Arkadelphia, Arkansas, the answer may be "go to the local development bank." The Southern Development Bancorporation is a holding company for several for-profit companies and non-profit affiliates. Southern recently purchased controlling interest in an Arkadelphia bank which will make business and employment generating loans to Arkansas communities in several surrounding counties. Other members of the holding company will provide technical assistance to entrepreneurs and small businesses. Southern is an example of a good regenerative idea that can be of use to rural America even thought it was developed in radically different conditions. One of the partners in the holding corporation is Shorebank Corporation of Chicago, Illinois, umbrella for America's first development bank, the South Shore Bank. South Shore was a neighborhood with all of the urban problems imaginable—disinvestment by banks and industry, crime, drugs, and unemployment. The South Shore Bank was started by community organizations that wanted a financial institution that would invest in their neighborhoods and businesses. Community residents participated in the panels that made decisions on who would get loans, ensuring that those loans would benefit the community more than they would outsiders.

The Winthrop Rockefeller Foundation recognized that rural America shares many of the negative effects that economic disinvestment has created in urban areas. The same community-based approach used in Chicago should work in Arkansas. The foundation and other Arkansas investors provided funds for the purchase of their own bank. By teaming up with Southshore to help manage it, Arkansas organizations can gain the expertise to broaden the impact of their already significant regenerative activity. This is an example of how a local community can assess its capacity and make the best possible partnership with someone from another area to complement at.

Regeneration and Public Policy

Regeneration is less dependent on policy than on a spirit of change. We can think of regeneration as a seed and policy as a kind of weed control to keep the new life from being choked. There are, however, some fundamental principles by which policies can be channeled in regenerative directions.

First, policy makers should look to see if there are policies favoring the use of external resources that discourage the use of local capacity. These should be changed. For example, policies that promote the production of cheap commodities for export discourage both the development of local markets for produce in the U.S. and in the Third World. African wheat growers cannot compete with artificially low prices, and family farmers cannot afford to produce such cheap wheat. Both would benefit from a better mix of production for local and export markets.

Second, thinking on public policy has to include those dimensions that foster the building of community spirit as well as local economies. Often it is difficult to determine where social consensus ends and policy begins. Both can be altered for the better if the following basic points are kept in mind:

(1) Communities are not just economic entities, but have important social, cultural, and spiritual dimensions as well.

(2) People can go beyond identifying problems and point to positive and constructive solutions. The outlook is hopeful.

(3) Change begins with small steps.

(4) "Policy" is not the primary focus, people are.

(5) Imagination and creativity are important. People shouldn't be afraid to "reinvent the wheel" if the old ones aren't working so well.

(6) People can identify common ground and build cooperation, appreciate diversity, and move beyond an adversarial approach where possible.

(7) Using the language that comes out of common experience, people can redefine the concepts of progress, development, growth, security, health, and wealth in more positive ways.

(8) Local people are the only ones who can really decide what is best for their communities.

Finally, policies must allow for the long time required for real regeneration to take place. Just as a pine forest cannot regenerate overnight, community regeneration takes time. Where outside resources are necessary, communities should not be forced to move quickly by restrictions on the means put forth to assist them. In regeneration, patience is a public virtue.

Regeneration is a powerful force for healing in nature and in society. But we have to look for that ability, nurture it, allow it to emerge. We can do that as citizens, as farmers, as public officials. And if we all do it, we can regenerate rural America.

Notes

1. Regeneration is a comprehensive word which has distinct meanings in the fields of biology, physics, chemistry, engineering, computer science and

economics. Our construction of the term draws most heavily on its biological, economic, and spiritual connotations.

Within the life sciences, regeneration signifies "the replacement by an organism of parts of the body which have been lost or severely injured. The term is comprehensive and covers a wide range of restorative activities in a variety of organisms." *Encyclopedia of Science and Technology* (5th ed.), New York: McGraw Hill. 1982, p.465.)

Interestingly, this biological notion of regeneration may also be at the root of another word which embodies the fruition of hope, "renaissance." In his book, *The Idea of Reform*, Gerhart B. Ladner notes that J. Trier ". . . has shown that the metaphorical meaning of *renasci*" is not necessarily "to be reborn" but may be "to grow again," the metaphor being taken from the realm of the horticulturist and forester, from tree life, where the "danger" done by cutting (pruning) results in new growth, in a "Renaissance."

2. Clements, F.E. *Research Methods in Ecology*, Lincoln, Neb.: University Publishing Co. 1905.

3. Cairns, John Jr. (ed.) *The Recovery Process in Damaged Ecosystems*, Ann Arbor: Ann Arbor Science Publishers Inc., 1980.

4. Some pioneer plants appear to commit suicide by autotoxicity. That effect is reported by R.E. Wilson and E.C. Rice in their paper, "Allelopathy as expressed by *Helianthus annus* and its role in old field succession," *Torrey Botanical Club Bulletin* 95: 432-448 (1968). J. McClromich reports a similar observation in "Succession," *Via* 1: 1-16 (1968).

5. Our use of biological metaphors in our development of the regeneration concept should not be confused with the attempt to align ourselves with any branch of the field known as social or human ecology, although our concepts of pioneer enterprise and regeneration may be of interest to those engaged in these disciplines. The social ecologists' emphasis is on communities as territories within which a population is in competition seemed too incompatible with our views to make social ecology our intellectual base. Ours is a less rigid, scientific comparison of the social and natural worlds than the attempt to relate people and nature using metaphors from nature. For further reading on the origin of social ecological thought, see Doggan and Stein, *Social Ecology*, Cambridge, Ma.: The M.I.T. Press, Massachusetts Institute of Technology, 1969. See also, Alihan, Milla Aissa, *Social Ecology: A Critical Analysis*, Morningside Heights, N.Y.: Columbia University Press, 1938.

6. For an excellent analysis of the harmful effects of transplant industries, see Jane Jacobs' *Cities and the Wealth of Nations*.

References

Alihan, Milla Aissa. 1938. *Social Ecology: A Critical Analysis*. Morningside Heights, N.Y.: Columbia University Press.

Cairns, John Jr. (ed.). 1980. *The Recovery Process in Damaged Ecosystems*. Ann Arbor: Ann Arbor Science Publishers Inc.

Clements, F.E. 1905. *Research Methods in Ecology*. Lincoln, Neb.: University Publishing Co.

Doggan, Mattei and Stein Rokkan, (eds.). 1969. *Social Ecology*. Cambridge, Ma.: The M.I.T. Press, Massachusetts Institute of Technology.

Encyclopedia of Science and Technology (5th ed.). 1982. New York: McGraw Hill. P. 465.

Jane Jacobs. 1984. *Cities and the Wealth of Nations*. New York, N.Y.: Random House.

Ladner, Gerhart Burian. 1967. *The Idea of Reform*. Revised edition. New York, N.Y.: Harper and Row.

McClromich, J. 1968. "Succession." *Via*, 1: 1-16.

Wilson, R.E., and E.C. Rice. 1968. "Allelopathy as expressed by Helianthus annus and its role in old field succession." *Torrey Botanical Club Bulletin*. 95: 432-448.

15

Waking the Owl of Minerva: Constructing a Future for Rural America

Lawrence Busch

For the past several decades, the declining power of rural people has been accepted as virtually inevitable. As the society we live in becomes more complex, it is assumed that power will continue to gravitate to urban centers. As Warner has cogently argued:

> The shift of power and resources increasingly into the hands of the corporate actors (both public and private), . . . has probably reinforced the declining power, involvement, and representation of rural people in the major decisions affecting their lives (1974: 309).

It is the thesis of this chapter that this decline is in part due to the loss of a positive image of the future. Without that image, rural Americans can do little to influence the decisions that affect their lives. Furthermore, it is asserted that social scientists have an important role to play in constructing a new image.

First, the role of social scientists in constructing the future is discussed. Next, an effort is made to examine various current theoretical perspectives on rural-urban relationships. The image of the future they implicitly present is analyzed. Then, a variety of rural problems are discussed as they relate to rural-urban relations and an outline of a new, explicit image of the future is presented. Finally, a specific example is provided of how this image might be applied to rural America.

Constructing the Future

In Hegel's theory of history, even though ideas are the *primum mobile*, the force that brings about all social change, the power of ideas is always revealed to us after the fact. Hence, we have Hegel's dictum that "the Owl of Minerva takes its flight only when the shades of night are gathering." When the day is done, when the material consequences of an idea are apparent, then one can see its true significance.

Despite the strong materialistic bent that Western society has since taken, this notion persists. It is assumed that any projection of the ideal, unless strictly an extrapolation of present trends, is at best "unscientific" and certainly hopelessly "utopian." Indeed, the peculiar thing about Hegel's dictum is that it leaves even an idealist powerless to change an inexorable, though dialectical, course of events.

Behaviorism and positivism have strengthened this belief. The behaviorist position, simply put, is that changes in the environment (i.e., stimuli) are responded to in a behavioral way. Although ideas, norms, and values, may enter into the situation, they are viewed as epiphenomena, of little help in explaining change. The positivist position, not incompatible with that of the behaviorist, also emphasizes the material. Positivism, however, makes a rigid distinction between what is and what ought to be. It puts forth the goal of science as the study of what is and excludes values from the scientific process. While few social scientists would consider themselves to be value free, in the sense that their own values play no role in their research, most still accept the positivist distinction and try to study "what is" instead of "what ought to be." Yet, can we exclude the study of what ought to be from social science?

Alfred Schutz (1967) has noted that, as individuals, we are conscious of an action only if we contemplate it as if it were over and done with. That is to say, thinking is proleptic;[1] we think in the future perfect tense. We constantly take the probable future (as we perceive it) into account, in coping with the present. To put it another way, all being is also becoming. What is *implies* what ought to be.[2]

There are two major implications for social scientists that can be derived from this. First, the subjects of social research, namely people, do not in their everyday life make *clear* distinctions between what is and what ought to be. When faced with a change in their environment, they do not mechanically respond in a certain way. Rather, they examine proleptically the consequences that the change may have for them. That means, they take the likely course of events into account when evaluating the present. For example, if I use a certain route to get to work, but find it blocked today, I will interpret that event in light of my desire to arrive at work. Then I will revise my course of action accordingly. Of course, people in similar material circumstances may be more likely to respond in a specific way, but only because material conditions of their existence tend to give them similar images of the future.

Moreover, on another level, there is a kind of social prolepsis, a shared image of the future, that is common to all social institutions within a given society. This image provides its adherents with a meaningful social existence. It is the underlying ideal toward which social action is directed. It is the moral imperative that holds the social world together (cf. Polak 1961).

A second implication for social scientists, is that their endeavors constitute a moral science. As Kenneth Boulding puts it, "as science develops it no longer merely investigates the world; it creates the world it is investigating" (1969: 3). That is to say, not only the choice of research topics, but more fundamentally, the very process of "doing science" is value laden and future-directed.

The very process of constructing a theory involves the attachment of "ought" to "is." As Kuhn says: " The success of a paradigm . . . is at the start largely a promise of success discoverable in selected and still incomplete examples" (1970: 23-24). It is just that, a promise, a set of propositions about the way the world *ought* to be. For example, Parson's claim that all structures are designed to fulfill certain functions, is really a claim for what ought to be: structure ought to follow function. But, indeed, as his critics have pointed out, this ideal is not always met in practice.[3]

Furthermore, the methods we use allow us to sift out what is knowledge from what is not. For example, if I wish to use current statistical techniques I must exclude those data that are not quantifiable. Moreover, method asserts that the world must have a particular form in order to make the type of knowledge we seek possible (Wolin 1969).

In short, if it is conceded that people act proleptically, both individually and socially, then we must include that understanding in our formulation of social theory. Furthermore, since we are a part of what we study, we should be aware of the prolepsis inherent in theory itself.

To do otherwise is simply unscientific for it dogmatically ignores variables known to be related to human behavior.

It appears, therefore, that social scientists have an obligation to constantly re-examine social institutions to see if they live up to their goals, and to see whether the goals themselves remain meaningful. This is not to say that social scientists should hold themselves up as the arbiters of public morality. Instead, we should make clear the alternatives that might be, and let the public decide which ones they find meaningful. The purpose of this chapter is to do just that. Let us begin by examining the proleptic images implicit in three theories of rural-urban relations.

The Relationship Between Rural and Urban Areas

There are arguably three major schools of thought on the relationship between rural and urban areas: Human Ecology, Dependency, and Central Place Theory. Each of these schools concedes that urban places have an advantage over rural places, though they differ on the nature of that advantage. Let us briefly examine each of these perspectives.

The human ecology school is ambivalent about the degree to which the metropolis dominates its hinterland. This ambivalent relation was apparent in the first ecological analysis of metropolitan regions, N.S.B. Gras' *An Introduction to Economic History* (1922). First, Gras argues:

> Just as villages remained when town economy prevailed, so do towns remain when metropolitan economy comes into existence. Towns remain, but in economic subordination to the metropolis. They continue to play a part, but as tributaries to a larger center (185).

Then several paragraphs later, he asserts that "interdependence of the parts is really the key to the whole situation" (187).

McKenzie, a decade later, asserted that "The metropolitan region represents a constellation of centers, the interrelations of which are characterized by dominance and subordination" (1933: 70). In 1950, Bogue made an empirical test and concluded "that the metropolis . . . exercises an organizing and integrative influence on the social and economic life of a broad expanse of territory far beyond the civil boundaries, and thereby dominates all other communities within the area

(1950: 6)." In a more recent work, Hawley has lent his support to the notion of dominance (1971).

Though lately of lesser concern, central place theory has previously been recognized and employed by rural sociologists to study relations between rural and urban areas. In C.J. Galpin's classic work, he employed central place theory to analyze the relationship between a Wisconsin community and its hinterland. What specifically concerned Galpin was that the farm surplus was being used to create city institutions without any similar institutions being created for the farm population (1915). In a more recent study by E.A.J. Johnson, incorporating the work of the German geographers Christaller and Loesch, it is asserted that domination exists only when the market structure is essentially dendritic in form (1970). Put another way, Johnson believes that a well-integrated hierarchy of central places reflects an equitable balance of socio-economic power.

The dependency school has also noted the tendency toward metropolitan domination. However, its proponents have adopted a neo-Marxist argument: ". . . the capitalistic world, or one might say the entire capitalist society, is inexorably divided into exploiting developed metropolis and exploited underdeveloped periphery" (Frank 1969: 226). Though Frank develops this theme with Latin America in mind, others have applied various versions to the United States (cf. Bonilla and Girling 1973; and Blauner 1972). In general, dependency theorists have examined urban-rural relationships in terms of class and stratification, as opposed to central place theorists and human ecologists who have concentrated upon spatial structure.

Upon comparing the three models we see that the first two assume that urban-rural relationships will always be benign while the third assumes they will always be exploitative. The first two frameworks tend to examine spatial organization as a natural system and pay scant attention to the voluminous literature on economic and political concentration (e.g., Blair 1972; Domhoff 1970; Epstein 1969). On the other hand, dependency theorists have virtually ignored the impact of new technology, and economies of scale on the organization of space.

In contrast, however, there is substantial agreement among the three perspectives that the United States is becoming more integrated politically, economically, and socially, while a regional division of labor becomes increasingly apparent. Whole states are increasingly dominated by the production of a single commodity. Rural and urban areas are becoming less distinct; communication networks at once bring about and maintain increased centralization and national integration.

In short, the proleptic images implicit in each of the three theories are remarkably similar. In human ecology and central place theory the image is of a generally positive future, while in dependency theory the future is negative. In all three frameworks, however, there is a certain sense of determinism. By refusing to state explicitly what the future ought to be, the proponents of these theories project the present into the future. Unlike the ever-changing social world, the world as they describe it is fixed. The sense of becoming that gives meaning to human interaction is necessarily excluded from their image. The proleptic quality which is inherent in all social life—indeed, the quality that defines the limits of our very consciousness—is denied.

Some Signs of Malaise

Until recently, it had been considered virtually inevitable by both social scientists and the general population, that urbanization would increase, that the complexity of industrial society would demand a continued concentration of industry in urban areas, and that rural areas would socially, economically, and culturally follow the lead of the metropolitan areas. While some of the hegemony exercised by metropolitan areas has been exploitative—witness the Railroad Barons' gouging of western farmers about the turn of the century—it has been accompanied by a tacit acceptance on the part of rural society of metropolitan dominance. As Nolan and Heffernan (1974) have noted, rural development has been viewed as bringing urban industry to rural areas, as a repetition of the urban development process.

As a result, the United States, and much of the world, is today suffering from a spatial overdivision of labor, combined with a dangerous overcentralization of political and economic power. Whole sections of the nation have been reserved for the production of a few items: Michigan for autos, California for vegetables, the rural South for textiles. From the point of view of human ecology, this spatial division of labor is highly unstable. Disruption of the distributive system is felt nationally, when in previous times only local problems would have resulted. Hence, we have national shortages when something goes awry. And since the problems are national, decision-making power is eroded at the local level while it is increased at the national level.

From the point of view of central place theory, the kind of graduated hierarchy of central places suggested as an ideal by Johnson does exist, but only as a spatial pattern. The near-autonomy of each level of hierarchical organization, typically the case in biological hierarchies, is lacking. Instead, the spread of modern communication and transportation networks has permitted the concentration of decision-making power at the top.[4]

To dependency theorists, the ills described are a result of Western capitalism. Yet, there is absolutely no doubt that the imbalance described above is as much a characteristic of the Soviet system as of that of the West. For example, a recently built truck factory in the Soviet Union was expected to provide all the large trucks that nation uses! Hence, regardless of the names we attach to the world's socioeconomic systems, they share this commonality. The spatial overdivision of labor and the overconcentration of political and economic power are ubiquitous.

In short, whether we view society through the perspective of human ecology, central place theory, or dependency theory, we are confronted with a situation that is highly unstable and conducive to crisis. A more complete evaluation of the relationship between rural and urban areas, an attempt to construct a new image of the future, is in order. What, then, can we posit as a new image of the future for rural America?

Some Suggestions for Optimizing Rural Values

How can we re-interpret traditional rural values within a new context? How can we put new meaning into rural life? Can we provide a guide to help solve the problems that currently face rural America? Three interrelated goals appear to me to provide a potential answer to these questions: Ecologism, Participation, and Self-realization. They are not proposed as givens, but as hypotheses. Let us briefly examine each of them.

Ecologism

Clearly, no future society can exist without a greater concern for the environment. Ecologism is a way of looking at the world as a single self-contained whole.

For the last several hundred years, we have used the earth's resources as if they were infinite. Our economics does not assign a value to resources. The value of the minerals and fossil fuels of the earth has been completely discounted. The price of a barrel of oil or a ton of coal for the most part reflects the cost of mining and processing and the oligopoly profits of the oil and coal companies, as compared to the minuscule value assigned to the commodity itself. As a result, future generations have been robbed of a substantial proportion of the earth's resources.

Ecologism is an understanding of the simple but profound fact that human life is part of a delicate ecological balance that we are increasingly capable of disrupting. This is not to say that we should revert to the life of some "noble savage." This is not a call for a return to nature, to some never-never land of the mythical past. That is neither desirable nor possible. Nor is it a suggestion that we are ultimately doomed to live in a world of scarcity. That is likely to lead to unfreedom, to constant crisis, to the restriction of alternatives. Rather, liberation lies in our mergence with the environment. To the extent that we minimize our use of, and find substitutes for, non-renewable resources, to the extent that we build up rather than deplete the soil, to the extent we put back into the ecosystem at least as much as we remove, to that extent we can be free to be what we wish to be.

Ecologism literally means "the doctrine of the house." To this may be counterposed the notion of ecocide, or "the destruction of the house." Since we all live in the house, and no other house exists within commuting distance, only the former option is rational or desirable. Nor is there an option of building our own house—the technological fix. It is sheer madness to suggest that we are capable of providing our own system, independent of nature. One need only examine the life support systems used by astronauts to realize how infinitely complex and exceedingly flexible is the natural life support system that we live in. The sooner we shed our visions of grandeur, the better.

Ecologism also implies the replacement of pyramidal structures with networks. Instead of perceiving ourselves at the top of a pyramid, we need to begin to view ourselves as parts of a series of networks. We must come to the realization that as a species we are not at the center of the biosystem but a single interdependent part. So with our social structures: we must shed notions of dominance and subordination and replace them with that of interdependence. Rural areas must develop the institutions they need to put themselves on an equal footing with urban areas.

Ecologism then, is acting according to the realization that we have limits, that we are neither omnipotent nor omniscient. We must begin to accept responsibility for the consequences of our (individual and collective) actions. Acceptance of that responsibility will allow us a freedom we have never known before.

Participation

The concept of participation has a long history in rural America. Rural Americans have traditionally banded together for a variety of reasons. Town meeting democracy, where all could actively participate, survives to this day in some places. Voluntary associations, popular with Americans when de Tocqueville wrote, are still to be found in great numbers.

Participation means different things at different levels. To groups, participation is intimately bound up with self-determination. It is the right of every cultural, linguistic, ethnic, and geographic community to make its own internal decisions and to participate in those decisions which affect it but must be made at a more global level. It is the right of a group to have its own unique, distinctive identity.

To individuals, participation is the right to a part in shaping and reshaping the institutions of one's immediate environment. It is the constant active engagement in the process of decision making, in the family, in the workshop, in the community, and in any and all other institutions.

Participation is not representation. To vote for a representative is to surrender one's right to decision making, to delegate it to another. Participation involves taking an active part in decision making, not the submission of a proxy. While representation was an enormous improvement over autocracy, it has outlived its usefulness. With the development of enormous populations and representative bodies that have to examine thousands of bills, representation has become simply a new form of legitimated remoteness. A replacement is long overdue.

Effective participation, as described here, must rest on the equalization of power, the elimination of hierarchy. If a group of people are engaged together in any kind of institutionalized activity, but only one person has the authority to make decisions, clearly no decision-making power is left for the other members of the group. It is irrelevant to argue that the person in authority may delegate some of his or her power, for the delegator will still retain the right to nullify the adverse decisions of subordinates. In short, true participation is impossible in a hierarchical system.

Although Durkheim was examining the process of making contracts, his observation is equally true of participation in decision-making: "In order that equivalence be the rule for contracts, it is necessary that the contracting parties be placed in conditions externally equal" (1964: 384). Full participation can only occur within an environment of equality.

Self-realization

The final, but equally important, concept necessary to a new proleptic image is self-realization. It can be defined as the process whereby individuals attain a fuller comprehension of themselves. In practice, it means that people should be free to learn, to explore, to create. It means the re-synthesis of manual and intellectual labor, of work and play. It means the end of the formal separation between learning, working, and resting.

This, of course, is exactly what the rugged individualism of the last century was all about. The frontier farmer was able to develop a host of manual and intellectual skills. He or she was able to directly influence, if not control the decisions that affected his or her daily life. While his life was not easy, it was *his or hers*.

Today, of course, there is little room for such rugged individualism. The unexplored fertile fields no longer exist. Hence, we are confronted with a new challenge: we must design new institutions that once again align social and individual goals.

In the recent past, the division of labor has meant the division of people. While many benefits derive from the division of labor, there is no longer any reason why anyone should be expected to perform the same task, using the same part of him or her self, every day. This can and does lead to the repression of a large portion of all of us.

It is within our means now to eliminate meaningless labor, to cybernate many unpleasant tasks, and to spend the time thus saved in an enormous burst of creativity. Several thousand years ago Aristotle wrote:

> For if every instrument could accomplish its own work, obeying or anticipating the will of others . . . ; if in like manner, the shuttle would

weave and the plectrum touch the lyre without a hand to guide them, chief workmen would not want servants, nor master slaves (1905: 31).

We have the capacity to achieve just that today.

The three goals of ecologism, participation, and self-realization are not unrelated. On the contrary, they are as intimately related as the parts of the ecosystem itself. Unless all three lead in the same direction, no society based on them could long survive.

All three goals are democratic. All three celebrate life, encourage awareness. If participation does not lead to self-realization, it is unlikely to be valued. If ecologism does not provide us with a greater understanding of the nature of human beings and our place in the universe, then neither will it be valued.

These three goals also stress the absolute quality of circumstances, the uniqueness of situation, the relativity of time and space. They include the recognition that the needs of all are best satisfied by the encouragement of diversity. They stress harmony in both senses of that word, as concord and as a group of different voices put together.

Finally, it is important to note that all three goals are processes rather than finite ends. Ecologism is a never-ending process of maintaining and rebuilding the environment. Participation is involvement in the ever-changing realities of daily life. Self-realization involves the never-ending growth of human faculties. These goals have no ends.

Furthermore, these three goals should not be considered as merely an idealist scheme. They imply the utilization of certain concrete means for their achievement. They are meant to be what Mannheim called a relative utopia (1936). That is to say, some measure of each of them is readily achievable now and does not depend on some future event that has yet to take place. While it is impossible to provide more than a sketch here, it appears necessary to provide an example of what means might be employed to further these three process-goals in rural America. One such means is an industrial organizational system called Workers' Self-management.

An Application

Hansen has noted that although only 500-750 new industrial plants open annually, there are over 14,000 development organizations attempting to attract industries to particular communities (1974: 42). It is clear from these figure that (1) a great deal of time, effort, and money is wasted in futile attempts to attract outside industry, and (2) rural communities see no alternative to dependence on large (and typically metropolitan) corporate actors as a source of employment. Workers' self-management offers a potentially viable alternative to this situation.

As developed by Vanek (1970; 1971; 1975; 1977), workers' self-management (WSM) is an application of democratic theory to the workplace. It is a hybrid between the traditional production cooperative and the capitalist firm. Its foundations rest squarely on the notion of (1) direct participation by all, and (2) a convergence of individual and organizational goals.

Specifically, two organizations are established, a self-managed corporation (SMC) and a supporting corporation (SC). The SMC is a one-plant industrial organization employing any number of workers. Workers initiate and implement decisions of a non-routine type based on the principle of one-person, one-vote. Routine decisions are delegated to a manager who is a member of and responsible to the firm. The specific details of the decision-making process might vary from firm to firm and would be spelled out in a written constitution and by-laws. All new workers hired by the firm would become members with full rights.

The key to such an SMC is obviously financing. Unlike the producers' cooperative where members must directly finance the firm, the SMC is financed through a supporting corporation. The SC acts as a vehicle for raising funds to operate one or many SMCs. The SC is managed by a board of directors elected by the members of the SMC. It borrows money from banks, government agencies, and/or individuals at the market rate of interest for a period equal to the estimated time needed for the capital equipment of the SMC to depreciate to zero. In other words, if the SMC wishes to buy ten machines at $1,000.00 each, and it is expected that each machine will have a life of ten years, then the SMC borrows $10,000.000 to be repaid with interest in equal installments over ten years. When the loan is fully paid off, the equipment will have no further value.

The reasoning behind this unique financing system is simple. First, it insures that workers' shares in the SMC will always remain valueless. In a successful production cooperative, shares typically rise in value to a point where new workers cannot afford to enter the firm.[5] However, under WSM, entry and exit remains a simple matter throughout the life of the firm.

Second, workers, as individuals, may invest any portion of their salary that they wish in the supporting corporation, at the going rate of interest. Thus, self-financing at an artificially deflated rate of interest does not occur.

It is also important to note that the SC and the initial funding source do not have the power to influence or intervene in the affairs of the SMC. That is to say, the separation of ownership and control is complete and institutionalized. Only in the case of bankruptcy can the owners intervene in the daily operations of the SMC.

While no firms exist that exactly meet these criteria, experiments in varying degrees of worker participation have been conducted in a variety of places around the world. Industrial organizations in some parts of the United States (Bernstein 1974), Spain (Whyte 1988), Yugoslavia (Blumberg 1968), Israel (Spiro 1956), and Sweden (Karlsson 1973), among others, incorporate substantial portions of the model proposed by Vanek. A Report of a Special Task Force to the Secretary of Health, Education, and Welfare some years ago reported that "in no instance of which we have evidence has a *major* effort to increase employee participation resulted in a long-term decline in productivity" (1973: 112). Typically productivity increases of five to forty per cent have been recorded.

Additionally, there is substantial evidence to link participation in decision-making with increased job satisfaction and decreased alienation. Paul Blumberg writes:

> There is hardly a study in the entire literature which fails to demonstrate that satisfaction in work is enhanced or that other generally acknowledged beneficial consequences accrue from a genuine increase in workers' decision-making power (1968: 123).

WSM should have particular appeal in traditionally non-industrial areas such as parts of Appalachia and the Ozarks where private firms find the labor force to be "undisciplined." Since WSM allows workers to set their own hours, their own work pace, and their own vacations, it would be likely to be adaptable to the cultural patterns of these areas.

Additionally, worker-managed firms are not likely to move out of town, as the branches of large corporations often do. Nor are they as likely to pollute, since it is typically their own community that would be polluted. They are likely to be more innovative, as was the American farmer of the 19th century, for the benefits of labor-saving devices accrue directly and immediately to everyone. Self-managed firms are likely to require less management personnel since organizational and individual goals are convergent.

Of course, WSM is not a panacea. It will not solve all our problems. It is simply one means. It offers the possibility for increased participation, for self-realization, and for concern for the environment. It is one way of replacing metropolitan dominance with interdependence, and thus revitalizing our rural areas. Another means is the development of decentralizing technologies, particularly in the field of energy supply and telecommunications. A third means might be a reorganization of local governments along more participatory lines. Still another means might involve innovations in land-use planning.

Federal, state, and local government are now spending millions of dollars through myriad agencies to attract industry to rural communities. Millions more are being spent to provide unemployment benefits and welfare compensation. WSM offers a means for substantially reducing this often futile effort, and for providing people with the means to help themselves. The three process goals of ecologism, participation, and self-realization offer a positive image of the future for rural America, an end to urban dominance. Let us wake the Owl of Minerva and consciously construct a meaningful future for rural America!

Notes

1. The term prolepsis, literally to think in the future perfect, was brought to my attention by Jon Hendricks.

2. This is not merely a semantic issue. It is virtually impossible to conceive of a conscious action that does not require thinking about what ought to be.

3. It may be argued that Parsons took Weber's notion of an ideal type and, instead of using it as Weber did, as an ideal, used it as an image of the real.

4. The term hierarchy has a vastly different meaning for biologists and ecologists than the one typically attributed to it by social scientists. No authority relations are implied in the biological model (cf. Koestler 1967: 59 ff).

5. This is exactly what has happened to the plywood cooperatives in the northwestern United States. Share values have approached $35,000. See Bellas in Vanek (1975).

References

Aristotle. 1905. *Aristotle's Politics*, translated by Benjamin Jowett. Oxford: Clarendon Press.

Bernstein, Paul. 1974. "Run Your Own Business: Worker-Owned Plywood Firms," *Working Papers.* 2: 24-34.

Blair, John M. 1972. *Economic Concentration.* New York: Harcourt, Brace, Jovanovich.

Blauner, Robert. 1972. "Internal Colonialism and Ghetto Revolt," *Poverty of Progress*, Milton Mankoff (ed). Pp. 216-230. New York: Holt, Rinehart, Winston.

Blumberg, Paul. 1968. *Industrial Democracy.* New York: Schocken.

Bogue, Don J. 1950. *The Structure of the Metropolitan Community.* Ann Arbor: University of Michigan.

Bonilla, Frank and Robert Girling. 1973. *Structures of Dependency.* Palo Alto: Stanford University.

Boulding, Kenneth. 1969. "Economics as a Moral Science." *American Economic Review.* 59: 1-12.

Domhoff, G. William. 1970. *The Higher Circles.* New York: Random House.

Durkheim, Emile. 1964. *The Division of Labor in Society.* New York: Free Press.

Epstein, Edwin M. 1969. *The Corporation in American Politics.* Englewood Cliffs, N.J.: Prentice-Hall.

Frank, Andre Gunder. 1969. *Latin America: Underdevelopment or Revolution.* New York: Monthly Review Press.

Galpin, S.J. 1915. *The Social Anatomy of An Agricultural Community.* Madison, Wisconsin: University of Wisconsin Agricultural Experiment Station. Research Bulletin 34.

Gras, N.S.B. 1922. *An Introduction to Economic History.* New York: Harper.

Hansen, Niles M. 1974. "Factors Determining the Location of Industrial Activity." *Rural Industrialization.* Pp. 27-45. Ames: Iowa State University Press.

266

Hawley, Amos. 1971. *Urban Society.* New York: Ronald Press.

Johnson, E.A.J. 1970. *The Organization of Space in Developing Countries.* Cambridge, Massachusetts: Harvard University Press.

Karlsson, Lars Erik. 1973. *Experiences in Employee Participation in Sweden:* 1969-72. Ithaca: Cornell University Program on Participation and Labor-managed Systems, Mimeo.

Koestler, Arthur. 1967. *The Ghost in the Machine.* Chicago: Henry Regnery.

Kuhn, Thomas. 1970. *The Structure of Scientific Revolutions.* Chicago: University of Chicago Press.

Mannheim, Karl. 1936. *Ideology and Utopia.* London: Routledge and Kegan Paul.

McKenzie, R.D. 1933. *The Metropolitan Community.* New York: McGraw-Hill.

Nolan, Michael F. and William D. Heffernan. 1974. "The Rural Development Act of 1972: A Skeptical View." *Rural Sociology.* 39: 536-543.

Polak, Fred. 1961. *The Image of the Future.* Leyden: A.W. Sythoff. 2 vols.

Report of a Special Task Force to the Secretary of Health, Education, and Welfare. 1973. *Work in America.* Cambridge, Massachusetts: MIT Press.

Schutz, Alfred. 1967. *The Phenomenology of the Social World.* Evanston: Northwestern University Press.

Spiro, Melford E. 1956. *Kibbutz: Venture in Utopia.* Cambridge, MA: Harvard University Press.

Vanek, Jaroslav. 1970. *The General Theory of Labor-managed Market Economics.* Ithaca, N.Y.: Cornell University Press.

_____. 1971. *The Participatory Economy.* Ithaca, N.Y.: Cornell University Press.

_____. 1975. *Self-Management: Economic Liberation of Man.* Baltimore: Penguin.

_____. 1977. *The Labor-Managed Economy.* Ithaca, N.Y.: Cornell University Press.

Warner, W. Keith. 1974. "Rural Society in a Post-Industrial Age." *Rural Sociology.* 39: 306-318.

Whyte, William F. 1988. *Making Mondragon: The Growth and Dynamics of a Worker Cooperative Complex.* Ithaca, N.Y.: ILR Press.

Wolin, Sheldon S. 1969. "Political Theory as a Vocation." *American Political Science Review.* 63: 1062-1082.

About the Contributors

Edward J. Blakely is currently Chair of the Department of City and Regional Planning at the University of California at Berkeley. He is well known for his work on community development and local economic development theory and practice. He has served on the Board of Directors of the Community Development Society and the American Planning Association.

Lawrence Busch is Professor of Sociology at Michigan State University. His most recent (co-authored) book is *Plants, Power and Profit: Social, Economic and Ethical Consequences of the New Biotechnologies* (Blackwell Press). He is continuing his research on other issues of agricultural science and development policy.

Frederick H. Buttel is Professor of Rural Sociology; Faculty Associate, Program on Science, Technology and Society; and Chair of the Biology and Society Major at Cornell Univesity. He is currently President of the Rural Sociological Society and co-author, with Gilbert Gillespie and Olaf Larson, of *The Sociology of Agriculture* published by Greenwood Press, 1990.

Emery N. Castle is Chairman, University Graduate Faculty of Economics, at Oregon State University. He also is Chairman of the National Rural Studies Committee which is supported by the W.K. Kellogg Foundation. He is a Fellow of the American Association for the Advancement of Science, the American Agricultural Economics Association and the American Academy of Arts and Sciences.

Mark Drabenstott is Vice President and Economist with the Federal Reserve Bank of Kansas City, where he heads the Regional Economics Group in the Economic Research Department. Dr. Drabenstott has spoken to business, financial, and policymaking audiences on public policy issues across the nation and is the author of numerous articles on such subjects as farm policy, rural development, farm exports, and agricutural finance. He currently serves as Chairman of the Federal Reserve System Committee on Agriculture and Rural Development.

Lorraine Garkovich, is a professor in the Department of Sociology, College of Agriclture, University of Kentucky. Her research has focused on the consequences of population change for rural communities and patterns of family and work roles in farm households. She has recently written a book, *Population and Community in Rural America*, and her research has also appeared in *Rural Sociology*, the *Journal of the Community Development Society*, and *Population and Environment*.

Gilbert W. Gillespie, Jr. is Research Associate in the Department of Rural Sociology at Cornell University. He has had a longstanding interest in issues relating to agriculture, rural development, and the environment. He recently co-authored *The Sociology of Agriculture*, published by Greenwood Press in 1990.

William R. Gillis is Director of the Center for Rural Pennsylvania. The Rural Center is an agency of the Pennsylvania Legislature providing a focal point for rural policy development.

W. Richard Goe is Senior Research Scholar in the Center for Economic Development, School of Urban and Public Affairs, at Carnegie Mellon University. He is the author of a forthcoming book entitled *Information and the Development of the American Food Production System* (Ablex, 1991). His published research falls under the areas of agricultural and rural development, the political economy of information technology and the consequences of economic restructuring for metropolitan regions.

Martin Kenney is Associate Professor of Sociology in the Department of Applied Behavioral Sciences at the University of California, Davis. He is the author of two books, *Biotechnology: The University-Industrial Complex* (Yale, 1986) and (with Richard Florida) *The Breakthrough Illusion: Corporate America's Inability to Link Innovation and Mass Production* (Basic, 1990). He is the author of articles that have appeared in *Economic Development and Cultural Change, Rural Sociology, Research Policy,* and *Sociologica Ruralis*.

Karen Lehman is a community regeneration consultant with The Minnesota Project, a nonprofit rural capacity building organization. She is also a contributing editor to *Regeneration*, published by Rodale Press.

Donald W. Littrell is Associate Professor, Department of Community Development, University of Missouri-Columbia, and State Extension Community Development Specialist. He is well known for his work in training and development of civic education and leadership programs. He is a founding member and former board member of the

International Community Development Society, and a Fulbright fellow to Thailand.

Doris P. Littrell is Director of Extension Teaching, University of Missouri-Columbia. Her work has centered on adult/continuing education and higher education administration. She is former president of the Missouri Community Development Society, is active in the International Community Development Society, the National University Continuing Education Association and other adult education associations.

Kenneth E. Pigg is Associate Professor, Department of Rural Sociology and Extension Specialist in Community and Rural Development, University of Missouri-Columbia. He has contributed to several journals with articles on community development and program evaluation. His work also emphasizes program development in communities and professional education in rural community economic development.

Glen C. Pulver is Professor Emeritus, University of Wisconsin-Madison. His field of specialty is community economic development policy and he has worked closely with governmental bodies, private businesses, economic development committees, organizations, agencies and educators throughout the United States.

Robert Rodale was Chairman of the Board and Chief Executive Officer of Rodale Press, Inc. in Emmaus, Pennsylvania for nearly twenty years. Throughout his career, he worked to develop, promote, and gain acceptance for innovative ideas in the areas of farming and gardening, food and nutrition, and health and fitness. He established the Rodale Research Center for the study and demonstration of regenerative agricultural techniques and the Rodale Institute, a nonprofit educational, research service organization dedicated to finding ways to use existing resources to make agriculture more profitable and biologically sound. Unfortunately for the future of rural America, Robert Rodale was killed in an automobile accident on September 20, 1990.

Jim Seroka is a professor of political science at Pennsylvania State University at Erie, Pennsylvania. He is editor of *Rural Public Administration* and has contributed to numerous professional journals, including *National Civic Review, Journal of Planning Literature,* and *Journal of the Community Development Society.*

Sonya Salamon is Professor of Family Studies, University of Illinois at Urbana-Champaign. Her research focuses on family farmers, land tenure and rural communities in the Midwest.

Seshan Subramaniam is a doctoral student in political science at Indiana University and received an MPA degree from Southern Illinois University in Carbondale, Illinois.

Jerry L. Wade is Associate Professor, Department of Community Development and State Community Development Specialist, University of Missouri-Columbia. His work emphasizes program development for communities and professional education in community economic development.

Kenneth P. Wilkinson is Professor of Rural Sociology at Pennsylvania State University. He teaches, conducts research projects and writes on community action and social change in small towns and rural areas. His recent work examines trends molding the future social well-being of people and communities in the rural areas of North America and Europe.

Index

285